D0034456

NOTHING
TO LOSE,
EVERYTHING
TO GAIN

NOTHING TO LOSE, EVERYTHING TO GAIN

Being Black *and* Conservative *in* America

Kathy Barnette

CENTER
STREET®

NEW YORK   NASHVILLE

Center Street
Hachette Book Group
1290 Avenue of the Americas, New York, NY 10104
centerstreet.com
twitter.com/centerstreet

First Edition: February 2020

Center Street is a division of Hachette Book Group, Inc. The Center Street
name and logo are trademarks of Hachette Book Group, Inc.

The publisher is not responsible for websites (or their content)
that are not owned by the publisher.

Print book interior design by Timothy Shaner, NightandDaydesign.biz

Library of Congress Cataloging-in-Publication Data has been applied for.

ISBNs: 978-1-5460-8575-1 (hardcover), 978-1-5460-8577-5 (ebook)

Printed in the United States of America

LSC-C

10 9 8 7 6 5 4 3 2 1

Carl, Kayla, and Carl Jr., your presence in my life is visible proof and a daily reminder that I am highly favored by God. You three are my joy. I could not have done this without you.

I love you.

CONTENTS

Introduction 1

1. Nothing to Lose, Everything to Gain 11

2. Living Outside of the Liberal Box 35

3. I'm Black, but I'm Not a Democrat 51

4. What Does It Mean to Be Black in America? 65

5. Culture of Poverty 89

6. The Patriotism of Slaves 119

7. The Black Harbinger of America's Future 133

8. Yes, Racism Exists. What Do We Do about It? 151

9. The Importance of the Black Vote 171

10. Socialism Is Slavery 187

11. A Lesson from the Jews:
    Mourn, Fight, Move On 213

12. My Hope for the Black Community 229

13. We Are Victors, Not Victims 255

    Thank You, Little Black Girl 266

    Acknowledgments 268

    Notes 270

INTRODUCTION

We are all the sum of many parts, places, people, and experiences that together make us who we are. We are not our own. For me, the words and deeds of past generations still speak in my life today. Like handprints in dried cement, I am a composite of indelible impressions made by many people, some of whom I've never met.

I was reminded of this when someone once asked me, "Kathy, who has influenced you to become who you are?" Given my background and ethnicity, the questioner wanted to know how I, a black woman, had arrived at the conservative convictions I wear so loudly and proudly on such topics as economics, politics, theology, and culture.

At the time, I hadn't given the question much thought. So, with the sincerest heart I replied, "Jesus!"

In my mind, it almost seemed as though my journey had been a natural progression of things—becoming a Christian at nineteen, finishing college, marrying the love of my life, buying our first home, having children, planning play dates. It all seemed so natural. After much reflection, however, I realized it is anything but a natural ebb and flow of life that has landed me where I am today. Many times I had to swim against the current, and I had to do so alone.

At that particular moment the question was asked, I had never stopped long enough to examine all of the odds that were stacked against me. The odds surrounding my birth. The probabilities associated with an impoverished start in life. The impossibilities of me ever overcoming the pervasive and false narratives that would have me believe that because I'm black, I'm a victim. After much time and with great consideration of my journey in life, I realized my answer to the gentleman was incomplete.

In part, it was a true response. But not in whole. With the benefit of some time to contemplate the question, I now realize the correct answer is that many people have influenced me.

So before we jump into chapter 1, let me first walk you through a few of the influences and people who have had some part in me becoming who I am. This book is birthed both from my past and from my hope for the future, especially my hope for the future of black America.

TIME ON THE FARM

I grew up on a very small farm in southern Alabama in a one stop-sign town in a restful and rustic corner of the world. Among many things on that farm, we raised pigs and chickens, and since we always had a raccoon or two in the backyard, I guess we raised them, too. There were about ten families in our small community. None of us were rich. In fact, we were what's known as dirt poor. Yet, without question, I had the best childhood ever. I often lament not being able to give my own children such a childhood.

As a child, I never knew just how poor we really were, nor did I even think of us as poor. When my grandmother Hattie would ask me to help her in the garden, I thought she just wanted to spend quality time with me. I never knew it was for our survival. If we ever wanted greens or beans on our plate, it had to come from the effort of our own two hands.

From these people in our community—*my* people—and from that small spot on the map, I learned the valuable lesson of what it means to be a part of the black community. I learned it has nothing to do with the style of my hair—whether it's natural or processed. I learned that sharing in the black community has nothing to do with how far my son's pants sag, or if I speak just the acceptable amount of broken English, or if I vote in a certain predictable way. Nor is my membership in the black community predicated on how easily I can tie my emotions back to slavery or how much of a victim mentality I can adopt because my ancestors didn't have the advantages I have today.

Instead, I was taught that the black community is a village. We're not invisible. We see each other. We're not alone. We share a common destiny. Our fate, in many ways, is tied to our collective success. We're all engaged in the same battle. We take care of our own. I remember that when I was a child, if I did something less than honorable while I was away from my family, rarely could I make it down the hill from church and back to my grandmother's house without at least six of the ten families reporting my mischief to her before I walked through the front door.

I learned I did not belong to myself. I didn't even belong only to my parents. I was obligated to live well because to do otherwise reflected poorly on our village. I was obligated to be respectful to my elders—never would a child dare call an elder by their first name. It was always "Yes, ma'am" and "No, sir." We gave deference whether it was earned or not.

As the granddaughter of farmers, I saw my grandparents up early working in the fields, sowing seeds with full expectation that their efforts wouldn't be in vain. I saw my grandfather slaughter a hog and then go from house to house sharing portions of his bounty with others. It wasn't uncommon to awaken in the morning to find anonymous bunches of collard greens on our front porch. One family borrowed sugar, another borrowed rice. We *shared*. We often had extra people at the dinner table. I had more play cousins than I could count. We were all a part of a larger family.

My brothers and I lived with my mother and maternal grandmother. Among the many luxuries we lacked was the comfort of running water. In addition to having to traipse out to a dark and gloomy outhouse in the backyard that promised to suck me in if I sat on it, we also had a well on the side of the house for our drinking water.

That well was revered by children and adults alike. It was old. It seemed to me as a child that one false move would cause that decrepit contraption to crumble and I would fall to my ultimate demise. It dared me to come closer. It beckoned me to look over its rickety railings into the dark chasm below. Every child I knew passed by it with at least a ten-foot margin of space.

You can imagine my wild-eyed amazement when I saw my paternal grandfather, Charles, sitting in a chair, dangling over the mouth of that well, being lowered down into the belly of the beast. Our eyes met. *No, Granddaddy!* were my unspoken words. He just looked at me and smiled. Soon he was out of my line of view. This went on every day for about a week. Every morning he would disappear into that well and in the evening he would reemerge.

Apparently, the well was running dry and needed to be hewn out to produce more water. My grandfather was the only one who knew how to do such a thing—or at least the only one brave enough to venture twenty feet beneath the earth's surface. But day after day, I saw my grandfather being lowered into that well not to reappear until late in the evening. No currency was ever exchanged for his services. My maternal grandmother was in need and my paternal grandfather could help. That's all he needed to know.

Although my material wealth was less than nothing, I never felt lack. Most importantly, I never thought of myself as a victim because of my impoverished circumstances or because of the racism that permeates the history of the South. From the many examples of the people I knew, and the experiences I had, I grew up earnestly believing that if I sowed seeds of great quality, my efforts wouldn't be in vain. Sadly, my grandfather and grandmother died before they could see the fruits of their labor. But I and many others are that fruit.

This was the black culture I knew. A culture steeped in personal accountability. It was a culture that taught us to work for what we wanted, to be respectful, and to share with others. It taught us that we were not our own. We belonged to a larger body of people for whom we were to live lives of integrity, bring honor to our family, and take care of one another.

Everything my mother and grandmother had, they poured into my brothers and me. They poured into us love, respect for ourselves and our fellow man, laughter, and joy, and they introduced us to Christ.

However, they could not pour into us what they themselves did not possess. I routinely say that I didn't grow up in a home where my parents read the *Wall Street Journal*, discussed their latest stock picks, or sat around the fireplace chatting about their purpose in life. For the majority of blacks in Nichburg, Alabama, and surrounding areas, the goal of each day was sheer survival— food, clothing, heating, and keeping the lights on were on the top of our minds. Planning for the future usually stopped at the purchase of life insurance, if that.

Yet despite that meager beginning, now as an adult I see ever so clearly how God carved out a path for me to walk. I see how God had a bigger purpose for my life than my environment would have predicted. Bigger even than the dreams I harbored as a little girl.

I can remember walking down a long plum bush–lined street to the mailbox each day, watching the cars zoom by, daydreaming about faraway places and living a life that would be unthinkable for a little country girl from Nichburg, Alabama.

Many years, careers, and adventures have passed since I was that little pigtailed girl with a bad speech impediment but those precious years are a "part of my sum."

This is who I am.

THANK YOU, LITTLE BLACK GIRL

Another factor that has helped determine who I am relates to an image I've held in my mind for many years. It's an image of this little black girl being chased through the woods as dusk turns into an eerie darkness. I see her running, stumbling as she desperately looks behind her. I can hear her slave master's taunts; she's breathless, scared, and alone. I see her, and my heart aches for her. I see her, and I can't help but feel a sense of connection with her. I recall her as if I've met her, though that's impossible, for this little girl is my mother's mother's mother. Although generations stand between us, our connection remains unbroken.

I resemble her. I am her seed, after all. Our two stories have some distance between them, but they are not completely severed. This girl toted my water to freedom. The price she paid has forever indebted me and every other American—white and black people alike. This is an indebtedness that can only be repaid in our worthiness. Am I, a black woman, worthy of the price she paid? Although

I can never meet this little black girl, I've become acquainted with her many ways through the seed of my mother—Mamie Jo.

LITTLE MAMIE JO

In addition to being raised as what many would consider "disadvantaged," I'll add one more stumbling block to success: I'm the by-product of a rape. Because of the strength and determination of my mother, the circumstances surrounding my conception and birth are not the end of my story . . . or hers. When adding up the sum of who I am, I have to include the influences of my mother, Mamie Jo.

I see little Mamie Jo, twelve years old, full of promise. Or at least filled with as much promise as a poor little country girl in southern Alabama during the late 1950s can have. My birth certificate lists her gender as merely "Negro girl." But that tells us nothing about Mamie Jo. It doesn't tell us that she was the result of a secret affair. It doesn't let us know she wasn't wanted by either parents, but instead was given away to a lady who was not of her blood—but who loved her as if she was her very own.

My mother was eleven years old when I was conceived. My father was twenty-one. I cannot imagine the pain and the confusion my mother undoubtedly experienced when at the age of twelve she was forced to marry the one who had inflicted so much suffering upon her.

Many twists and turns and years would pass, two little brothers would be added to our brood, but my father abandoned my mother shortly after they were married. One horrible relationship after another, and on her own, my mother became strong. She became a pillar of strength to me and to everyone who crossed her path.

No, life has not been a bed of roses for Mamie Jo. She has made her fair share of mistakes along the way. But, as I stand here, a full-grown woman with a family of my own, I am immensely impressed with my mother. She *believed*. She never gave up. She never stopped smiling. She never stopped striving for something better. She refused to be defeated. She refused to be a victim.

Like that little black girl from a bygone era, I can feel the weight of my mother's choices. She chose to survive the rape, to endure harsh treatment by men, to reject the lingering presence of hopelessness and fear. But why?

"Why" has to do with another who gave the ultimate sacrifice. Rejected, scourged, brutally beaten beyond recognition, eyes like slits, unrecognizable by those who knew Him best, through the streets of Via Dolorosa our Savior stumbled to His Crucifixion bearing just one thought in mind: you and me—and little Mamie Jo.

The circumstances surrounding Christ's death were unimaginable. Yet, He found time to think of me. Scripture declares in Hebrews 12:2, "For the joy that was set before him, he endured the cross . . . " (NKJV). *We* are the joy that consumed the mind of Christ on that harsh day. With His eyes fixed on us, Jesus suffered the cross, refusing to be ashamed. This is a love and a determination most cannot comprehend.

Yet, I see it in my mother. Similar to our Savior and like that little black girl I spoke about earlier, who I see in my mind's eye running from the taunts and maltreatment of her "master," I also see my mother, little Mamie Jo. My mother refused the shame. Although her circumstances were unbearable, my mother saw the joy that was set before her, too. She peered into the future and saw me. I am my mother's joy.

THE WHITE HAND ON THE DOORKNOB

Fast forward many years and Mamie Jo's prayers for me, her

daughter, have had a profound effect on any success I've had or will have. In the Amplified Bible, we read in Revelation 3:8, "I know your [record of] works *and* what you are doing. See! I have set before you a door wide open which no one is able to shut."

If we see ourselves as victims of adversity, racism, or impoverishment, we'll never notice the doors that God is opening. Or if we notice them and turn away because we see a white hand holding the door open, we'll leave that open door for someone else to walk through and smugly decry our victimhood.

I'm firmly convinced God, and God alone, opens doors of opportunities for us to walk through. He certainly has for me. But for every door of opportunity God opened up for me in my professional life, with one exception, there was a white hand holding the doorknob.

Because of these white hands who helped open doors for me, I would be a fool to reject all white people as racist. Believe me, I know racism. I grew up in the Deep South during a time when racism was epidemic. Yet my personal experiences and the experiences of many others tell me I would be a fool to say, "All white people are evil." It's just not true.

Are there racist white people in the world? *Yes.* But are there racist black people, Hispanic people, Asian people, Russians, Europeans, and Middle Easterners? Yes.

In all honesty, I've experienced far more discrimination from those who share my melanic pigmentation than from any other ethnicity. I've had more black people reject me based on, for the most part, things I cannot control. I've been told my voice sounds too "Valley girl" or too white because my diction is clear and my vocabulary is expansive. I've been told that my complexion isn't dark enough or I'm not light-skinned enough or the texture of my hair isn't ethnic enough or my impoverished start in life should hold me back or my political views are too conservative, and on and on and on.

I've learned a couple of things along the way, chief among them that I must always be true to myself. It is not my job to make others feel good about my existence or try to appease their insecurities because I've simply walked into the room. As a child, I often felt unprotected. As an adult, I've learned that one of my first responsibilities is to take care of little Kathy Jean. To be true to her. To advocate for her. As Frederick Douglass said so aptly, "I prefer to be true to myself, even at the hazard of incurring the ridicule of others, rather than to be false, and incur my own abhorrence."[1]

I've also learned it's less than prudent to judge a whole race of people by our limited interactions with some. Regarding race, people are entitled to their opinions, regardless of how misguided and antiquated their opinions might be. In today's America, other people's opinions do not cost us our lives by hanging on a cross or being lynched as it did several decades ago. Their prejudiced opinions don't prohibit us from voting or stop us from providing for our families. Their biases can't prohibit us from working hard, dedicating ourselves to a task, and making something of our lives.

We in the black community are no longer slaves. Yes, other people's opinions can make life more challenging. But we are free. Our futures are our own. We have one life to live. I want mine to count. I think you want yours to count, too.

Let's make it happen.

1.

NOTHING TO LOSE, EVERYTHING TO GAIN

I remember the days preceding the 2016 presidential election. I remember the night I stayed up late to watch then candidate Donald Trump speak at yet another packed rally in Akron, Ohio. It was a sea of red MAGA hats and flailing arms of enthusiasm; a deluge of Trump/Pence signs; and spontaneous breakout chants of "Trump! Trump! Trump! Trump!"

To a non-liberal, it was exhilarating! The energy in the jam-packed arena was raw and infectious. I could almost feel the thunderous applause. I can't recall ever witnessing such displays of genuine enthusiasm for a Republican presidential candidate—for any presidential candidate, for that matter. Their excitement was palpable.

Up to this point on the campaign trail, candidate Trump had made all sorts of promises. Big promises. Promises that if enacted would be revolutionary by any standard. Interestingly enough, however, none of his many promises pandered to any specific ethnic group. Instead, at this point, his promises generally aligned with his pledge to make all American lives better. To "Make America Great Again."

There was a promise to "build a wall" that would protect our porous southern border.

He also waxed strong about the dangers of undocumented Syrian refugees streaming into our country unchecked, and he promised to temporarily suspend travel from select countries known to harbor "radical Islamic terrorists."

Then he promised to produce the "magic wand" President Barack Obama could never seem to find during his eight years in office and use it to bring manufacturing jobs back to America. He promised to impose tariffs on imports from China and force them to play fair in the international marketplace.

He promised to renegotiate the North America Free Trade Agreement (NAFTA) to better serve American interests.

He promised to stop the uptick of terrorist attacks in our own country that had almost become pervasive. Up to that point, we had had the Pulse Nightclub shooting in Orlando; the San Bernardino shooting; the Prophet Muhammad cartoon stabbing in Garland, Texas; and the Boston Marathon bombing. We had seen vehicles being weaponized and driven into crowds of unsuspecting people. It seemed as if terrorist attacks might become our new normal. We were all unnerved.

He promised to appoint conservative judges to federal benches and to the Supreme Court.

He promised to get us out of the lopsided Iran nuclear deal.

He promised to pull the plug on the wealth-siphoning climate change initiative known as the Paris Agreement.

He promised to drain the swamp in Washington, DC; to repeal Obamacare; to fix the Department of Veterans Affairs; to cut taxes; and for good measure, to decimate ISIS while he was at it.

His to-do list, if he was elected president, promised to be long and seemingly never-ending. All of it was politically incorrect. It promised to be an uphill battle to bring any of these measures to pass, given our own thoroughly reluctant government and the lack of support abroad.

We didn't care, though. We drank up every promise he made like a parched desert floor. We were so elated to have someone finally speaking for *us* on a national platform. His provocative rhetoric to "Make America Great Again" gave us all hope that our country wasn't truly lost after enduring eight long years under what the Obama administration characterized as "fundamental change." We were exhilarated.

Then the unimaginable happened at that rally. Suddenly, things became more personal. There was a shift in the atmosphere. In the midst of citing his long list of promises to "Make America Great Again," he paused. All of the promises he had made up to that point weren't directed to any one specific group of people. All of his promises had been bold, but now he was about to become even bolder.

Among this sea of white faces, he addressed his next remarks to the black community, the voters who have historically voted Democrat since the days of President Lyndon B. Johnson. But that didn't matter to Mr. Trump. He went off script and spoke to us personally. It was no canned speech. This wasn't the usual pandering we've all come to expect on campaign trails.

I can't remember a time a Republican candidate had ever done such a thing. Candidate Trump wasn't willing to assume that *my* vote, as a black person, was a foregone conclusion resting comfortably in the back pockets of Democrats. The realization of what happened then still excites me today.

First, delineating Hillary Clinton's horrid track record in the black community, candidate Trump with great stealth traversed the rugged and dangerous terrain of many urban cities before concluding with his appeal that has now become a rally cry for many black Americans:

> Our government has totally failed our African American friends, our Hispanic friends, and the people of our country. Period. The Democrats have failed completely in the inner cities. For those hurting the most who have been failed and failed by their politicians—year after year, failure after failure, worse numbers after worse numbers. Poverty. Rejection. Horrible education. No housing, no homes, no ownership. Crime at levels that nobody has seen. You can go to war zones in countries that we are fighting and it's safer than living in some of our inner cities that are run by the Democrats. And I ask you this, I ask you this—crime, all of the problems—to the African Americans, who I employ so many, so many people, to the Hispanics, tremendous people: What the hell do you have to lose? Give me a chance. I'll straighten it out. I'll straighten it out. What do you have to lose?

What passion! What conviction! Who has ever made such a plea to the black community? Who has ever spoken so frankly on behalf of black people?

He continued:

> And you know, I say it, and I'm going to keep saying it. And some people say: "Wow that makes sense." And then some people say: "Well, that wasn't very nice." Look, it is a disaster the way African Americans are living, in many

cases, and, in many cases the way Hispanics are living, and I say it with such a deep-felt feeling: What do you have to lose? I will straighten it out. I'll bring jobs back. We'll bring spirit back. We'll get rid of the crime. You'll be able to walk down the street without getting shot. Right now, you walk down the street, you get shot. Look at the statistics. We'll straighten it out. If you keep voting for the same failed politicians, you will keep getting the same results. They don't care about you. They just like you once every four years—get your vote and then they say: "Bye, bye!"[1]

It has been said that insanity is defined as doing the same thing over and over again and expecting different results. This "insanity" is the trance of madness, the dance of absurdity the black community has engaged in for generations with the Democrat Party. We've been locked in a Texas two-step with the Democrats since the days of President Johnson. And for all of our traipsing around we've gotten very little in return, while they continued to secure the White House with our vote.

If, only for a moment, we could allow ourselves to move beyond any knee-jerk reactions to hate the man as the media and their Democrat enablers would have us to do, we would clearly see what then candidate Trump was offering to the black community is actually one of the most unracist postures a white politician can take. If there is any offense to be taken it should be to the realization that we've been duped by the Democrat Party. Then candidate Trump calling a thing a thing is no reason to take offense. Only speaking plainly will set us free. To look beyond the color of my skin and to look beyond your preconceived ideas about me has proven to be a Herculean task even for some of the most well intentioned.

Consider the posture one must take in order to come to the black community and consider them as equals, to approach the black community as one having something of real worth to offer them. This is a posture those within the black community have rarely seen a white politician assume. To be elevated from the proverbial back pockets of Democrats and engaged as equals isn't a common behavior experienced by most blacks when interacting with white politicians on either side of the aisle. We're often seen as victims, helpless creatures forever needing the liberal white politician to rescue us. Trump's posture was a welcome change.

In true Trump fashion, he created a marketplace of sorts. We have problems. He has solutions. We have the power of the black vote. He wants to get into the White House. Just like that, a marketplace was created, and he spent the better half of his first term putting down collateral to secure the black vote for future conservatives who will bring workable solutions to the problems the black community faces. All candidates make promises. We in the black community have seen that over and over again. But once elected, will that candidate follow through?

To some, then candidate Trump's words were seen as wicked and divisive or, at best, simply ill framed. But to me and many others in the black community, his words sounded like a gauntlet being thrown down. As if a line was being drawn in the sand.

Never in my lifetime that I can recall has a politician spoken so clearly, so succinctly. Nothing was left to the imagination. No interpretation was needed. He said exactly what he intended to say. Many in the media and Democrat leaders immediately criticized the vagueness of his promises, as if they expected him to produce a ten-point plan to remedy generations of neglect right then and there, something the Democrats had certainly never done themselves.

Some voters might not have liked his tone then, and while time has done nothing to alleviate their dislike for how he says things, his actions after the election have improved the lives of many Americans, not least among them the black community.

As Mr. Trump asked us: What do we have to lose except for high crime rates, poor school conditions, and high dropout and illiteracy rates? What do we have to lose except for neighborhoods that have become shooting galleries and havens for some of the most debauched minds, high unemployment, and low homeownership rates? What do we have to lose except for our young men to drugs, gangs, and the grave? What do we have to lose except for our young daughters ending up as single moms dependent on welfare or walking the streets in search of a john?

Sound ominous? It is and worse.

THE OMINOUS BY-PRODUCT OF DEMOCRAT POLICIES: FATHERLESS HOMES

Dr. Martin Luther King Jr. accurately proclaimed, "Nothing is so much needed as a secure family life for a people to pull themselves out of poverty."

Nothing brings greater security to a family than having one father and one mother in a committed and married relationship. Can you imagine what would happen in black communities if we raised our children in stable, loving families where dads modeled leadership and responsibility to their sons? This alone could dramatically prevent much of the desolation we find rampant in cities such as Chicago, Baltimore, and Washington, DC. This alone would eradicate so many of our problems in the black community. It would significantly curtail the family instability, inadequate housing, and food insecurity felt by many in the inner cities.

The family is the bedrock of any society. The strength of a nation is equal to the strength of its families. Weaken the family unit and you weaken the linchpin that holds society together. History tells us that one man and one woman coming together to create and nurture a family is vital to any society. Too many of any other kind of family unit weakens it all.

Let's consider some statistics: economically speaking, 34 percent of single mothers raising a family live at or below the poverty line compared to only 6 percent of married-couple households living below poverty level.[2] In 2017, 58 percent of all poor children lived in families headed by a single mother.[3] Undeniably, marriage is associated with wealth, attaining a higher education, homeownership, personal security, and stability.

Socially speaking, kids growing up in a fatherless household are more likely to be physically and emotionally abused. They're more likely to use drugs, smoke, engage in underage drinking, become sexually active, perform poorly in school, and behave more aggressively.

According to the National Fatherhood Initiative, 60 percent of rapists, 72 percent of adolescent murderers, and 70 percent of long-term prison inmates are men who grew up without a father in the home.[4]

Still in doubt? Consider that according to the US Department of Health and Human Services (USDHHS), 90 percent of homeless and runaway children are from fatherless homes, 71 percent of pregnant teenagers lack a father, and 75 percent of adolescent patients in chemical abuse centers come from fatherless homes.

According to the US Department of Justice, 45 percent of drug abusing or dependent state prisoners lived in single-parent households while growing up.[5] A 2017 report shows that 89 percent of youth in custody in the juvenile justice system grew up in a mother-only household.[6] According to USDHHS, a fatherless child is twice as likely to drop out of high school, twice as likely to end up in jail, and four times more likely to need help for emotional or behavioral problems compared to a child who grew up with a father in the home.

The statistics tell us 63 percent of youth suicides are from fatherless homes, and 71 percent of high school dropouts come from fatherless homes.[7]

Houston, I believe we have a problem.

These statements aren't merely my opinion or a figment of my imagination. They are facts. Former president Obama himself said that "a child who grows up without a father is 20 percent more likely to have a run-in with the law."[8]

His acute awareness of this was just another reason I was sorely disappointed with his presidency. He grew up in a fatherless household but was able to attain the most coveted, influential, and powerful seat in the world—the US presidency. What a platform he had to share with millions of young black boys on how to beat the odds. What a tremendous megaphone he had at his disposal to speak on the importance of getting an education, speaking fluent English (not Ebonics), networking with influencers who may not look like you, making a difference in your community by getting involved in constructive ways, staying clear of the prison system, learning and practicing the unwritten rules of common behaviors in our society, getting married to one woman, and raising your own children with her.

I don't recall a time he had this frank and open conversation without disguise, without subterfuge, without an agenda to demean the United States in the process. I don't recall a time he spoke plainly to those who suffer the most from the exact same upbringing he endured.

The fatherless rate in our country is pandemic and does not just affect the black family. Fatherless homes are an increasing problem that transcends race, national origins, and socioeconomic status. Fatherless homes are not just a black issue; they're an American issue. We all have a stake in the America we're creating for our children and grandchildren. We're in the midst of a national epidemic—one that could prove fatal unless we're willing to take the medicine that will effect an adequate cure.

Though white families suffer from the wide-ranging consequences of fatherless homes as well, I believe no community of people is harmed more by this deadly virus than the black community. The depressing statistics aren't a source of pride. This isn't something we want to come in first at doing.

We're acutely struggling as a community in this area. What's more, this fatherless epidemic touches every other aspect of life. Not one aspect of our lives is left undisturbed by an absent father.

Black children are 55 percent more likely to live in a single-parent home than a white child (21 percent). In essence, one out of every two black kids we see is growing up in a fatherless home, compared to one out of five white kids, one out of three Hispanic kids, and one out of thirteen Asian kids. This is tragic on every level. Although fatherless homes affect every community, it's at an epidemic proportion in the black community. How in the world can we transcend such a widespread delinquency that's disproportionately larger in scope relative to other communities? It feels almost insurmountable.

Married-couple households make up approximately 80 percent of homes among whites and Asians. They make up 62 percent of Hispanic homes. But this bedrock institution only makes up 44 percent of black homes—less than half!

Family breakdown is the number one issue plaguing the black community. Not police brutality. Not racism. Not overprivileged white people. Not even lack of money. It's one man and one woman *not* committing to cast their lot together in raising up their own family. This is the black community's number one problem.

Because so many in the black community are running around chasing after every whiff of "racism," we haven't identified and catapulted this issue of reckless abandonment of the black father to the forefront in our nation. Without doing so, how can we ever hope to resolve it or direct resources to understand it? How can we find a solution to a problem if we refuse to identify the problem accurately?

This is just one more reason liberal policies are destroying America, specifically the black community. Because of their incessant spotlight on nebulous issues such as white privilege and toppling Confederate statues, we, as a nation, aren't focusing on the real problem: the epidemic fatherless rate within black communities.

Feminists in particular might protest placing so much importance on the father in the home. For many, perhaps the father is just the DNA donor and nothing more. But, the facts are in on this one, ladies.

Having grown up in a fatherless home, I can attest to the emotional, physical, and financial instabilities we dealt with as a family—my mother, myself, and two younger brothers. I remember the extreme lack once we moved away from our grandparents' home. I remember sitting in the dark because my mother couldn't afford to pay both the rent and the light bill. I remember the empty refrigerator. The worn hand-me-down clothing. The undone hair. Being left unattended because my mother couldn't afford a babysitter and she needed to go to work to support us.

My family and I played the hand we were dealt. We banded together. We got through it all. Because of the foundation of love, identity, and common respect for ourselves and others instilled in us by our grandparents, my brothers and I did more than just survive. In many ways, we've thrived. We often joke about how impressed we are with ourselves in making it out and beating so many odds that were stacked against us. But this isn't the preferred scenario, and it's not the most likely outcome. In this regard, my brothers and I are the outliers. Nevertheless, I bear some unseen scars. I did not exit my at times tumultuous childhood completely unscathed.

My mother and father separated when I was very young. He not only left our mother; he abandoned his children as well. Because of doting grandparents, memories from my early child-hood are happy ones. However, much like an iceberg, the deeper complications of not having a father in the home was not evident on the surface. One of the deepest unseen scars fatherless chil-dren must deal with is their lack of identity. The father, typically, gives us our last name. In this way, he not only tells the little girl who she is; he tells her *whose* she is. She belongs to somebody, she's valuable, and she's protected—three things I did not feel very strongly as a little girl.

If I had had a father, he would have looked at my little broth-ers and taught them how to defend what is theirs. He would have shown them how he worked a nine-to-five job and brought the entire paycheck home to his wife. These are bedrock things. These are the no-brainers in life. They're foundational in every way. Yet so many children are missing out on these rudimentary lessons that are more "caught" then "taught."

These fundamental teachings are being left untaught and "uncaught" in the black community. Consider for a moment the staggering effect on a group of people where 70 percent of black children are born to unmarried mothers.[9]

Now, couple my lack of personal identity because my father was absent with my lack of ethnic identity due to the effects of slavery and the severing of my heritage, and we begin to see why our black youth is in crisis mode today. Many do not know who they are. Our black fathers are AWOL on an endemic level. The black community is a broken community. The cornerstone of our community is the family, and the black father is missing in action.

When our families are broken and unstable, it's next to impossible to pull ourselves out of poverty. While liberal leaders charter buses to take us to statue-toppling rallies, or lead us to howl at the moon because we don't like our democratically elected president, or encourage us to resist law enforcement officers, our black families remain in such poverty that single-mother families are four times more likely to receive food assistance (38 percent) versus a married couple (9 percent).

While Democrat politicians continue to propose one policy or program after another that fails to meet its objectives, tends to stifle job growth, and often enables bad behavior, the black father still isn't at home, and the black community continues to be decimated by these failed social and economic positions. In fact, these liberal policies often remove the black man from the home.

Knowing the answer to the age-old riddle of which came first, the chicken or the egg is of no great importance. Knowing if social conditions must change before economic conditions change or the other way around is of the upmost importance—especially if your aim is to wage war on poverty. Much of the Democrats' war on poverty has focused on easing economic conditions—providing subsidies in various forms—rather than raising the bar of expectation in black communities, namely advocating marriage as opposed to normalizing the prevalent concept of the "baby mama" versus the wife. (In case you're wondering, the chicken came first.)

Because most liberals have rarely met a government program they didn't like, we have spent trillions of dollars on subsidizing homes, creating an endless stream of programs, childcare, pre-natal care, and the like with very little impact on stabilizing the black family. What most liberals don't understand is that family instability in the black community is not a peripheral issue. It is *the* issue.

Welfare, for instance, has aided in creating a generational cycle of the erroneous image of the "strong black woman," who is single and oftentimes dependent on government aid and whose children frequently have more than one father. Welfare policies of the 1960s, not racism or a lack of jobs or the legacy of slav-ery, is the cause of the dysfunction in black communities. Charles Murray, a political scientist and libertarian, in particular argued that welfare money provided a disincentive for marriage.[10] With all of its benevolence, the government effectively became the black woman's "sugar daddy." He (the government) pays the rent, pur-chases the food, picks up the medical expenses, covers the light bills, gives a phone, and pays for internet service. Each of the 2020 presidential candidates espouses some form of global educa-tion from pre-K through twelfth grade, universal childcare, and unlimited abortions—all paid for by a doting federal government. After all is said and done, what does a woman need a man for? One of the greatest incentives to marriage is financial security. Instead of marriage, however, we see generation after generation of black children growing up imitating what they've experienced at home—multiple baby daddies and no father in the home. Fam-ilies shape children's character. Burgess Owens wrote, "Marriage orients a man and a woman to not only commit to each other, but to plan for their future."[11] It's not out of the control of a black man to commit to one woman. Similarly, it's not out of the control of a black woman to wait until she's married to bear children. It's just that the bar of expectation has been lowered in the black community to such a point where debased behavior is expected, and to see a black person behaving otherwise is considered an anomaly. Plus, we have a prevalent liberal ideology that financially rewards such irresponsible behavior. Why am I calling out Democrat policies and spending so much time on the high fatherless rates within black communities? Because we must diagnosis the problem in order to solve it, and it's in the government's best interest to make policies that address these issues in order to provide stability for the nation.

For the exact same reason our government has gotten involved in making sure our kids are educated. As we moved into the Industrial Revolution, it became crystal clear that it was in the nation's best interest to make sure we have a population who can read, write, and do simple arithmetic. As much as most of us love our independence and don't want the government to infringe upon it, we have all been the beneficiaries of this specific awareness on the part of our government.

As we see the growing and troubling trends taking place within our cities, we find that once more it's in the government's best interest to make sure the family structure is stable and able to thrive, and that there are no untoward obstacles—especially obstacles put in place by the very government that claims to want to help us—standing in the way of this stability.

When we have more than one-third (36 percent)[12] of blacks living in urban areas and roughly 70 percent of both blacks and Hispanics living in cities and inner-ring suburbs[13] governed primarily by Democrats, you have to look at the policies impacting their lives. According to the Pew Research Center, "twice as many urban voters identify as Democrats or lean Democrat (62 percent) as affiliate with the GOP or lean Republican."[14] How is it that so few in the black community connect the dots between the types of politicians they elect and the quality of life they endure? These Democrat-controlled cities are rife with crime, lack of job opportunities, failing schools, poor or inadequate housing, and low homeownership rates.

The tenaciousness of racism during slavery and the Jim Crow era was easily identifiable to any honest observer as being responsible for the radical divisions in society during the late 1960s, effectively creating one society for the white man and another for the black man. The Kerner Commission examined the causes of civil unrest in black communities and delivered its conclusion to President Johnson. The report named "white racism"—leading to "pervasive discrimination in employment, education and housing"—as the culprit dividing the nation along color lines.[15]

Over fifty years later and after tremendous sacrifice on the part of all Americans to give the black community both liberty and equality, what has been most shocking to me in the case of black homeownership is that we have actually lost ground relative to whites and have not even improved much compared to blacks in 1968. How is this possible?

According to the Economic Policy Institute, "One of the most important forms of wealth for working and middle-class families is home equity. Yet, the share of black households that owned their own home remained virtually unchanged between 1968 (41.1 percent) and today (41.2 percent). Over the same period, homeownership for white households increased 5.2 percentage points to 71.1 percent, about 30 percentage points higher than the ownership rate for black households."[16] So, after all of this time the black community has not improved its situation much, specifically so in cities that tend to vote Democrat. Minneapolis has the nation's largest homeownership gap (50 percent) between whites who own a home (74.8 percent) and blacks (24.8 percent)[17]—a city that leans liberal based on recent voting in national elections, federal campaign contributions, and consumer personality profiles.[18] It is followed by Albany, New York, with a homeownership gap of 48.8 percent between whites (68.9 percent) and blacks (20.1 percent)— again, a city that is comfortably liberal. Buffalo, New York, has a gap of 44.5 percent between whites (73.4 percent) and blacks (28.9 percent)—again, a comfortably liberal-leaning city. Are you seeing the trends? We can go on and on and the results are the same. For instance, Salisbury, Maryland, and Bridgeport, Connecticut, both have a homeownership gap between whites and blacks exceeding 40 percent, and both lean liberal politically.

Furthermore, according to Bureau of Justice Statistics, the average violent crime rate in urban areas is about 74 percent higher than the rural rate of violent crime and 37 percent higher than the suburban rate. Urban males will experience violent victimization at rates 64 percent higher than the average combined suburban and rural male rate and 47 percent higher than urban females. Furthermore, property crimes are generally higher against urban homes than against suburban and rural homes.[19]

So, when then candidate Trump makes the claim that "inner cities run by the Democrats" are more dangerous than countries such as Iraq and Afghanistan, he's not far off. And here lies the appeal of President Trump—and other conservative candidates— to the black community.

Given the abysmal failures liberal policies have had on the black community and in light of Trump's proposal to fix what ails us specifically, we have to repeat his challenging question: What have we in the black community got to lose? Nothing except failing schools, soaring unemployment rates, crime-ridden streets, regentrification of our communities, more favorable treatment under the law for illegal aliens than for black people due to sanctuary status, overflowing prisons, and perhaps above all, fatherless homes.

As deeply rooted as the support among the black community has been for failing liberal politicians, so too are the tone-deaf "solutions" posed by liberal office seekers. Even now, as we listen to the many promises being made by prominent Democrats, they're forever focused on assisting every other community over and above the black community and only regurgitating big-government solutions to our inner-city problems.

How will their promise to decriminalize illegal border crossings help our black communities? How will elevating climate change to a national state of emergency help us? How will eliminating fossil fuels, which would surely be an effective chokehold on our economy, help us?

The bottom line is, we have everything to gain and nothing to lose by heeding Mr. Trump's admonitions.

What has been the result of President Trump's proactive support for black communities?

Black unemployment, as a whole, has steadily declined to its lowest rate in history under President Trump's direction. Moreover and perhaps more impressive, the recent surge of minority women gaining full-time and higher-wage jobs has helped push the US workforce across a historic threshold. "For the first time, most new hires of prime working age (25 to 54) are people of color. Minority hires overtook white hires."[20]

The good news continues with even the spread between white and black unemployment shrinking to its smallest spread on record.[21] This didn't happen under President Bill Clinton's eight years in office. It didn't happen under President George W. Bush nor under President Obama. It happened under President Trump. He promised to do just this, and he kept his promise. What more does someone have to do to get us to vote for our *own* best interest?

Specifically to the black community, he promised to address prison reform, and *he did*. He enacted the First Step Act, which is already proving to positively impact the lives of those who are incarcerated. He promised to revitalize urban areas by directing and creating an environment that encourages capital investments into these areas, and *he did*. He signed into law Opportunity Zones, which encourage billions of dollars of investment into economically depressed communities. He promised to stand with historically black colleges and universities, and *he did*. The Bipartisan Budget Act of 2018 made over $300 million available to issue a full forgiveness of the hurricane relief loans provided to four such institutions after Hurricanes Katrina and Rita struck the Gulf Coast in 2005.[22]

THE THREE TYPES OF REPUBLICANS

President Trump has proven to be an extraordinary man with amazing stamina and broad shoulders capable of carrying the weight of his office. Many of us saw this during the primaries. Some of us saw it sooner than others. I was, admittedly, late to the party.

For many of us who are labeled conservative, we are fully aware that all Republicans are *not* equal. One need look no further than the policies they support.

During the 2016 presidential primaries to select the Republican candidate who would represent the party in the general election against Democrat contender Hillary Clinton, three Republican presidential candidates stood out for more than just their individual platforms. To me, they represented much more than themselves. They represented the very clear divide within the party.

Senator Ted Cruz, businessman Donald Trump, and Governor John Kasich, the last three candidates standing at the end of the presidential primary season, were a model image of the three types of Republicans.

First, the Ted Cruz Republicans, aka the "Cruz-ers," are some of the more staunch conservatives. They're unwavering in their faith to country, family, and God. They consider themselves Constitutionalists. They believe America is the greatest nation that has ever existed because it was founded upon the greatest political document ever written—the US Constitution. They believe we are to be governed by law and not the whims of men.

For much of the presidential primary cycle, I was firmly a Cruz-er. How could I not be? He was definitely my choice. But then Trump exploded on to the scene.

Trump Republicans are those who are sick and tired of being sick and tired. They're sick of the lies. They're tired of the false promises. They're weary of compromising deeply held principles. They're disgusted by the brazen criminality seen throughout the ranks of political leadership and their friends who are on both Wall Street and K Street. They've become weary of those who say one thing in public only to turn tail and run in a completely different direction after the slightest pushback. They're annoyed by Republican leadership pandering to wealthy donors and placating the average voter. They believe their country has been hijacked by would-be global tyrants. They're repulsed by the attraction to socialism they see among otherwise reasonable people. They believed firmly that it would take a type-A personality to kick open doors and clean house. They're not interested in the home-bred politicians. They wanted something different. They wanted the brassy businessman, Donald Trump.

Last, there are the Kasich Republicans, the ones often called RINOs—Republican in Name Only. They are *not* true believers in conservative principles. They have a nodding acquaintance with conservatism and are not hard-pressed to champion conservative principles in the marketplace for the sake of votes. They're not particularly disturbed that those conservative principles aren't being reflected culturally, economically, or politically. At best, they will espouse conservative principles when it's convenient to do so—if all the stars are aligned, the majority is in the bag, and there is no major risk to them. If it's convenient and personally beneficial to be a conservative, then they are. But overwhelmingly, these are not your die-hard conservatives. They're the ones who make backroom deals that leave our border walls porous. They make a big show of angst in front of cameras, but make their tee time with progressive donors. Their choices are primarily selected through the finely tuned prism of "What's in it for me."

Most of the self-described Cruz-ers and Trumpers, without much goading, would agree that Kasich Republicans comprised much of the Republican leadership within the party before President Trump. In truth, they're often considered Democrats in disguise. Although they're Republicans, a vote for Hillary would have been a vote for them, too. A vote for Hillary would have been a vote to maintain the status quo and maintain their hard-earned power and control.

They have a very relaxed view of the 2016 Republican platform, which states, "the Constitution was written not as a flexible document, but as our enduring covenant." Similar to Hillary,

Obama, and the majority of Democrats, RINOs, too, see the Constitution as a "breathing document" to be interpreted and reinterpreted to fit their ever-changing agenda, though they'd never admit to this out loud.

We know this to be true based on how they folded like a lawn chair when President Obama decided to sidestep the Defense of Marriage Act because it didn't agree with his *evolving* view of how he saw the world—an act that was a federal law passed by the 104th US Congress and signed into law by President Bill Clinton.

We saw this every time the RINOs allowed Obama, with his phone and pen in hand, to circumvent the separation of powers so clearly outlined in the Constitution and bypass Congress to create laws through his use of executive orders—laws such as Deferred Action for Childhood Arrivals (DACA), an immigration policy that Obama created out of thin air that allows some individuals who were brought to the US illegally when they were children to receive a renewable two-year period of deferred action from deportation and become eligible for work permits.

These fence riders on conservative principles can often be seen grinning like Cheshire Cats during photo ops after signing one unfair trade deal after another that they allow to pass and stand. Trade deals and accords like the North American Free Trade Agreement (NAFTA; 1993), United States–China Relations Act (2000), the climate change accord struck in the Paris Agreement (2015), and the disastrous Trans-Pacific Partnership (TPP; 2015)—all of these agreements impose on American jobs and flood the American market with cheap goods, while other nations either restrict or close their markets to American products and cripple America's ability to compete because of currency manipulations or unfair trade practices.

The Kasich Republican is motivated by power and control.

They typically come before the American people with pseudo anger over topics they know we're concerned about, such as the budget, healthcare, and the Iran deal (at the time). Then, with very little provocation by the Democrats, they buckle. A few national parks are closed and these RINOs cave in. Obama tells them they can only see the details of the monumental Iran deal in a closed and monitored room, where they can't take any notes, and would have a time limit on how long they could stay in before being escorted out. They rolled their eyes, stomped their feet, and threw their hands up in despair, and then they *all* acquiesced. Where was the resistance we've now become so familiar with since Trump's been in office?

There's no wonder in my mind why career politicians like former House speaker turned lobbyist John Boehner, Senator Ben Sasse, and Senator Jeff Flake all came out strong against then candidate Trump. Truth be told, they preferred him as a donor. President? Absolutely not!

Trump represented a threat to their power and control. They knew Trump would disrupt them doing business as usual. Trump's type-A braggadocian personality wouldn't allow him to appease them or go along to get along. Unlike most politicians, Trump wasn't bought and paid for by big money donors during the election. He was beholden to no one. They knew he would do things his own way, thus making him a threat—a threat that couldn't be tolerated.

These Never Trumpers were never going to support Trump. They were just biding their time for the opportunity to come out en masse to reject him. But Trumpers were never swayed in the least by the Kasich Republicans' beating of their chests.

In all honesty, I was not a Trumper initially. With the likes of former governor Mike Huckabee, neurosurgeon Ben Carson, and

Senator Ted Cruz, there was no way on God's green Earth I was intending to vote for the television and business mogul. We had just too many "good" options to resort to voting for him. Out of sixteen presidential candidates, Donald Trump was number 16 on my preferred list.

Praise God for second chances. Though I didn't vote for Trump in the primaries, by the time the general election rolled around I was firmly on the first car of the Trump train. It dawned on me as it did for many of his enthusiastic supporters in Akron, Ohio: "What do I have to lose?"

I've lived under the Cruz Republican and the Kasich Republican before, and not much ever really changed in the black community. So what did I have to lose by casting my lot in with Trump? Although I might not have said some of the things he said or I might not have said it how he said it, I agreed with pretty much everything he said on the campaign trail. He was speaking my thoughts. It became apparent to me that voting for then candidate Trump was really voting for my own best interest—not just as an American, but for the black community as well.

The only thing most blacks have to lose in leaving the Democrat plantation is their pride over staying longer than they should have. We should have left the party a long time ago. We were duped. But it can stop today.

Accepting what Trump has done is so much bigger than the man himself. He is just the one filling in the position for now. In a few short years, yet another political cycle will unfold. Hopefully with each new cycle we'll see a continuing shift in how we see ourselves in the black community—and, accordingly, how we vote.

After all, we have nothing to lose, at this point, and everything to gain.

2.

LIVING OUTSIDE OF
THE LIBERAL BOX

To truly be free, we must not allow others to define who we
are by telling us who they think we should be or what we
should think . . . or how we should vote.

To be free, we must not allow ourselves to be pigeonholed—a
strategy that is most profoundly seen among political and social
liberals. This stereotyping that causes knee-jerk reactions, particularly among the Left, is seen almost daily in the news.

Let's consider a prominent example from 2019. In an encounter between a young white man wearing a MAGA hat and a Native
American leader, the news media led millions of Americans to
believe the young man was confronting the Native American, rid-
iculing him with a smirk. But really, what did this boy do that
equates to the supposed racism of the event? What did a child
do to cause the liberal world—plus some ill-informed conservatives—to descend upon him and his classmates in a vicious and
accusatory manner? To call for doxxing him?[1] To threaten expul-
sion from his school?[2] To virtue signal their higher morality? To

wish for their and their parents' death?[3] To receive threats of being burned alive and hopes of them being "sexually assaulted by the clergy members"?[4] How did the Native American man, who was beating his drum in the young boy's face, become the declared victim in this story with little investigation and with absolute certainty?

Surely these kids must have committed the most egregious of crimes to deserve such a universal demand for their complete ruination. Unquestionably, this group of young white boys violated some cardinal rule of some sort to justify such villainous treatment.

No, as it would turn out, their only crime was being white males wearing Make America Great Again paraphernalia while attending a Christian conservative event. Or, as the co-host of ABC's *The View* Joy Behar, in a brief moment of clarity, would reveal, the reason the media and others jumped on the story was "because we're desperate to get Trump out of office."[5]

How did this happen? How did arguably reasonable adults lose all reason? How did the media's attack so thoroughly saturate every nook and cranny of our lives that adults were calling for these kids to be punched, raped, and even murdered? How did the wild mischaracterization of what happened between a group of white boys and a Native American man spread so quickly?

The answer is boxes. More specifically, the boxes of identity politics. We have all been influenced to one degree or another by this dangerous predisposition to pigeonhole the ones we want to identify—whether we agree with them or not, to put them into easily identifiable boxes.

Not even the staunchest conservatives among us have been completely untouched by the notion of identity politics. We all have allowed ourselves to be put in boxes.

These kids were falsely placed in the box of the white male

identity as the reason for their encounter. These boys were thrown under the proverbial bus by their own Catholic Church, their hometown mayor, many parents, the media, politicians, conservatives, and liberals alike. Not one person stopped long enough to say, "Wait! These are kids!" Most just saw boxes—WHITE. MALE. NATIVE AMERICAN. End of story.

Nathan Phillips, the Native American man and arguably the real agitator in this story, is a minority. According to identity politics, because he is a minority, that makes him the *greater* victim and to be believed. Nick Sandmann, the eleventh grader with the uncomfortable smirk on his face, is white and male—thus the presumed aggressor. As if Nick's plight couldn't get any worse, he dared to wear a MAGA hat. Poor Nick. There was absolutely nothing he could have done to rescue himself. The cards were stacked against him from the start. According to identity politics, Nick is guilty of whatever the crime—facts be damned. He's white. He's a male. He likes Trump. Case closed.

THE STRATEGY

The Democrat strategist asks, "Red and Yellow, Black and White—who's *more* precious in God's sight? Who's more valuable? Who's more worthy?"

To whom I reply, "Who are you to ask such a ridiculous question?"

Yet the question still stands in our society. What's more, the answer to this question has become the chief cornerstone of the Democrat strategy in winning the hearts and minds of *select* Americans, on every single political issue:

- Voting laws
- Healthcare reform

- Law enforcement
- Immigration
- Minimum wage
- Terrorism
- ICE
- Taxes
- Abortion
- Gender politics
- Trade wars
- Education

Each of these issues—and more—is constantly run through a political rubric heavily weighted in favor of identity politics above what's simply right and wrong. The wind of Democrat support is dissected, divided, analyzed, and broken down based on the quintessential worth of every person at hand *at that particular time.*

For many politicians—specifically those belonging to the Democrat Party—and even to many bureaucrats, you are only as valuable as a particular trait you possess can be manipulated and controlled (e.g., skin color, sexual orientation, gender, religion, nation of origin).

Don't believe me?

Days before the 2014 midterm election, then First Lady Michelle Obama, speaking to a predominately black television audience on TV One, declared, "That's my message to voters, this isn't about Barack. It's not about the person on that ballot, it's about you, and for most of the people we are talking to [that is, black folks], a Democrat ticket is the clear ticket that we should be voting on regardless of who said what or did this, that shouldn't even come into the equation."[6]

In other words, black folks, shut your mouth and just vote

Democrat—no one needs to spend time trying to persuade you or trying to woo your vote; just line up and do what you're told.

The first African American First Lady then went on to joke with the host, Roland Martin, about black folks going out and eating some fried chicken[7] after they cast their ballot for the Democrat Party. She might as well have encouraged us to eat a slice of watermelon while we were at it. Had Donald Trump dared to utter such a racist trope, I can imagine people setting their hair on fire and running through glass pane windows in horror.

When has there ever been a time when we, as a nation, were told that it doesn't matter what a politician says or does? Or is it just for black folks that it doesn't matter how many promises have been broken or lies have been told to secure our vote? Is it only black people who are encouraged to check their brains outside the ballot box?

Well, I'm one black woman, among many, who patently disagrees with Michelle's assessment of my role in our constitutional republic. I reject her low opinion of the worth of my vote.

I am not a slave. I am not in a box. My vote is valuable. My vote deserves to be wooed and pursued with great vigor. My vote does not belong to any one specific party. I get to set the priority of my vote—not Michelle. As Oney Judge Staines, one of President George Washington's runaway slaves, remarked in an 1845 interview, "I am free now, and choose to remain so."

It's important for us all—especially the black community—to be reminded that not all overseers on the slave plantation were white. There were also black overseers they called drivers. Their job was the same as the white overseer—that is, to keep black folks toeing the line.

Yes, I'm black. But I'm not a Democrat. I'm more than the sum of my individual parts. Conservative. Veteran. Woman. Christian.

Black. Suburban. Middle class. Impoverished beginnings. Hail from the Deep South. College educated. Fatherless child. Wife and mother. Each is a part of who I am. Each contributes to my makeup. But not one, alone, tells you who I am.

This truth applies not only to the black community. It's equally true for each box labeled by the Democrat Party. It's true for the box labeled SEXUAL ORIENTATION. It applies to the box marked IMMIGRANT. It affects the container stamped FEMALE. POOR. PRIVILEGED. WHITE. JEWISH. COLLEGE EDUCATED. SUBUR-BAN. INNER CITY.

How did we become boxes on a political scorecard that's often used to manipulate our votes rather than shape policies that positively impact all Americans? This is the $50 million question.

My babies grew up reading Dr. Seuss's books and singing his songs. I can still see them running through the house reciting his funny little pithy sayings. None was truer and more packed with wisdom than his adage that went, "Today you are You! That is truer than true! There is no one alive who is You-er than You!"[8]

We have lost our personal identity in this political whirlwind of a culture we live in today. I'm conservative. I'm liberal. I'm a Republican. I'm a Libertarian.

No! Dr. Seuss had it right. I am *me*. You are *you*. We are more than political pawns. We don't belong in boxes. We are Americans. We are mothers, brothers, fathers, and sisters. We are rich, poor, and in between. Above all, we get to chart our own course in life, which is a rare privilege not shared by most in this world.

The right of self-determination is a powerful concept our Founding Fathers knew well. This was the one defining idea that separated America from every other nation: the idea that Americans get to decide how they will live their lives—not politicians, not bureaucrats, not even kings and queens. Instead, the idea was formulated that we, the people, elect from our peers, representatives who legislate in ways that allow us to live out our lives the way we see fit.

But stop and consider just how far we've fallen from what the Founders first believed. Americans, today, are tenderly being led by the nose as asses are[9] led to the slaughter by means of identity politics. The incessant categorizing and labeling of people may help the political strategist to whip up emotions and rally those who gladly wear the "victim" button. But in so doing, they're deepening the divide between Americans. Categorizing people dehumanizes us all. Each of us is more than the color of our collective skin or our education level or where we worship.

Divisive labeling is an attempt to diminish my voice, my vote, my vision as to who I am and how I want to live my life. It does that to all who fall prey to the deceptive voices undermining our true identity.

One of those deceptive voices is the *New York Times*. They, too, have fallen prey to liberal ideology. Their 1619 Project, which claimed to observe the four hundredth anniversary of the beginning of slavery in America, is actually a ruse to rewrite America's history in order to substantiate their wild-eyed position of control over how we think about ourselves as blacks and as Americans. According to the project, the beginning of American history is not 1776, but 1619, when American slavery began. As economist and syndicated columnist Walter Williams—a black man—explains, "it aims to reframe American history so that slavery and the contributions of black Americans explain who we are as a nation."[10]

If the *New York Times*' little pet project is correct, then who are we as Americans? Why do we salute the American flag? Why can I not sit through one rendition of our national anthem and not cry? If America was formed simply for our Founding Fathers to have a place where they could conduct acts of slavery undisturbed and not for some noble or altruistic purpose—say, freedom—then who are we? And if the *New York Times* is the first publication to make this claim in such an official way and we buy into this twisted way of viewing our world, then they win the right to tell us how we should now think about other issues they deem worthy of revision.

In a leaked town hall meeting, a reporter from the *New York Times* asked the executive editor, Dean Baquet, why the *Times* doesn't integrate the message of the 1619 Project into every single subject the paper covers, declaring, "I'm wondering to what extent you think that the fact of racism and white supremacy being sort of the foundation of this country should play into our reporting . . . *I just feel like racism is in everything* [emphasis added]. It should be considered in our science reporting, in our culture reporting, in our national reporting. And so, to me, it's less about the individual instances of racism, and sort of how we're thinking about racism and white supremacy as the foundation of all of the systems in the country."[11]

One of our foremost media outlets has now taken the lead in indoctrinating the public through the falsification of the history of this country. This reporter's question isn't far off base. If you follow the rhetoric of the Left, this is the natural conclusion: "racism is in everything."

There are some people who automatically think they know all about me when I walk into a room because of what they see. Without knowing my name or even saying hello, there are many who think they can look at the color of my skin and immediately know who I voted for in the last presidential election. Because I'm a woman they assume I voted for Hillary Clinton. But because I'm a woman and did *not* vote for Hillary Clinton, Michelle Obama assumed I voted against my own voice.[12] Michelle Obama, speaking on CNN, said any woman who votes against Hillary is voting against her own voice. Because I wear a cross on my lapel, some may call me narrow-minded. Because I had an impoverished childhood in the Deep South, some assume I couldn't possibly have become successful through my own efforts and the God-given opportunities that have come my way. They may not believe I was able to achieve a measure of success without money from the government in the form of some sort of handout.

To be honest, I actually understand why some people would look at me and wrongly assume they know my political, religious, and cultural beliefs. I understand that they think because I'm black, there is an 85 percent chance I would be a Democrat.

And once upon a time I was—but I grew up and put away childish thinking. Childish thinking such as "If you're black, you must be a Democrat or else you're betraying your race." Or childish thinking like "Only racists are Republicans." Or, the most childish thinking of all, "The Democrat Party represents me," even though there is absolutely no visible proof that their progressive policies positively impact our lives. On the contrary, many of their policies and tactics have hurt black communities.

THE BLACK LIVES MATTER MOVEMENT

Take for example the rise of the Black Lives Matter (BLM) movement. The Democrat Party created the environment from which that movement emerged. Once on the scene, it was the Democrat Party that continuously fanned its flames, giving it oxygen, finding stories for it to exploit, and then, with the help of a complicit media, plastered those stories all over the evening news.

In its infancy, when it first reared its ugly head, before we all knew much about its origin, leaders, or agenda, one thing was clear to me. I remember the night when I rolled over in bed, looked my husband in the eyes, and said, "BLM is going to get you and our black son shot."

I meant it then, and I mean it now. BLM has done nothing to shine a light on the real plight threatening to destroy the black community. Where are the marches to combat the devastating effects of the high fatherless rate that's ravishing black communities—seven out of ten black children growing up fatherless? Where are the riots in the street for illegal immigrants moving into already at-risk communities, sucking up limited resources, receiving more favorable treatment under the law than the black citizens who live there, and stirring up even more violence?

And where is the unrest over Planned Parenthood facilities that are strategically placed in black communities, annihilating our little black boys and girls? For every 1,000 black babies born, 477 are murdered in their mother's womb. That's a 32 percent kill rate. Lynching has nothing on Planned Parenthood! Where is the outrage? Where are the demonstrations? Where is the revolt against the Democrat Party, which not only sanctions Planned Parenthood but funds it, applauds it, honors its racist founder, and goes out stumping for it?

In a 2009 *New York Times Magazine* interview, Supreme Court Justice Ruth Bader Ginsburg discussed her surprise over the court's 1980 decision to uphold the Hyde Amendment, which bans federal funding for abortion. Either candidly or unwittingly, she revealed her understanding of the purpose of *Roe v. Wade* and the mission of organizations like Planned Parenthood. She stated, "Frankly, I had thought that at the time *Roe* was decided, there was concern about population growth and particularly growth in populations that *we don't want to have too many of.* [emphasis added] So that Roe was going to be then set up for Medicaid funding of abortion."[13]

Wow! Consider this for a moment. Don't allow yourself to pass over it too quickly. Justice Ginsburg is no ordinary citizen. She cofounded the ACLU's Women's Rights Project. She is the woman displayed on a 2015 *Time* magazine cover as one of "The Icons."[14] She has been credited by *Glamour* magazine "for making the law of this country work for women.[15] She was heralded by the *New Republic* as an "American Hero."[16] She was swooned over by *Atlantic* magazine as the "American ideal of power and authority for millions of women and girls."[17] And her life story has been told in a 2018 documentary titled *RBG* as having an "exceptional life and career . . . becoming an unexpected pop culture icon"—a documentary that went on to be nominated for two Oscars.[18] She is a force to be reckoned with. When she speaks, we should listen.

Yet, her understanding of the purpose of *Roe v. Wade* doesn't seem to mirror what we consistently hear from pro-choice advocates today, does it? Today, we're reminded nonstop that the decision emanating from *Roe* was to secure a *woman's choice*. But Justice Ginsburg's remarks sounds like *Roe* was more for the control of those considered "undesirable," not merely a woman's choice to do with her body as she pleases.

Furthermore, notice her understanding of where the funding was going to come from to accomplish this depopulation— Medicaid, a program that "provides health coverage to low-income people."[19] In other words, poor people.

According to the Kaiser Family Foundation,[20] 21 percent of those enrolled in Medicaid are black, while 40 percent are white. However, this doesn't show just how much of the total black population is affected. In comparing the number of blacks on Medicaid relative to the total black population, we see that 36 percent of all black people in America are on Medicaid, as opposed to just 15 percent of the white population.[21]

You can begin to see the enormous impact on the black community that Justice Ginsburg's understanding of abortion and Planned Parenthood, an organization that has a 32 percent kill rate of black babies, has on it. The results have been devastating.

However, even after Justice Ginsburg's interview echoed the founder of Planned Parenthood's racist sentiment to control the population of the "undesireables," so-called black leaders continue to support the organization as if nothing has been spoken. Even after Justice Ginsburg gave a twenty-first-century voice to the organization's historical intent, movements like BLM continues to collaborate with the organization.[22]

But if BLM really cares about black lives, why are their resources and tools on Planned Parenthood's website for those who intend to "mobilize students and local communities through dialogue" about the past, present, and future of black people?[23] Really?

Instead of tearing down statues of Robert E. Lee, BLM should instead concern themselves with the inordinate number of blacks living in inner cities. Toppling Confederate statues does nothing to improve my life today, nor does the presence of those statues do anything to impede my life. Neither will tearing down Robert E. Lee's statue do anything to improve the lives of the overwhelming number of black people living under conditions the elitist mainstream media and liberal politicians would never find themselves in.

If BLM really cared about black lives, they would focus on why the majority of black people live in some of the worst conditions and why these areas are all run by Democrats. BLM, in their effort to reduce what they call the pandemic of police brutality, would do well to focus on the Democrat leaders who have represented these dilapidated inner cities for decades and, instead of making improvements, they have watched conditions only get worse. The late representative Elijah Cummings comes to mind.

What have we black folks received from giving the Democrat Party our loyalty at a voting rate as high as 90 percent at times? Our schools are still some of the worst schools in the nation, our communities are some of the deadliest in the nation, and our black children are being gunned down by black thugs, while others are ripped from their black mother's bellies by abortions at an alarming rate.

In light of all this, are we just supposed to keep our mouths shut and continue to vote Democrat, as First Lady Michelle Obama alluded to? Should we just adopt the false narrative that our plight is all the "white man's" fault? Should we believe that all policemen are power-hungry and eager to gun down black men although the stats don't support such a narrative? In light of what we know and what many are experiencing in their own lives, should we believe that voting Democrat will solve all of our problems? We have supported the Democrat Party for the past five decades. How many more decades are we willing to gamble away?

Some may wrongly assume that the false narrative that because I'm black, I must vote Democrat, is pushed and peddled by mostly white people alone. But in reality, the false narratives are thrusted upon us and forever perpetuated by so-called black leaders in our community as well. You know of whom I'm speaking—Al Sharpton, Jesse Jackson, Oprah Winfrey, Barack and Michelle Obama, Maxine Waters, Marc Lamont Hill, John Lewis, Jay-Z, and so many more who would keep us in lockstep with failing liberalism. What these purveyors of division are peddling is the racist belief that all blacks are the same—that we are all undifferentiated black souls.

One thing is for sure: America isn't perfect. She has many problems. But she is our home—home to all of us. Like those who came before us, it's high time that we who believe in the power of the individual over the power of the state begin to fight for a destiny for our children that's greater than our own. We can start by denouncing and renouncing identity politics. We must get out of the box of liberal expectations if we want to keep our freedom and achieve our own personal greatness.

Old white men from long ago affirmed what seemed apparent to them when they declared "all men are created equal . . . and endowed with certain unalienable rights," rights incapable of being alienated or sold and transferred to another.[24] These same words were used to free millions of people from the bondage of slavery less than a century later. In short, those old white men of long ago believed in the *individual* human worth.

Being black and a proud American isn't an oxymoron and doesn't make me an outlier. At one point, I must admit, it was somewhat comical to enter into any political discussion when I knew people would assume, based on my appearance, that they knew exactly what I was going to say or on which side of the political ideology I would align. They would be utterly shocked and knocked onto their proverbial heels once I opened my mouth.

In today's cantankerous political environment, it's no longer humorous. It's deadly serious. It's either willful ignorance we must deal with or something much more sinister. The categorizing of people into boxes as though herding cattle is both wrong and manipulative. Yet it has proven to be an effective tool in the hands of those bent on leading the rest of us by the nose and telling us what to think and how to vote. It works only because we allow it. It works because we all—black, white, yellow, brown—give it permission to work.

Yes, I'm black. Yes, the color of my skin has contributed significantly to who I am. But the color of my skin is not all there is to me. The black community is a microcosm of what Democrats—namely white liberals—are doing to the larger American community. The failed liberal policies that have been perfected in pillaging black communities are now spilling over into the larger American community—with the same results. Democrats promise to do exactly what they have done in the black community—ravish it, control it, define it, and exploit it.

I have stepped out of the box of identity politics. It started with knowing my true identity. Do you know your true identity? Or have you allowed yourself to be defined by the empty promises of politicians?

Your answer matters.

3.

I'M BLACK, BUT I'M NOT A DEMOCRAT

was born into the Democrat Party just as much as I was born into brown skin. For me, there was no distinction, no point of separation. There was never a time I recall deliberating my political options. Just as I had no thought of changing from brown skin to white skin, there was never a thought given to changing political parties, either. It just wasn't a consideration or conversation I ever remember having with anyone. I was a product of identity politics. I was securely in the "box" marked DEMOCRAT—worse yet, I didn't know why.

It's shocking to me now to recall that the idea of *not* being a Democrat never even presented itself as a possibility during my formative years. I was not hot nor cold. I was worse, I was indifferent. I'm black, therefore I must be a Democrat. Right?

Most assuredly, blacks know that as a community we are as diverse as a box of chocolates—pun intended. There are some light-colored ones. Some darker ones. Some smooth ones. And a few nuts in the bunch. All 30 million plus of us hail from divergent backgrounds, contrasting experiences, and varying socioeconomic factors. We're not all poor. We haven't all grown up without a father in the home. We don't all live in the hood. We don't all speak Ebonics fluently. We can't all dance. We don't all have bad credit, either. We are not all undifferentiated black souls, as some people may think.

The DNA of resiliency still flows through our collective bloodline. We've all inherited some degree of ingenuity. But we don't all see the world in the same exact way. We don't all have the same experiences. We're individuals. Some are more informed on political issues than others. Some are more liberal than others. Some are as pragmatic as an accountant with a pocket protector.

Given our stark differences, one should expect variances in how we vote as well. So why isn't that the case? Why do we overwhelmingly vote Democrat, as if there are no lines of demarcation among us, as if we're all one big homogeneous blob of cells acting as one?

I think part of the explanation is this notion many blacks have that America, as a whole, is not their own. Never formally tutored in the idea of alienation but instructed in it in countless subtle ways nevertheless, most blacks look around and see a majority white-occupied America. They see this daily in the corporate world, in education, banking, suburbia, most of the media, and most definitely in the Republican Party, and they deduce from this that America has no room for them, or at a minimum, they are merely second-class citizens. This is in stark contrast to the "big tent" slogan of the Democrat Party, where anyone and everyone is supposedly welcomed, embraced, and celebrated.

I think another reason the lines of demarcation that delineate how diverse we are as a people are often blurred is due to all of the energy propelling some of the false narratives that are swirling all around us. False narratives such as white privilege. False narratives like extreme and targeted police brutality against the black community. False narratives that the Republican Party and specifically President Trump is racist. All of the energy propelling these false narratives and perpetually thrusting them in our faces on a daily basis is a major distraction that often impedes the black community from considering the whole story. With all of the mayhem we see around us, we've lost sight of the fact that we are not *just* black. The color of our skin isn't all that defines us. Yes, I'm black. But I'm also an American.

Today, a black person admitting they don't vote at all barely raises an eyebrow. Being a black Democrat and not voting is equally tolerable. But outright leaving the Democrat Party is unthinkable. Worse yet, voting Republican is anathema. Telling other blacks you didn't vote for Barack Obama in either presidential election is akin to cursing your own skin.

The intolerance shown toward a black person who dares to make an autonomous vote, unencumbered by society's expectations, is driven by mainstream media, hammered by political pundits, and reinforced by convenient statistics. Blacks are at risk of being shunned by other black folks for noncompliance. If you're black, you must vote Democrat or risk becoming an outlier. Noncompliance is not allowed. Period. End of discussion.

Being black and voting Democrat are synonymous in many circles. It's like trying to split the unsplittable. That's why it's such a challenge for some blacks to fathom the idea that you can be black and *not* a Democrat. And it's not just blacks who think this way. Many whites also have a difficult time understanding why a black person wouldn't vote Democrat.

Recently I've seen numerous white political strategists balk over the idea of blacks not voting for a Democrat candidate. I've literally seen them offer up a snarky laugh at the suggestion. I've never once heard them provide a valid description of what the Democrat candidate will offer the black community that would obligate them to vote for him or her versus voting for President Trump, who has reduced black unemployment to its lowest rate in history in addition to finally bringing forward much-needed prison reform. Reports about the First Step Act say that blacks are benefiting overwhelmingly from the justice reform pushed by the Trump administration.[1] President Trump worked with Senator Tim Scott (who happens to be a black Republican) to add an incentive in the 2017 tax cut law that could direct as much as $100 billion dollars into designated Opportunity Zones, where the poverty levels are as high as 30 percent.[2] This measure is already working and proving it has the ability to turn the tide in economically depressed communities.[3] The political pundits prefer to ignore these facts and smugly throw out the assertion that blacks leaving the Democrat Party is too ridiculous of an idea to consider. These naysayers always seem so assured of themselves, never once considering just how insulting their wrong-headed assumptions are—as if my vote and I are securely in their back pocket.

Regardless of the party's policies, its agendas, its platform, its moral decline, or the lack of its community responsiveness, the encoded message is that if you're black, you must be a Democrat. To do, think, or say otherwise is to reject your own race. And that is unacceptable.

No other ethnicity in America has such a restrictive standard held over them in order to participate as a full member of their community as the black race. An almost unbendable rule is the requirement that you maintain your status in the Democrat Party—it doesn't matter if you vote or not. As a black person, your status as being a part of the Democrat Party is enough to maintain the unspoken but very real expectation of all blacks being a Democrat. It also serves to demonize any black person who dares to step off the Democrat plantation.

Whereas it may be profitable or even considered a compliment for a white person to reject their whiteness and claim to be black (e.g., Rachel Dolezal), it's the highest form of infidelity for a black person to even appear as though they're rejecting their *blackness*. Of course, a black conservative is in no way rejecting their ethnicity, but to their critics, their motivation is of no importance. The very idea is enough to warrant rejection, alienation, and the constant barrage of the commonly used labels of "coon," "Uncle Tom," "sellout," "house servant," and worse.

You think I'm exaggerating? During the 2016 general election, I lost all of my black friends save two of my dearest friends from high school—Candace and Tisa. Believe me when I say I felt alone and isolated. I can't count the number of tears I cried. I felt the weight of others' attempts to marginalize me—rolling their eyes when I walked into the room, their elevated sensitivity if I said anything amiss, their dismissive attitude, hushed whispers, and the not-so-quiet silent treatment. I felt it most acutely when their not-so-subtle snubs were also directed toward my two little ones. To this I often reminded myself of the conversation Booker T. Washington had with Frederick Douglass when he was forced, on account of his color, to ride in the baggage car of the train. When some of the white passengers went to console him one said, "I'm sorry, Mr. Douglass, that you have been degraded in this manner," to which he replied, "They cannot degrade Frederick Douglass. The soul that is within me no man can degrade. I am not the one that is being degraded on account of this treatment, but those who are inflicting it upon me."[4] Likewise, I came to realize I wasn't the one being marginalized when rejected by longstanding friends. It reflects more poorly on them than on me.

Although the rejection stung, I increasingly realized over time these people didn't hate me. As implausible as it may sound, they hated what I stood for—that is, the right to think and choose for myself. The ideas I represented and the change in thinking I was asking them to consider was intimidating to many, new to others, and a threat to the established order of some.

I love a quote frequently attributed to Harriet Tubman, the great Underground Railroad conductor and abolitionist: "I freed a thousand slaves. I could have freed a thousand more if only they knew they were slaves." Whether an accurate quote or wrongly attributed to her, it's true today within the black community. I've long understood that we don't know what we don't know. Instead of inquiring and wanting to know more, to be increasingly well informed, many people—not just blacks—have a knee-jerk reaction to balk at the unknown.

AMERICA'S HISTORY IS MY HISTORY, TOO

The city of Philadelphia is replete with one historical museum, trail, and storyline after another. Living right outside the birthplace of freedom and the Liberty Bell, I've visited many historical sites. In fact, during our first year after moving to Philly I often joked that my family and I overdosed on history. What an amazing place. It was in Carpenters' Hall that the first Continental Congress showed unity in their determination to defy Great Britain and declare their independence. It was in Independence Hall that our Founding Fathers convened to hammer out our Constitution, creating the first constitutional republic. Many slaves traveled to Philadelphia on the Underground Railroad to seek their freedom. I still can't get enough of visiting the Liberty Bell and hearing the same stories over and over again about the many attempts made to fix the crack in it, the same crack that now serves as a reminder that liberty isn't perfect and must be continually sought after by all people. Or stories about how General George Washington's men put up a valiant fight to recover the historical Cliveden mansion that had been overrun by the British. It's not just history. The trials, the wisdom learned, and the battles they overcame point to the way forward over our own hurdles as a nation.

Upon entering any of the historical residences of significant figures, a striking fact catches your attention immediately. The first room in each house has a massive library. Books lined the walls, often extending from the floor to the ceiling. During each tour, the docent would dutifully remind us that these great men read every single book on the wall. Great men (and women) are always consuming knowledge, acquiring it, using it, or packaging it to be sold.

I share—even though it may be on a much smaller scale—this insatiable need to be informed. So I'm always in a quandary when I meet people who don't know something that could be beneficial to their own well-being only to discover they don't *want* to know. They actually get mad if you try to impart information to them or try to convince them to think differently by providing clear facts that challenge their assumptions. It's not an overstatement to say I've met many people like this over the years. It's truly puzzling to see others willingly reject the opportunity to learn something that could drastically improve their lives.

While my friends' arrows were directed toward me, I wasn't their intended target. Their ad hominem attacks felt personal at the time and often were fashioned as such but were really designed to distract and detract from my message.

However, though these were my friends, when it came right down to it most of them didn't really know me—at least not as well as they should have. If they really knew me, they would know their words couldn't degrade me. How could they? I was a black conservative before being a black conservative was openly discussed in the black community. This was when being a black conservative was the equivalent of being a black unicorn—a mythical creature.

Thank God that although unicorns are a myth, black conservatives are not. Though still a minority—and considered an oxymoron—we are on the rise. Because of the tangible effort of President Trump and artists like Kanye West making black conservatism "cool" again, there is a quiet but ever-growing conservative movement among black Americans. This reality will surely catch some political pundits off guard. I just hope I'm somewhere in the room to see their smug grins dissipate. It's becoming more common to see a young black person openly and proudly speak about issues from a conservative, not liberal, viewpoint.

It's stunning to many to see a black person declare their respect and admiration for this great country. Challenging blacks' blind loyalty to the Democrat Party has rarely been done straight on. Those who did it were often sidelined by their limited platform compared to the overshadowing platforms of the Al Sharptons and Jesse Jacksons of the world, who have been generously catapulted into stardom and promoted by a complicit liberal culture.

It may seem surprising, but being shunned by some in the black community has had a positive effect on me. It's prompted me to seek out what it truly means to be black. It's led me to a better understanding of my place in America. It's taught me to move beyond *just* the color of my skin when adding up the sum of my worth—a lesson I believe all Americans can benefit from.

One of the most inescapable realities that's come into focus on this journey is the realization that America is just as much my *own* country as it is my fellow white American brothers' and sisters'. White America has no greater claim to this country than I have. Studying American history and embracing the roles my ancestors played in building this country has allowed me to walk into a higher degree of understanding about who I am—both as a black woman and as an American. I don't need to ask permission to occupy the space I'm in. Neither does any black person. I don't walk with hat in hand, begging to be admitted into the American Dream. I *am* the American Dream.

Think for a moment about the building of this country. If you're a black American descended from slaves, you, like me, have a huge stake in this country. Our ancestors shed blood and much sweat toiling for the country we live in today. Yes, it was unwilling servitude, but doesn't that make it all the more our duty to redeem their labors by taking advantage of the opportunities we now have? What does it say about our attitude toward their part in building America if we resort to the modern version of slavery under liberalism? I think it says we don't fully appreciate what they went through. For me, that's unacceptable. This way of thinking runs entirely opposite to what is espoused in the Democrat Party, specifically among black people. We're incessantly told that we're victims and that others (whites) have more privileges than us. As such, we're led to believe that we're inferior, and since we can't help our current state of being, we might as well not even try. This defeatist thinking has only brought hopelessness and despair to the black community—just enough hopelessness and despair to inevitably lead black voters to blind allegiance to political candidates who promise what they cannot deliver and make promises they have no intentions of fulfilling.

Why do we excuse such nonsense? Especially within black circles, they will vehemently defend the undefendable lack of response from their Democrat leadership. They make excuses justifying the contemptuous treatment they receive from the Democrat Party. They will sling personal attacks against a trusted friend in order to defend trash-lined streets or the shooting-gallery neighborhoods they live in. They know the liberal policies being espoused in no way benefit their community. Yet, they soldier on in their loyalty to the party.

Why they accept such scornful treatment is beyond my comprehension. It's sheer foolishness. But somehow we've convinced ourselves either that this is as good as it gets or that we don't deserve much more or even that we've made these elected politicians our gods. I believe we've forgotten that hope for the individual—black, white, or any other color—comes from within, realizing our true worth does not—and cannot—come from Washington, DC.

We're reminded from one political speech to the next, from one BLM protest to the next one, that all our problems stem from the white man and the white man's systems. We're told *they* are the ones victimizing us. We're continually given example after example of how past slavery still marginalizes us today.

Recently, I had a young black military officer who is in a loving marriage, has some of the most beautiful and happy little kids, and is also a homeowner lament to me about how he will never experience the American Dream because of the color of his skin. *Really?*

I inquired of him, "What do you think the American Dream is exactly?" His wife has chosen the wonderful occupation of staying at home to raise their young family, and they are both college educated. How is this *not* the American Dream? He had no meaningful response. In fact, he looked somewhat surprised that I asked him to explain what the American Dream is if what he had wasn't it.

His rationale runs counter to what most would intuitively expect. I believe most people would point to the circumstances of his life as an example of someone living the American Dream—

homeowner, military officer, intact family, and college educated. Having had the opportunity to travel to many parts of the world, I'm fairly confident I've met people along the way who would trade places with him in a New York minute.

Unfortunately for my young black friend, he can't see the forest for the trees. He can't see the wealth of opportunities he has inherited simply by being an American. He can't see them because of the false narrative that blacks are perpetual victims. Unfortunately, he's not alone in this. Most can't see what is right in front of them. Regrettably, they can't appreciate it, either.

I feel confident that this young man will come into the light. But many who share in his misguided way of thinking may never come out of the shadows of hopelessness. They may very well live a life of self-fulfilling prophecy of feeling as though they don't belong in America and that they are always on the outside looking in. They feel this way all because of a false victim mentality. Sadly, this mentality is too often passed down from the adults to the upcoming generation. And the cycle goes on.

MY JOURNEY OFF THE DEMOCRAT PLANTATION

I remember when I walked into the voting booth to cast my very first vote. I was so excited to finally take part in this wonderful rite of passage. I took it seriously. I studied the candidates. I researched the issues. But I didn't know what I didn't know. At the time I didn't know the odds had been stacked against me as I walked behind the curtain to cast my first vote. I didn't know about all of the unspoken subliminal messages that had penetrated my conscious perception along the way—namely, if you're black, you *must* vote Democrat. Regrettably, I wasn't weighing different ideas or feelings about which political party I would support. Sadly, I voted a straight Democrat ticket. I did so not because the Democrat candidates were particularly a better option. I did so because it was expected of me. Yes, I had studied the issues and the candidates, but I had done so through the eyes of the black community's expectations of me.

As I see it today, voting is a personal and intimate decision, right up there with spiritual decisions and the serious life-changing decision of selecting your future spouse. It's not just the pulling of a lever or the pushing of a button. It's so much more. It's peering into the future and saying *This is my contribution to society*—as an American and to the world.

Especially in these tumultuous times, voting is akin to literally shaping the world for the next generation. The outcome of the next election will decide if we have the right to secure our southern border as President Trump is presently doing or if we will decriminalize illegal border crossing as eight out of the ten 2020 Democrat presidential candidates pledged they would do. The latter option aligns perfectly with what Mexico's president, Andrés Manuel López Obrador, suggested, that America is not just for Americans but for migrants as well.[5] Voting for one party or the other will determine if we renew the disastrous Iran deal or if we continue to apply pressure on the number one state sponsor of terrorism.[6] Will China be allowed to continue to pollute our planet at record levels, create unfair market conditions by unfairly subsidizing state-backed companies, and steal innovations through forced transfers of proprietary technology, or not? Will we continue to engage North Korea head on, or will we resort to failed dark-curtain politics, thinking we can shut them out of the world stage and shame them into compliance? Will America become a socialist country with the complete government takeover of our healthcare, education, and job creation?[7] Our individual vote, no matter how anemic one may think it is, will decide these issues and so much more. All tallied up, our votes become a collective affirmation as we cast our lot and fate with one another.

This is what it means to vote. And this is why it's so astonishing to me that we, in the black community, ever voted over 90 percent for one political party. We are presently dealing with very weighty issues in the world. Are we really this unified in how we see them? Or do we need to reevaluate our personal priorities and vote accordingly?

Fortunately, the tide turned for me. While I was in college I had my first inclination to get involved in politics. I remember walking into some random Democrat campaign headquarters with the idea of volunteering. As I sat across from the candidate, it was then that I had my very first thought about whether or not we actually agreed on the issues. The thought was unplanned and caught me off guard. I remember not being able to exit his office fast enough. It was the first time I can recall ever thinking about my *own* personal convictions relative to a candidate's platform. That thought would linger for many years to come, from one political season to the next, until I could no longer ignore it.

Leaving the Democrat Party has caused me to realize I am no one's victim. More importantly, as part of the journey of leaving the Democrat Party, I have come into the full understanding that not only *can* I be both black and a proud American, but that *I am* both.

Today, I have no crisis of identity, only a growing awareness and appreciation for the opportunities before me. I contrast that awareness with the chains that were once on my ancestors' legs, arms, and neck, and realize that similar chains have now been placed on many black Americans' brains today. Frederick Douglass, reflecting on his fortunate circumstance of not being bequeathed to his cruel master's equally cruel and drunkard of a son, said that had circumstances been different he would not be seated by his own table, enjoying freedom in a happy home and writing his first book. Instead, he would have "been confined in the galling chains of slavery."[8] He would be distressed to know that today the chains still exist and are often self-inflicted.

But this isn't just a problem for black America. As Americans, all of our fates are intertwined. If my side of the boat goes down, your side will go down as well. The journey of a thousand steps begins with knowing who you are and holding on to it as tightly as you can.

A white woman pompously informed me once, "Kathy, you're black." "Yes, I am," I responded. Unperturbed, she continued to chastise me for supporting President Trump, because I'm black and, according to her, he's a racist. With a smile on my face, I calmly explained that I'm much more than the color of my skin. In fact, the color of my skin does not speak to my intelligence at all, nor does it tell anyone anything about the content of my character. It's only one of *many* aspects about me. It's not the *only* thing about me.

Because I'm black, I am expected by many in our culture to think a certain way, to act a certain way, and to vote a certain way. That, as I explain to my self-proclaimed "tolerant" white friend, is the very definition of "intolerance."

Though we are a tapestry of cultures, ways of thinking, ideologies, and languages, we are all being woven together into a single America. We are truly one. Being an American is just as much a part of my identity as my being black.

God had to go through a tremendous amount of work to get me here. But I made it, and I'm determined to live my life out loud and according to my own convictions. Like the Liberty Bell, our nation is imperfect. Freedom isn't perfect. It's messy at times. But it's for each of us to participate in it vigorously, rigorously, and with full autonomy.

It's in our *own* best interest to do so.

4.

WHAT DOES IT MEAN TO BE BLACK IN AMERICA?

Much time has passed since my formative years. The black culture has radically changed since then. It's become almost unrecognizable to me.

Here is the problem in a nutshell: There is a culture of poverty[1] that has spilled over from the ghettos of America and is now affecting the broader black culture. This pattern of behavior, way of thinking, felt experiences, and belief system that was once quarantined in pockets throughout inner cities is now being adopted by the larger black culture as their own identity—to their detriment and *our* detriment as a whole.

We see black businessmen in expensive suits living in multi-million-dollar mansions protesting inequality. It's not uncommon to see black, college-educated military officers and homeowners with stable families bemoaning how the effects of slavery continue to marginalize them and prevent them from the full realization of the American Dream. We see black sports and entertainment stars behaving badly, becoming role models of who our children should *not* become. We see black Americans identifying with someone living a "thug life," notwithstanding the fact that they have never even been to the hood before and don't know even one "thug" by name.

This culture of poverty permeating the black community can't be enumerated in dollars and cents alone; it must also be measured in terms of lack and absence.

The lack is partly one of a clear vision of what *could* be. The absence is one of not understanding what has been lost. The concept of village—even community—is gone or on life support at best. Black America is floundering as a people. We're running to and fro from one hyperbolic factless agenda to another—toppling Confederate statues, kneeling during the National Anthem, rallying for and identifying with repeat criminal offenders, and shaming top-tier black athletes to forgo the advantageous opportunities they've earned to attend top-tier universities just because they happen to be predominately white. Instead, they're encouraged to attend historically black universities *solely* because those schools are predominately black. Yet none of these activities strengthen our community, none of them move us out of generational poverty or put our children into thriving circumstances—and perhaps most tragic, none restore our broken families.

Why are black Americans, as a rule, circling the wagons around some of the most debased ethics imaginable? Why are we so defensive about attitudes and behaviors that our predecessors would have covered their heads in shame over?

Why have we allowed the basest among us to define the black experience? We've taken on some of the most reckless and reprehensible attributes of humanity and displayed them as our own. We've been reduced to a people often characterized by a culture of saggy pants, crime-ridden communities, low-performing schools, broken English, rap music, pot smoking, and vulgarity-slinging loudmouths with chips on our shoulders.

If you think I'm exaggerating, close your eyes and think back for a moment. During her 2016 presidential campaign, who did then candidate Hillary Clinton bring to the stage in Cleveland, Ohio, to help her connect with her young audience—a city with a black population of roughly 51 percent?[2] Who did she trot onto the national stage to show just how hip she is, to demonstrate how connected she is to what's plaguing our society, and to express how *down* she is for the people? Jay-Z![3] Beyoncé! Chance the Rapper!

Jay-Z is a multimillionaire who has won his fortune by concocting and bundling up some of the vilest sentences, labeling them as rap music, and displaying it as his experience of the black community.

He strolled out onto Hillary's campaign stage before the nation, an audience filled with black people, and repeatedly used the N-word! Hey, Jay-Z, *I'm* black. What does throwing around the N-word on stage at that political rally have to do with *my* vote? It's reprehensible that someone would think this was a great idea to introduce during a pivotal campaign to get out the vote just two days before the general election. It's reprehensible that the larger black community just grinned, did a jig, and came alongside this foolishness. But it's also revealing in how we think about ourselves as a black community and what others think about us as well.

I'm an earnest believer that we teach people how to treat us. What have we taught a significant segment of our political class about who we are that would allow Hillary to think it was a fantastic idea to trot out something as demeaning as a rap concert in order to woo *our* vote? When she visited her Wall Street friends, did she offer them a rap concert? How about tickets to see Celine Dion perform? No! She came before them with logic and concrete promises. It's insufferable, at times, to stop and consider other people's opinions about the black community. Often we're viewed with such contempt and, unfortunately, not always unwarranted.

We in the black community must first value ourselves before we can demand that others assign some higher worth to us. We must demand more by voting our convictions and not solely relying on words to express our worth.

Clearly Hillary knew of the great lack and struggle in the Cleveland area. Surely she knew that the area near Cleveland State University, where the free concert was held, is approximately 70 percent black, while the state of Ohio is roughly 80 percent white. Certainly she knew that the people her multimillionaire guests were gyrating in front of live under a poverty rate that is almost five times (65 percent) that of the national average of 13 percent.[4] Unquestionably she knew the unemployment rate of those living in this area is almost 1.5 times (6 percent) that of the state of Ohio (4 percent). Without a doubt her research showed her that the fatherless rate is at an epidemic level in this community. Female heads of households with no husband present are a staggering 48 percent versus the national and state average of roughly 17 percent. Consider the ramifications of this for a moment. Almost half of the homes in Cleveland's 44115 zip code are fatherless. How do you overcome this? With a rap concert? I don't think so.

Given all that she or her aides undoubtedly knew, how in the world did they decide to have a concert where the N-word was slung around like water from a leaky faucet? How could that possibly offer hope to improve the lives she wanted to connect with and get out to vote for her? In short, it didn't.

Unfortunately, there's an intense and swift aversion toward anyone who veers off script and shines a spotlight on the deplorable behavior of politicians like Hillary Clinton. But as a black woman raising black children and hailing from a black family, I have a personal stake in how the black community fares in this nation. I have a vested interest in the rise or fall of the American black community. My children will inherit what I leave behind. Although this is often a difficult conversation to have, loaded with the usual landmines scattered indiscriminately around, it's a conversation we must have. The black community is in deep trouble. I fear we cannot survive this level of foolishness from our elected representatives much longer. But they have no impetus to change if we don't change how we view ourselves.

A journey of a thousand miles starts with us knowing who we are. Since the color of our skin seems to be so primal to most, it behooves us to know what it means to be black and to pass this learning on to the next generation.

COLOR, CONSCIOUSNESS, CULTURE

I often take my young children back to that small rural town in Alabama where I grew up. Once I asked our local country sage, "What does it mean to be black?" His answer startled me for a moment in both its simplicity and sophistication. He wisely answered that being black can be defined as "color, consciousness, and culture."

Color in that to be black, you must share the darker pigmentation. Although even this basic definition of being black has been misappropriated previously by people like former MSNBC host Melissa Harris-Perry and Rachel Dolezal, the former NAACP chapter president who resigned after she, a white woman, was accused of pretending to be black.

On her show, Harris-Perry inquired, "Is it possible that she might actually be black?"[5] This, even though both of Dolezal's biological parents are white. Even throughout this hyperbolic media-frenzied story, we discovered that with many people it's not enough to *just* identify as being black but that you must genetically be so as well.

Consciousness is the state of being aware, of being awake, of knowing what's happening around you. Or, as liberals like to say, "being woke."

Due to all the energy behind the BLM movement, NFL players kneeling, the false narrative that the Republican Party is racist, we've become distracted. The net result is that the black community isn't *awake*. We have fallen asleep at the wheel. As a community we aren't focusing on what really matters.

Yes, I'm a part of the black community. But I'm also an American. W. E. B. Du Bois talked about the two souls or the double consciousness of the black person in his classic book *The Souls of Black Folk*. Du Bois wrote this book just forty years removed from the Emancipation Proclamation.

As assistant labor secretary Daniel Patrick Moynihan, under President Lyndon B. Johnson, put it, "Lincoln freed the slaves. But, they were given liberty, not equality. Their continued fight has been for equality."[6]

Imagine if you can, that yesterday you were a slave, and today you're told you're free. What does that mean? For many, it meant being tossed off their owner's plantation and expected to stand on their own two feet—the same two feet that previously belonged to their white master. You're now expected to compete with your white counterparts as equals. But how can you? You don't even speak the language well. You have no wealth, no property, no education, no self-identity—you don't even have your own last name, and in some eyes you're not even fully human.

In the making of our identity, part of us is claimed by our country, part by our parents, and part by our friends.[7] But not for the slave. His country has never really accepted him as its equal. His mother was sold years ago. And his friend has no more to offer him than a pebble in his shoe—a constant source of frustration.

If you can imagine that, you can begin to understand what Du Bois meant when he referenced the black man's experience in America as a two-ness of souls. "This double-consciousness, this sense of always looking at one's self through the eyes of others, of measuring one's soul by the tape of a world that looks on in amused contempt and pity. One ever feels this twoness—an American, a Negro; two souls, two thoughts, two unreconciled strivings; two warring ideals in one dark body."[8]

He goes on to say that the black man "would not Africanize America, for America has too much to teach the world and Africa. He would not bleach his Negro soul blood in a flood of white Americanism, for he knows the Negro blood has a message for the world. He simply wishes to make it possible for a man to be both a Negro and an American."

It's unfortunate that still today we're contending with these rudimentary precepts. This warring within the soul is just as much foisted upon black people by other black people, as it is by the larger society and their unreasonable expectations that black people should act a certain way and vote a certain way. It's shameful that after over one hundred years we're still contending with the concept of equality.

As both a member of the black community and an American, it's repulsive to think that I must choose between the two. Yet to many, I must choose to either be proudly black or proudly American. To claim both is anathema, or to be censured, at least, by a whole swath of society.

Sorry, but I would find it hypocritical to cling to my blackness and yet disparage and mock everything American, while at the same time enjoying as many of the fruits of being a citizen of America. Likewise, I would find it more than strange to see someone deny the fact that they are black and *just* an American.

None of this suggests that racism doesn't exist or doesn't matter. It *does*. None of this suggests there isn't a distribution problem in the number of black Americans occupying senior positions. We still have way too many "firsts" in our community in this day and age, and we still have "only one" of us sprinkled scantily here and there throughout corporate America, the media, and politics.

I remember being the first black person to work at Bank of America Capital Asset Management out of the St. Louis office a couple of years after I graduated from college. I remember feeling the weight of the black community riding on my shoulders, thinking that if I messed up, they would probably never hire another black person again. Whether that's true or not is of little consequence to the one carrying the burden.

I also remember thinking that I wasn't old enough to be the first black person doing anything today in America. Yet this is a constant reality even today—a reality that's changing, but it must be encouraged to continue to change.

I'm not suggesting we pretend to be blind to the realities that surround us. Instead, what I'm suggesting is that we take a "now what" attitude. Someone is mean to you? Okay, now what? Someone appears to be a racist? Okay, now what? Someone is actively trying to limit your upward mobility in the office? Okay, now what?

Taking a "now what" attitude has the potential to propel us in taking personal responsibility for our own lives and the lives of our fellow brothers and sisters and forcing us to continue moving forward. I don't have time to wallow in adverse circumstances and lick my proverbial wounds if I'm constantly thinking, *Now what should I do?* We can't control other people, but we can control ourselves, our thoughts, our behaviors, and what we decide to do next. But to do this will mean taking the spotlight that's still shining squarely on slavery and instead shine some of that light onto our present and future conditions. We can't move forward by keeping our eyes fixed on the rearview mirror.

It will also require that we stop being jealous of each other within the black community. We often act like crabs in a bucket, constantly pulling the other down. Jealousy is the lowest common denominator of emotions. Instead of asking how a successful friend came up and out of a dire situation or how she prevailed over insurmountable odds, black folks have a tendency to not ask. Instead, they choose to malign the one who shows any signs of autonomy.

I've learned many things along the way. One is that you cannot be black and conservative or show any outward signs of appreciating President Trump while having thin skin, too. You must toughen up. I've also learned that it's easier to stand in the crowd than it is to step out and be yourself. I'm just not built to blend in that way.

America, though imperfect, still remains the consummate light on the hill for all nations who look to her for direction, hope, and dignity. During my ten years in the military, I pledged my life, and I continue to pledge my life today to keeping that light aflame for the next generation. Encouraging apathy, disdain, and disrespect for our nation actually undermines the future of the black community—actually every community, but especially those communities already at risk and vulnerable. Encouraging our children to disrespect police officers will not work in their favor. Coming alongside white liberals and joining them as they malign the only president since Abraham Lincoln to work so diligently in righting the wrongs committed against our community is sheer stupidity. We've demanded for years that someone engage prison reform in a way that meaningfully impacts the black community. President Trump has. We've demanded for decades that our politicians bring thriving businesses and investments into our poverty-stricken communities. Championing measures such as the Opportunity Zones that directs billions of dollars specifically into communities where the poverty rate is in excess of 30 percent, Trump is proving that he heard us and is responding. Since the time our nation started recording unemployment numbers, we've pointed to the unemployment gap between white people and black people as proof positive that white racism exists. President Trump's economic measures are having a positive impact on reducing that gap for the first time. When we sit and consider all of these things and more, how does it benefit our community to rail against this president? How does it move us up and forward by attacking him with harsh, often insulting language just because white liberals and so-called black leaders tell us he's a racist?

Our little black children, by the grace of God, will grow up someday. They will become the next generation of parents, tax-payers, lawyers, doctors, accountants, engineers, and law-abiding citizens of this representative form of government. It behooves us to get this right, to get back what we've lost as a black culture, to fix the brokenness within our own communities, and to recognize and support those who are working in our favor.

Last, but not least, is *culture*. The black community has a culture. It has a sum of attitudes, beliefs, and ways of thinking and behaving that distinguishes us from any other group. This summation of our culture is to be celebrated, not berated.

I can pick out the Italian family in the crowd, mostly because of certain ways of behaving that distinguish them from most others—

the number of them during family events, the types of food they serve, the increased volume in the room as they laugh, eat, and play.

There are attributes we unconsciously assign to groups of people. It's not racist. It's how God designed us.

We each have schemas or ways that our brain naturally walks through life organizing everything we see, taste, smell, hear, and touch. Our schema is like a large database in our brain. It's like a file cabinet. Every new experience or interaction goes into a file for later recall and informs us how we are to react when met with that interaction or experience again.

Have you ever walked into a room, smelled a familiar smell, and been immediately transported back in time? Well, that's your schema at work—recalling and attaching very real good or not-so-good emotions to that smell.

In the black community, when an outside event happens, we interpret that event based on all the things we've filed away, consciously and unconsciously, in our schemas.

During the time I was growing up in the very rural and very Deep South, blacks knew exactly what to do when a police officer pulled them over. Immediately, your hands went to ten and two on the wheel. Head forward. "Yes, sir" and "No, sir" were your replies as you were asked if you could hand over your papers. If there was a problem, the solution was not to fly off the handle, cussing and fussing and flipping out in some disturbed rant. There were just one too many dim-lit woods to take such a risk, and you knew one too many stories.

Instead, I can still hear my grandma Hattie sternly instructing my uncle Jimmy that if anything went awry, "You know how to read. Read their name and take down their badge number. We'll go down to the courthouse in the morning to file a complaint. But don't act a fool."

This way of behaving toward the police in the Deep South wasn't completely unfounded then, and we have seen more than one example to conclude that it's not completely unfounded today. Although I'm not old enough to have felt the full weight of Jim Crow laws in Alabama, by the time I came along there was still just enough of the lingering residue on the faces of my most beloved grandparents for me to know Jim Crow was no gentleman. He was an unrelenting brute.

Racism still exists. Bigotry is real. Hate is evil and can be as immovable as a parcel of land. Racism isn't germane to a particular skin color or political party. It will live in any willing host.

The culture of the South, specifically our interaction with the police in the South, weighs heavily on the culture of the black community. Our experiences of the Southern culture led us to adopting certain attitudes, certain ways of behaving and thinking when it comes to interacting with the police that would distinguish us from any other group of people. It also explains why the decibel of our sensitivity toward police brutality is usually turned all the way up.

There are legitimate reasons why we often raise our eyebrows in response to certain behaviors we see in the broader culture. There's a legitimate explanation for why blacks often cry foul when we see a police officer using excessive force. We're almost wired to do so. I get it, and I don't protest it too loudly. I understand.

What I *do* protest are black parents condoning their black children acting like a bunch of fools with a police officer—being loudmouths, acting belligerent, not cooperating, resisting, and fleeing a situation. What exactly are they expecting their child to receive at the end of their riotous behavior?

I had this conversation with one of my dearest friends. She posted a picture of her suburban son on Facebook looking not so clean-cut. Honestly, if we were walking at night and about to pass one another, I would strongly consider crossing the street. His appearance was somewhat shocking as he had veered from the oh-so-sweet two-year-old I had met many years ago. He deviated strangely from the meek and mild ten-year-old I once knew, and even the fourteen-year-old I had just seen a couple of years previously.

Eventually, I called my friend, and as always, our conversation turned to our children—how they're doing and what they're up to these days. She began to tell me about a run-in her son and several other kids had had with a police officer at a swim party. Although I was living in another state at the time, I knew immediately the confrontation she was referring to because it made national news. It was horrible. It was a situation that appeared to escalate wildly due to the unruly behavior of the very young and very large crowd of black teens. They were boisterous, rowdy, and uncontrollable. The police officers appeared completely frazzled and overwhelmed by the belligerent crowd. The kids were argumentative, aggressive, wild-eyed, and unruly. It was a chaotic mess.

As a parent, the potential of what could have happened unnerved me. But when my friend began to justify the unruly kids' behavior I became unglued. I listened to all of her many reasons why she condoned her child behaving in such a disrespectful and downright dangerous manner in protest to what she believed was police brutality or excessive force against black people in general. She cited cases like Trayvon Martin, Eric Garner, and Michael Brown as her examples of such extreme brutality.

After listening, I asked my friend just one question, "Do you want your child to come home tonight?"

She paused. So I asked again, "Do you want your child to come home tonight?"

"Yes, of course!" she bit back impatiently.

"So teach him what your parents taught you!" I replied.

It's not rocket science. Police officers carry guns. They're licensed to use those guns. Their mandate is to control the situation. They will not be outshouted or out-manhandled. They will not turn around and go home. They will get control of the situation one way or another.

My dear friend is typically a very reasonable person. We call her the mother of our little group of girlfriends. She's successful. She works in corporate America. She's college educated, has an intact family, and lives in a beautiful home in the suburbs. Yet she felt justified in her foolish stance. Worse yet, she encouraged her only child—her only son—to risk his life for a cause whose premise is false.

I also protest the amount of attention the black community is placing on the topic of police brutality as if it's the number one reason the black community is suffering as it is. My dear friend surely believes this to be the case. However, statistically speaking, police brutality isn't even in the top five things decimating the black community.

Here are the facts. According to the 2018 FBI Uniform Crime Report, the total number of black deaths by homicide were 7,407.[9] Of that number, 229 blacks were fatally shot by the police.[10] That's roughly 3 percent of black homicides being attributed to police shooting. But, wait—there's more. Out of the 229 blacks who were fatally shot by a police officer in 2018, only eighteen were unarmed.[11] The eighteen do not distinguish between those who violently resisted arrest and those who did not. So now we're talking about 0.002 percent, not 100 percent, not even 3 percent.

If the narrative is that on every street corner a police officer is standing there waiting to shoot a black man, the facts just don't support that story line. My friend is putting her only child in harm's way because of a false narrative fueled by those who have a very large megaphone.

With emotionally charged topics such as police brutality and our schemas almost being wired to see racism immediately, we often depend on uninformed emotions to direct our opinions. But at some point, we must look at those pesky things we call facts if we truly want to bring change to the black community.

The final thing I protest when it comes to the damage being done to the black culture is how black parents are perpetuating the victim mentality onto yet another generation. This was on full display when parents allowed a youth football coach to lead their group of eight-year-olds in taking a knee before one of their games. When one little boy asked why they were doing this, another little one spoke up saying, "It's because the police is killing black people and no one is doing anything about it."[12]

I went on *Fox & Friends* the very next day to debunk this false narrative. This should send chills down our collective backs as parents. These are children! They are only eight years old.

There are a million and two things in the world I believe we can teach our children, things that are rich and full of color, full of character, full of substance and beauty. So why would parents do the unthinkable by teaching their eight-year-olds that they are seen as inferior? Why would parents teach their babies that because of the color of their skin they will be targeted and seen as less than their white counterparts?

Whether the parents knew it or not, this is exactly what they were teaching their most precious assets. I vehemently protest the extension into yet another generation of black people this "woe is me" victim mentality.

Although many of us may be wired to see racism on every street corner, we must force ourselves to examine facts or lose much more than we could ever possibly gain from protesting an issue that isn't as significant as some would have us to believe.

White plantation owners strongly depended upon older black slaves teaching the younger black slaves their place in life. It saved the white man a tremendous amount of time, energy, and money to not have to break in the uppity black slave himself. Here we see it being done once more under the guise of social justice. Black parents teaching their black children that the world sees them as inferior. Seeing those little eight-year-olds kneeling should be heartbreaking to anyone.

Our black babies, the lucky ones whose lives are *not* snatched away by Planned Parenthood, are our future. The Black Lives Matter movement has done a great disservice to their futures by making sure they walk into their tomorrows feeling inadequate, inferior, less than, and like second-rate citizens. BLM isn't alone in their efforts, though. White liberals, politicians, and so-called black leaders who claim to speak on behalf of the black community for their own gain make sure the next generation of black people know their place in our society. According to these same people, the black person's place is one where he or she consistently waits on someone other than themselves to rescue them.

My first military reserve assignment was with a Criminal Investigation Detachment unit. At the time, I was the only black person in the unit, and I was, by far, the youngest by at least fifteen years. Every person besides myself and one other had worked in law enforcement in their civilian life.

I remember attempting to debate one of the police officers with all the worldly wisdom an eighteen-year-old could muster. I was arguing what I thought was true. I had no research to back me up. My opinions were all steeped in personal stories, uninformed thoughts on the matter, and innuendos.

I was contending that stereotyping people is racist. He patiently began to inform me that I was wrong. "Everyone stereotypes," he declared.

I would later learn how schemas work in the brain. However, at that time, he went on to explain that only when we use stereotypes to inform us how we should treat people is it called racism. Racism is when we allow ourselves to respond to any particular group of people based on stereotypes or preconceived thoughts without getting to know the individual person.

In all of the BLM malarkey, parents have forgotten their first obligation: to raise up your child in a way that will produce a good life filled with joy, laughter, and success.

As a man thinks, so is he. As such, it should come as no surprise that our consciousness informs our culture. Our culture being the outward, physical manifestation of what we believe and how we see ourselves. If I see myself as a victim of circumstances that I have no control over, the way I think, how I act, what I say, and how I interact with the world around me will reflect the way I see myself. To see oneself as a defeated victim is setting oneself up for failure.

Victims find a way to be content with their circumstances. We often see some people who have been victimized overcome their circumstances. We often call them "heroes" or "survivors," in recognition of the strength of character that was needed to forge ahead when it could have been just as convenient to simply give up—to just settle.

The black community doesn't have to be victim to what may be seen as inequalities. We're more than equipped to overcome any circumstances. We have the blood of overcomers streaming through our veins.

Giving my life to Jesus Christ at the age of nineteen and committing myself to truly living a Christian life that would entail more than regularly attending church services and spouting off select Scriptures drastically changed the course of my life. Determining early on that I would learn to see people as God sees them and that I would love them right where they stood were all foundational concepts in helping me to think beyond just myself and to think higher thoughts about myself and the world around me. This decision was pivotal in turning my own life around, setting me on a productive path, and teaching me that my worth was more than the color of my skin.

The other thing that altered the course of my life was when I decided to finish my college education and get my first degree, which was a bachelor's degree in corporate finance. The results from accomplishing this were remarkable and swift. I often tell young black people about the jobs I was able to get before I walked across the stage to get my degree compared to those jobs I was able to get immediately after. It was as different as night and day. I went from settling for a job that paid $9.50 an hour with no benefits to a salaried position with both benefits and upward mobility.

I'm convinced that the ticket for most blacks to rise above what they may perceive as racism is education. What some call white privilege could very well be a lack of sufficient skills on the part of the minority. What many blacks feel is an act of discrimination based on the color of their skin could really be the inferiority of their education compared to another who is more qualified. I often say, once you've got it on your resume, no one can take it away from you. Education is a game changer! This is true for anyone, but it's especially germane to the black person with no wealth or significant network or contacts to lean upon.

One of my younger male relatives decided to drop out of high school. The only reason I could detect for this irrational decision was simply because he was lazy and didn't want to do what was required to pass his classes.

My conversation with him was to the point. I pulled out the United States Department of Labor unemployment report. His eyes went wide, and his mother mouthed the words, "Thank you" as she exited the room. She knew I had it from there.

The particular report I pulled that day broke down the unemployment numbers based on race, gender, age, and education. I walked through the numbers with him.

Total unemployment for someone without a high school diploma is 5.6 percent versus 4.1 percent with a high school diploma. With some college, the rate drops to 3.3 percent, and with an earned bachelor's or higher degree, the rate drops to 2.1.

I then moved on to the unemployment rate for a black person with no high school diploma being 10.4 percent, more than double the rate of a white person with no high school diploma at 5.1 percent. The spread between the two groups makes a noticeable drop when both get at least a high school diploma—going down to 6.7 percent for a black person versus 3.5 percent for a white person.

Here's where it gets interesting. As a black person goes on to obtain a higher and higher level of education, the spread between the rate of unemployment compared to his white counterpart continues to shrink significantly, approaching parity when the black person obtains a bachelor's or higher degree. A black person's rate of unemployment goes from 5.2 percent with some college but no degree to 2.9 percent with a bachelor's or higher degree, compared to a white person's rate of unemployment going from 2.9 percent down to 2.0 percent, respectively.

I had this conversation with my young male relative while we were under the Obama administration. During this time, a black male between the ages of sixteen and twenty-four with just a high school diploma had an unemployment rate of 39 percent, compared to his white male counterpart of 17 percent—again, more than double the rate. With some college, the rate dropped to 11.7 percent versus 6.2 percent for a white male the same age.

Again, the Labor Department breaks out the unemployment numbers by age, gender, race, and education. The one thing my young black male relative was able to control he had decided to flush down the toilet.

He can't control his age or when he was born. He can't control his gender, either. He had no say in the color of his skin. All of the above were decided for him.

One of the controllables in his life is his level of education. One of the greatest things blacks can do to improve their own situation, to not be perpetual victims as some would have us to be, is to decide to control the controllables. Our level of education is controllable. If I can come from a pig farm in southern Alabama and find a way to go to college and finish college, just about anyone else can in America.

It was remarkable to read about Frederick Douglass's winding path to learning how to read and write. It was not a direct route. But it was a determined path he decided to embark upon when he realized that the pathway from slavery to freedom was education.[13] Brick by brick, step by step, every word he learned brought him closer to leaving the chains of slavery. It was true for a slave. It remains true for every American today.

In summing up what makes our culture, I would be remiss if I didn't give a hat tip to one of the greatest influencers in the black culture. No, unfortunately it's not education. No, it's not the black father. There's a seven out of ten chance he's absent from the home. I'm talking about the TV—every house has at least one of them.

The television—the one-eyed brain condenser—enjoys a prime spot in the homes of most families in the United States. For better or for worse, the TV is here to stay, and it has become a vital source of information for all. Unfortunately, it has become the surrogate parent in many households.

One show after another instructs our kids on the latest must-have accessories, the latest fashion statement, the dangers of drinking and driving, and even how to ask a girl out on a date. The TV is also being used to instruct us on who we are as a person, our worth as an individual and what value system we should adopt—what's in and what's not.

For years, the black family has sat around the TV to gauge our place in society. Many decades ago two white men donned black-face and became Amos 'n' Andy on the radio and in film. It was clearly racist, and even when it became a TV series in the 1950s starring an all-black cast set in Harlem's historic black community, it was lambasted as nothing but racist stereotyping and was eventually taken off the air. Other TV shows of that era weren't much better. *Beulah* ran in the early 1950s with three actresses playing the lead over the course of three seasons, all caricatures of black people. But these shows were a reflection of their times, portraying where we were on black relations in this country.

It took a few more years for Hollywood to try again. But in the late 1960s we saw Diahann Carroll as *Julia*, a nurse and a single mother whose husband had been killed in Vietnam. Again, a reflection of the times after the 1964 Civil Rights Act was signed into law and during the tumultuous days of picket signs, when rebellion hung low in the air.

Later, other sitcoms came along to document our rise in American history and show our elevated place in time. With *The Jeffersons*, we thought we too had moved on up right along with

George and Weezy. *Amen*, *Family Matters*, *Good Times*, and, of course, *The Cosby Show*—all were signs of their times. All portrayed successful black families, and all starred strong, proud, and hardworking black fathers in the home. It was a reflection of our culture in the black community at that time.

Today the fall of the black family is being chronicled once more. The decimation of the black community is evident, in part, in how we are portrayed on TV.

My family and I rarely watch a live program on television. Most of what we watch are prerecorded shows. One of the many conveniences of watching prerecorded shows is the ability to fast-forward past commercials. During one particular show, I allowed the commercials to play as I was home alone and walking from room to room picking up as the show played in the background.

Suddenly, a commercial came on advertising an upcoming music award show that would be airing on Black Entertainment Television (BET). It took the third time the commercial was aired for me to fully understand what was happening.

During the commercial, the snappy jingle that kept playing repetitively in the background was, "This is what it means to be black. This is what it means to be black. This is what it means to be black." There were no other words sung. There were no other words spoken. I stopped what I was doing to pay closer attention to the commercial, and as the song played on, images of black women scantily dressed flashed across the screen, derriere uncovered and on full display. As the song played on and you see multiple camera lights flashing, suddenly young black men draped in gold chains, wearing expensive watches and clean sneakers, and adorned in oversized leather jackets posed for the cameras.

"Is this what it means to be black?" I thought. They certainly said so and said so often.

We have lost our identity. It would behoove us to start the work of rediscovering who we are. Unfortunately, this crisis mode status appears to be going undetected by most so-called black leaders in our country.

We have become a very self-focused society with very little personal ambition. This is seen in the black community as it is in any other. We must get rid of the *me* mentality that causes us to perpetually look in the mirror, forever seeing just ourselves, what we have, and what we don't have to the exclusion of what's happening to the community on a collective basis.

We must begin to consider what's beneficial for the whole, not just for me, me, and me. We must lay down our selfie sticks and look around our community. We must become more than just social media warriors and enter into the battle to turn our community around. We must relearn what it means to be black—it goes deeper than the color of our skin.

The black community is not separate from the rest of America. We are Americans, too. What happened to the black community happened to the rest of America at the same time. Slavery did not just happen to the black community. It degraded the souls of the white community, too. Blacks did not save themselves from slavery alone. We were in lockstep with many in the white community. The civil rights movement saw young white men getting on Freedom Ride buses heading to the Deep South to register black voters. The issues we contend with are not just black people's issues. They are all of our issues. As one group fails, it spills out into every other community. Until we lay aside our personal agendas, our me mentality, we will never be as great as we can be.

We are indebted to those who have come before us to live well. This is an indebtedness that can only be repaid in our worthiness.

Am I, a black woman, worthy of the price paid by those who have come before us? We are all a part of their legacy.

The black race owes those little black girls and black boys who came before us an enormous debt, a debt we have yet to repay in full. In fact, all Americans today owe every American who came before us and toted all of our collective water to freedom. We did not get to where we are today by ourselves. We all stand on the shoulders of every American who ever threw their hat into the ring and fought for our collective liberty and equality.

We have an obligation to live well. We have an obligation to take back our true identity. That is how we will repay them. This is how we will learn what it means to be black. In turn, we will live well. We will live as victors . . . not victims.

5.

CULTURE OF POVERTY

Many politicians treat poverty as if they're simply dealing with poor people who are just wannabe rich people looking for resources, skills, and job opportunities. But money alone can't solve the problems that plague us. Our troubles are much deeper and more menacing than what extra money can solve.

In reality, instead of being simply money-poor, we've become mind-poor as a nation. This insidious and poisonous way of thinking has seeped beyond the borders of America's slums and ghettos and now has crossed social, economic, and ethnic lines. Or, as Oscar Lewis said in his classic book *La Vida*, we have a culture of poverty problem.

No matter how much money is thrown at this problem, it's becoming clear that money alone can't address the issues that plague most ethnic communities—or any community, for that matter. Money can't correct the mind-poor thinking that permeates every nook and cranny of our culture today. In fact, most government programs that involve the pouring of money alone into the pockets of those where a culture of poverty already exists only end up serving as a Band-Aid over a gaping open wound. We need a serious fix, not another bandage.

Throughout Middle America there are growing pockets that are culturally bankrupt, teetering on insolvency not due to a lack of money only but due to poverty of thought. Once, this culture of poverty resided primarily in the slums of America—affecting only the hard-core poor. Once, the culture of poverty possessed a distinctive cultural profile, a way of life passed on from generation to generation, characterized by unstable families, high rates of illegitimate births, poor self-esteem, traumatic childhood experiences, and low levels of voting and political participation.[1]

Today, this bankruptcy of culture is being normalized throughout Middle America, consuming more victims as it moves along. Not only is it spreading, but it is being intentionally elevated from the slums where it has thrived for generations and mass-marketed to a large swath of the middle class.

This culture of poverty is resistant to money alone. Raising taxes to create yet another government-subsidized program can't resolve the scarcity in traditional American values. Those values make up our culture, strengthen it, and bind us together as fellow brothers and sisters. Those traditions are the ideals for raising up the next generation of Americans. They contain ideas that elevate our thinking about who we are and what our country has to offer us—and what we can offer it.

THE VALUES THAT SUSTAIN US

The importance of Judeo-Christian values as the dominant value system in our country in order to maintain a civil society is not a new concept. More than ever before I'm teaching my children that truth not only matters, but that it exists. That morality matters—

knowing the difference between right and wrong matters. More than ever before I'm being intentional in teaching and demonstrating to them how to think logically rather than being manipulated by their own untamed emotions.

As our culture increasingly goes the way of consenting to some of the most foolish, dangerous, and downright debased ways of living, such as a jury awarding a mother the right to continue the gender transitioning of her seven-year-old son despite the father's protest,[2] it is ever more clear to me that a return to moral discipline and principles of virtue is necessary to bind our society together. Not multiple baby daddies. Not a divorce rate teetering on 50 percent in some states.[3] Not a growing absentee father epidemic impacting all communities. Not killing our children in the womb. Not deciding to take a knee in protest against the country when the national anthem is played.

Oh, how I wished our nation was bursting from the seams with young people like Nathan Hale, the young, twenty-one-year-old Yale graduate who volunteered to go behind the British lines in 1776 to spy for information on their movements. He knew the penalty for doing so was death. When he was discovered by the British and sentenced to die by hanging, his last words reportedly were "I only regret that I have but one life to lose for my country."

A lack of good morals and a lack of those values that properly bind our society together are corrupting and destroying good order. There are such things as good and bad; everything is not relative. There are some absolutes in this world. And it's in our nation's best interest to understand the difference between the two and to fight for the better one.

Black Lives Matter, Antifa, and liberal progressive Democrats display a troubling degree of ambivalence toward our collective fate being tied to the welfare of this country. One of their purposes is to resist to the point of making "America ungovernable."[4] They seem to have no awareness that if America goes down, we all go down with her. It's not in *my* best interest to force myself into believing that America is totally depraved, unredeemable, and evil, that no good has ever come out of her, or that she is the consummate purveyor of hate.

After all, *I* am America. *You* are America. She does not exist apart from her inhabitants. We inform her character. If America is evil it is because *we* are evil. If there is something redeemable about America it's because of the individual values we, collectively, have agreed to follow. All things considered, we are her arms, legs, heart, and feet. If we accept a culture of poverty, we will see it continue to spread.

The effects of throwing cash at what is in reality a lack of values is similar to putting a broken arm in a cast before moving it back into position. Or like throwing precious pearls into a pig pen. Having grown up on a pig farm, I can assure you the pig has no ability to appreciate the pearls in its pen.

If the collective mind of America is in danger of being or already is broken in some regards, it must be reset before any amount of money or universal aid on the part of our government will make a difference. Throwing money at Antifa will not fix the problem. Throwing money at parents who are determined to transition their young children's gender will not fix the problems ailing our great nation. Not recognizing this blatant truth is the very reason our urban areas look as they do today, despite decades of government "aid."

We act like what liberal politicians are offering to the broader American culture hasn't been offered already, but we've seen this chapter and verse from their playbook before. They've already done in the black community what they are now offering to the broader culture, and it was and is a colossal failure of common sense. Instead of going to the root of the problems of the high fatherless rate or the broken education systems in these communities, liberal politicians and bureaucrats just throw money at the problem. More welfare, more housing assistance, more free programs, more universal aid, raise food stamp allowances, lock up and throw away the keys on criminal offenders.

We Americans are presently existing in the midst of a boisterous broken culture. We're bankrupt, but loud. Our values, our traditions, our national belief systems about who we are as Americans, how we see ourselves as citizens, what it means to even be a citizen, how we incorporate non-citizens, and our ways of behaving that distinguish us from other societies are all being redefined—dumbed down, as it were—leaning toward the most trivial definition of the words.

To illustrate the crisis of values we find ourselves in, we need look no further than our own US House of Representatives. Newly elected representative Rashida Tlaib, the first American Palestinian in Congress, prognosticated aloud regarding President Trump: "We're going to impeach the [MF'er]."[5] Unashamed, she doubled down on her prediction, declaring again seven months later "We're going to impeach the [MF'er], don't worry."[6] Where is the outcry condemning such debased rhetoric from a sitting member of Congress? Has this kind of behavior become the norm? We often hear calls for President Trump to act more "dignified," to behave in a way they consider more fitting for the office. However, Congress is a co-equal branch of the government. Where are the calls for Representative Tlaib to act decently? Instead, she sells "Impeach the MF" T-shirts at fundraising events.[7] As a co-equal branch of government she is obligated, as well, to behave with a sense of dignity. The hypocrisy of those who continuously call on

President Trump to behave a certain way is sickening when we consider the response such an expletive-laced comment would have received had it dripped from the lips of any white Republican during the Obama administration. A culture of poverty—mind poverty—is especially on display when it comes from our elected representatives.

Let's look at our justice system. A sitting judge of law and order was indicted for allegedly helping a twice-convicted illegal alien escape arrest by Immigration and Customs Enforcement (ICE) by surreptitiously escorting him out a back door while the ICE agent was instructed to wait in the lobby.[8] In 2018, Newton District Court judge Shelley M. Richmond Joseph and court officer Wesley MacGregor helped Jose Medina-Perez sneak out of the courthouse while the ICE agent waited for him in the lobby. Medina-Perez is a twice-deported illegal alien who had a fugitive warrant for drunk driving. He was in the judge's courtroom in order to be arraigned on drug charges. So underhanded were Joseph's actions that she, according to the indictment, requested the clerk to "go off the record for a moment," leaving nearly a minute unrecorded. Despite how one may feel about our immigration system, Joseph took an oath to uphold the law—not make it up as she sees fit.

Representative Ilhan Omar is alleged to have married her own brother in an effort to defraud immigration,[9] an allegation that has been widely discussed by conservative outlets, while rarely being reported on by liberal mainstream media. Representative Alexandria Ocasio-Cortez was a bartender before allegedly "auditioning" for her role of congresswoman. In 2017, her brother strongly encouraged her to attend an open casting call held by the Justice Democrats, who were looking to select potential candidates to run on their political platform of police reform, Green

New Deal, livable wage, guaranteed jobs, Medicare for all, and so forth.[10] Ocasio-Cortez fit the bill and now brilliantly "plays the part" of a liberal NY congresswoman.[11] At this writing, both are boisterous progressive members of Congress. Speaker Nancy Pelosi dismisses this progressive wing of her party as just being "like five people,"[12] but they and others of their progressive ilk are setting the agenda for the Democrat Party. Ocasio-Cortez alone has more Twitter followers than all of the 2020 Democrat presidential hopefuls.

Where is the investigative reporting? Where is the outcry over the potential stain or precedence being brought to our nation's capital?

Our culture is broken. The culture of poverty speaks to the difference between the reality and the idea of America as experienced by her citizens. There are those whose reality of America is very different from the idea of America, which says that a strong work ethic will allow you to carve out a respectable life for yourself. The idea of America being that life, liberty, and the pursuit of happiness is for all men and women. The idea of America says that hard work, intelligence, creativity, and a little bit of luck and intuition will allow you to leave a legacy for your children.

For those trapped in the culture of poverty, the reality of America is very different from the idea of America. Not only is it different in their minds; it's different in the urban areas in which they live, breathe, and raise up the next generation. In such communities, people feel disenfranchised from the privileges other Americans enjoy. They feel marginalized when they walk outside of their communities and venture into the banking system, voting system, educational system, commerce system, legal system, and the like. They live in what they would consider a bifurcated America—one for the haves and the other for the have-nots.

According to the latest American Community Survey, those living within urban areas are less likely to own their own homes, live in their state of birth, or have served in the military.[13] The aspirations most Americans see as common are not so common to them.

Their experience of America is much different from that of the larger society. They do not feel integrated into the larger culture. They feel ostracized, excluded from participating in the fabric of America. These feelings are either of their own making or made by others, but they exist nonetheless.

These victims of the culture of poverty feel no sense of identification with the great traditions or beliefs of America. They sense no duty to salute the flag, to stand for the national anthem, or to revere our Founding Fathers. Their feelings of alienation from the larger culture show up in abnormal, disruptive, and antisocial ways which only serve to extend their cycle of poverty and despair.

At one time in the past we could escape this disturbed pathology by simply choosing to not live close to it, making sure we lived outside of the limits of these urban areas, and making sure our children weren't in the same school district where it exists. Today, it's virtually impossible to ignore it, avoid it, or not get caught up in the tangle of pathology associated with the culture of poverty, mainly because of the mainstream media's obsession with reaffirming its existence on TV or by activists and liberal politicians obsessed with fanning the flames of this disturbed nature. The unhealthy way of thinking that's a part of the culture of poverty has expanded beyond the corners of urban areas.

The goal is to manufacture a problem even if most of us don't see one. Disturbingly, most see Middle America as a part of the have-nots now. According to most politicians, activists, and those

in the mainstream media, the battle is now between the one per-
centers and the rest of America. That's a pretty large gap.

Many of us—particularly in the minority community—have
been lumped into the have-not group and told almost daily that
the odds are against us and we don't belong. No matter how good
life may be going for us right now, we're told we're at the bottom.
No matter how financially sound we feel right now, we're told we're
missing out on something more. Because of the color of our skin,
the *New York Times*' 1619 Project urges us to view everything in
America through the lens of racism. We're constantly exposed to
the pathology of the "victim" group and in danger of being drawn
into it—and along with us, our children.

As blacks, we can't discuss how much better our lives are
under President Trump's administration than it ever was under
the Obama administration. We're led to believe we must kow-
tow to the false narrative that political conservatives are racist.
Most blacks feel compelled to overlook the drug needles lining the
curbs of their homes because to do otherwise would force them
to shine a spotlight on the failures of the Democrat Party. And
that, my friend, must never be allowed to happen. For example,
in October 2019 President Trump was given a "Bipartisan Justice Award" by the 20/20 Bipartisan Justice Center, a nationwide
coalition of black Republicans, Democrats, and Independents
focused on criminal justice reform. The largely black event that
was held at a historically black college is a highly sought after platform for candidates wanting to connect with the black community. Because the event deigned to honor President Trump and his
efforts to help black people who are disproportionately affected by
what is universally perceived as unfair criminal justice laws, presidential Democrat candidate Senator Kamala Harris decided not
to attend. Harris who is *not* an "African-American," (her father is

Jamaican and her mother is Indian), has cited as one of her many reasons for refusing to attend the event that as "the only candidate who attended an HBCU*, [she] knows the importance that these spaces hold for young black Americans."[14] It doesn't matter to Senator Harris, and perhaps in her mind it shouldn't matter to any black person, that President Trump has done something worthy of being honored . . . something that positively impacts the black community. It doesn't appear to matter to her that President Trump is doing for the black community what no other president seemed able to do, including our nation's first black president, Barack Obama. Many blacks are left to feel that although it is as a direct result of President Trump championing and later signing into law a measure "that has allowed thousands of non-violent offenders to gain early release from federal prison" we should not applaud him. Instead, we should continue to march to the beat that he is a racist. This is similar to white liberals overlooking the highly documented human feces lining the sidewalks of liberal bastions like San Francisco to instead criticize President Trump calling MS-13 members "animals" after they cut out the heart of a living person.

I was truly disturbed to see the pervasiveness of this moral decline when I overheard one of my dear uncles say he was "glad cops are being gunned down." He lives nowhere in proximity to the hood, where one might be less surprised to overhear someone make such a wicked statement. There was a sort of glee in his tone. I immediately chided him, crying, "No, uncle. Don't say that!"

From the front lines of the inner cities to the backwoods of Alabama, this notion of detachment from what is best for America and, by extension, what is best for me individually has seeped

---

* Historically Black Colleges Universities

out of the slums—I believe intentionally. Blacks are made to feel we're constantly at odds with the systems that traditionally have defined our nation.

It's not uncommon for me to have long discussions with educated people who have a riffraff mindset full of disquiet and rage against this nation. They're not the typical rioters and looters you may assume. No, many are simply middle-class folks who own their homes, are educated, and are raising families. What's disconcerting is that their rage is being directed against law and order, against traditional values, against the establishments that created those traditions, against patriotism, and against success above all. Throwing money at this only serves to mask the core rot.

Often, the pretext for this dangerous thinking is found in the fallacy of white privilege.

WHITE PRIVILEGE

The notion behind white privilege is one of the leading vehicles used to export the culture of poverty from the slums of America to Main Street. It's a vehicle crafted by white liberals and hand-delivered to a seemingly obliging nation.

To believe in the false agenda that fuels white privilege if I'm not white, I must believe I'm inferior to whites. I must believe that your white skin gives you privileges, freedoms, rights, honor, and advantages that my black skin doesn't afford me. I must believe that your white skin somehow gives you better access to a world I cannot enter. Ultimately, I must look at my black skin and see a traitor—denying me what your white skin so generously graces you with.

In a few words, white privilege offers me my own oppression. Connect the dots. Is it any wonder many blacks see themselves as victims? Is there any confusion as to why many blacks and other non-whites see themselves as mired down, cut off, detached from the promises of America's Declaration of Independence? Of course, I'm not referring to the perpetually peeved-off radicals who can never be appeased no matter what is said, done, or given to them. However, if the agenda that propels the false narrative of white privilege is the prevailing thought, is it really a riddle why some non-whites won't stand for the national anthem or honor our fallen soldiers?

How much money would it take to resolve this deficit? Or what values must we begin to reteach so that all of us feel a part of this American experience and won't fall prey to the notion that white skin is the *only* key needed to unlock privileges in this nation?

Labeling the agenda behind "white privilege" as false is not an admission that privileges in life don't exist. Of course there are privileges some have that others don't. My own children are far more "privileged" than I could have ever imagined to be as a young child growing up in the Deep South on a pig farm in southern Alabama. My children have a doting father, who is loyal to their mother and who is committed to his family. This fact alone catapults my children into a class of privilege relative to the 70% of black children who are growing up without a father and many of whom will sadly suffer the well-documented consequences from such.

In certain cases, those privileges could be based on the color of one's skin, as much as it could be premised on one's appearance, height, weight, age, accent, disability, wealth, education, or zip code.

Most privilege is based on wealth and celebrity and not skin color, alone; and many of the wealthiest and biggest celebrities push the agenda of "white privilege." Look no farther than the

2019 college admissions bribery scandal. Wealthy elites used their "privileges" to influence undergraduate college admissions decisions at several top American universities. These privileged liberals paid more than $25 million between 2011 and 2018 to the organizer of the scheme, Rick Singer.[15] Hollywood elite Lori Loughlin and her husband, fashion designer, Mossimo Giannulli paid $500,000 for their two daughters to be admitted into the University of Southern California.[16] Talk about being "white" and "privileged."

The agenda powering the white privilege deception is distinct from the overall concept of privileges existing, however. The false agenda behind white privilege is specifically used to accomplish several goals: (1) to evoke guilt and badger white people into submission, (2) to make those in the perceived "superior" group feel superior, and (3) to make those in the perceived "inferior" group feel inferior. It's not rocket science.

Booker T. Washington once aptly observed:

I have always been made sad when I have heard members of any race claiming rights or privileges, or certain badges of distinction, on the ground simply that they were members of this or that race, regardless of their own individual worth or attainments. I have been made to feel sad for such persons because I am conscious of the fact that mere connection with what is known as a superior race will not permanently carry an individual forward unless he has individual worth and mere connection with what is regarded as an inferior race will not finally hold an individual back if he possess intrinsic, individual merit. Every persecuted individual and race should get much consolation out of the great human law, which is universal and eternal, that *merit*, no matter under what skin found, is, in the long run, recognized and rewarded.[17]

What a profound observation, one that is especially needed in today's culture just as much as it was needed when Washington wrote it just a few years removed from the emancipation of slaves.

Stated less impeccably, Americans *are* privileged. One only needs to travel outside of this country to realize this truth. We may not all be an Oprah Winfrey or a Bill Gates. But with some hard work, intuition, and a little bit of luck, we can carve out a respectable life for ourselves in this country. Does this always happen 100 percent of the time? No. But it did for a poor little country girl from a pig farm in southern Alabama. In America, the odds are in our favor.

WHITE VALUES

Second only to the false narrative of white privilege is the notion that somehow white people are different from the rest of us. It's not often spoken, but lurking under the surface is an unsettling undercurrent that whispers, "Somehow white people want something different for their families than we in the black community want for our families." This, too, has been used to export the culture of poverty from the slums, where it may be less surprising to see certain patterns of behavior being acted out, and thrust upon the rest of us unchallenged. This vehicle has been used to create "protected" ways of behaving. To challenge some of those protected behaviors is to be immediately deemed a racist.

But what are white values? How do white people differ from the rest of us? How do the things they value differ from the things we in the minority community value? Can white values and black values be differentiated? If culture is the sum of shared attitudes, shared beliefs, and shared ways of thinking and behaving that distinguish one group of people from another group of people—as Americans from Iranians—then we should be able to make a clear demarcation between the major value systems of white people and those of others. Right?

To begin to understand this concept, I took to social media and asked my white friends to share their values. God, family, country were the values of most. Success. Raising productive citizens. Being a good spouse. Taking as many vacations as possible. Fighting for what is right. Education. Living debt-free. Being a truthful person. Cultivating good friendships. Working hard. Playing harder. Preserving the nation. Being loved. Being compassionate. Protecting the family. Leaving a legacy.

After a while, it became apparent that their values are also my values. I share these attitudes. I believe in these ideas. How I spend my time and money bears witness that the values of my white friends are indeed my values, too. They are also the values of most black people I know.

If these shared standards of living are not black values, then they should be. What higher principles are there than to be able to live according to your own conscience, be it a conscience that's birthed by the belief in a divine Creator or belief in yourself? What's more precious in this life than one's family? How do black values differ from these values? Again, if these are not black values, they should be. But I submit that we—blacks and whites—are not as different as some would have us to believe.

This false narrative has created prisons within our minds preventing us from raising the bar of expectations on what we, as a people, consider acceptable behavior within the black community. It prohibits us from calling out the lack of personal responsibility in lowering high illegitimacy rates by waiting to have children until we're married. It forbids us, as a nation, to call out certain ways of behaving as foul and aggressive. Instead, to dare to stand up, to dare to make policies that compel blacks to conform to a higher standard of thinking is to be accused of trying to make black folks "act white." As if low illegitimacy rates only help white folks.

It's in our own best interest to make sure our kids are attending safe and well-functioning schools. So why have we gotten comfortable with the chaos, violence, and confusion in many of our school systems that makes it virtually impossible for our children to learn? Why are we listening to liberal policy makers when the best they can give us to remedy our chaotic school system is to prohibit administrators from suspending students who disrupt school activities or otherwise willfully defy those in authority?[18] How is the best solution elected officials can come up with is to keep the disturbed with the sane? Is it better to coddle the disrupter than to create an environment conducive to learning for those who come prepared to learn? Isn't it all the more imperative within black communities to get rid of the disrupters so others can focus on learning?

Why are we listening to liberal policy makers when the best they can do is hire a professor to teach other professors how to grade students' papers based on the looney-tune logic that standard English, pure or correct English grammar, is racist? Rather than grade one's writing abilities or lack thereof on very clear rules of grammar, officials at American University hired Asao B. Inoue to instead teach their professors that what we consider to be correct English actually promotes white superiority. He is charged with the task of teaching faculty members to grade students based on how much effort they put into their writing and not on actual results. This is utter nonsense when we consider the overarching purpose of higher institutions of learning, or when we consider the readiness of our young minds when they enter the workforce, and especially when we consider that parents are plopping down nearly $50,000 a year in tuition to attend this university.[19] Surely their future employers will expect them to not only speak correct English but also communicate well in writing.

I can personally attest to how organizing my thoughts is directly linked to becoming a more effective writer. Understanding the difference between a transitive verb and an intransitive verb, how to use the proper verb tense, and how to modify a verb by adding a quality adverb has made it possible for me to effectively articulate what I'm thinking. It's one thing to think a thought. It's something completely different to speak that thought in a manner that solicits the kind of response you want. Diagramming sentences has become a staple in my children's homeschooling classes.

Undoubtedly, this error in judgment will hurt black students coming out of failing schools disproportionately more than white students. While their white counterparts will overwhelmingly be held to a higher standard as they come into these institutions with competent marks in this field of study, black students, like myself many years ago, will enter these higher institutions with below-competent marks and will be required to take remedial classes.

One study shows that 70 percent of black students entering a two-year institution take a remedial class.[20] According to another study, remedial classes "tended to have significant and large negative impacts on students who attended colleges with a high proportion of remedial students, on female students, on students who were younger than 25, and on Black students."[21]

Why have we grown comfortable with the endemic level of out-of-wedlock births within black communities? Slightly more than 50 percent of all homicide victims each year are black people, and 94 percent of the time, the perpetrator is another black person. Black-on-black crime is real and has become a deadly plague. Why has this become the norm in our communities? Why must we wait for the government or, in many cases as is in the mind of some, the white man to come in and fix our problems? Why must we wait for white folks to come save us? Why can't we save ourselves? First, we're told that all of our problems are a result of the white man interfering. Then, we're told that we must wait on the white man to come fix our problems. Sounds like insanity to me.

This isn't the case for the black community only. It's the same scenario playing out in predominately Muslim and Hispanic communities, as well. We're told we're xenophobic if we demand certain people assimilate into American culture, to adopt our norms and speak our language. Could I walk through Iran without a hijab? Or would I be forced to conform? Would I be forced to assimilate in Afghanistan? Or would I be able to exercise my own independence as a woman? In many influential circles, demanding that English be the national language in every city and state in America is now tantamount to being racist. Some behaviors are beneficial to adopt to maintain the identity of any nation— whether good or bad, whether wearing a burka or not, or demanding voter identification or not at all.

President Lyndon B. Johnson ran into this exact same illogic, proving once more there's nothing new under the sun, just old refurbished criticisms. President Johnson was accused of not being sensitive to ethnic values when he became aware of the systemic bankruptcy in culture that permeated the 1960s black inner-city family immortalized by the stains of slavery and Jim Crow laws that continued to create self-perpetuating cycles of poverty and despair.[22] Johnson introduced his new awareness in a speech delivered at Howard University in which he delineated plans he believed would promote genuine racial equality. His critics— both civil rights leaders and liberal whites—asserted that Johnson "found black families 'disintegrated' and their communities 'unstable' because they expected them to resemble white, middle-class families."[23]

"White values" implies that the black community is seen only as unstable and on the verge of breaking down because we expect them to resemble white, middle-class families, not because they are actually breaking down and unstable (which they are, by the way). That narrative promotes the idea that America is only willing to admit one "normal" standard for everyone; all others are wrong.

But any way you look at it, it's wrong to have multiple baby daddies. It's wrong that black fathers are disproportionately not staying home to raise their black children. It's wrong that the most dangerous place for a black child to be is in his or her black mother's womb. These are not white values. These are just the right values to have if you don't want to be exposed to the negative consequences of living otherwise. However, the virtue signaling of "white values" stops all legitimate conversations to address these real issues. Like a frog in boiling water, we are realizing too late that black values are American values.

All of this is the fruit of the culture of poverty.

ANTIFA IS CHEAPENING OUR CULTURE

I am a black woman married to a black man with two beautiful little black children. The color of a hood or a mask being worn by one determined to inflict terror is of little importance to me, except for the purposes of identifying to the police what the perpetrator wore. Black masks. White hoods. At the end of the day, what's the difference if their goal is the same?

The so-called anti-fascist group we call Antifa likes to think of themselves as the protectors of free speech, even while they shut down the free expression of those they self-righteously deem unworthy to speak. Both Back Lives Matter and Antifa are similar in that they fancy themselves as the liberators of those who have been oppressed by the evil white and privileged class while they, themselves, forcibly suppress any opposition to their own views. By definition of their well-documented behavior, Senator Ted Cruz has labeled them a domestic terrorist organization and called on all of Congress to do the same.[24]

Members of the Antifa movement wear black masks to cover up their shameful, illegal, and dastardly acts. Ku Klux Klansmen wore white hoods to hide their reprehensible deeds. Both groups would call themselves liberators. Both groups have used terror to achieve their goal of controlling the thoughts and actions of those around them. I don't recall Dr. Martin Luther King Jr. wearing a mask. Or President Abraham Lincoln. Or Harriet Tubman. They were the bona fide liberators of the oppressed. They had nothing to hide. There was no need for them to cower behind the mask of anonymity.

Americans who have had the unfortunate luck of crossing paths with Antifa or white supremacists, alike, are met with a rage they could not have anticipated. What difference does the color of their aggressor's mask make to them while they're being hit across the head with a bike lock? This happened to a Trump supporter by former East Bay college philosophy professor Eric Clanton, who was originally charged with four counts of felony assault with a deadly weapon. Professor Clanton's act of terror caused great bodily harm when he violently assaulted at least seven people across the head with a bike lock during a 2017 "free speech" rally in Berkeley, CA. Police "recovered U-locks, sunglasses, a glove, jeans and facial coverings consistent with items worn"[25] during the attack. A search of Clanton's home uncovered materials linking him to Antifa and other anarchist groups.

How does Eric Clanton's behavior differ from those of James Alex Fields Jr., the white supremacist who weaponized his car in August 2017 by plowing into a group of counter-protestors killing a 32-year old woman?[26] Answer: it doesn't differ. Perhaps to the political pundits it matters. Liberal media was certainly mute on spotlighting Clanton's offenses, while the Charlottesville attack was the leading story for months as proof intolerance still exist. But to most Americans hate is hate whether at the hands of a liberal or the alt-right. The sad difference today is that as a nation, we immediately condemned the actions of this white supremacist. Yet, we have had a difficult time rallying up liberals to condemn the actions of Antifa members who assault citizens for simply disagreeing with their views.

Whether it's a white sheet draped over the head of the KKK aggressor or a black mask donning the face of a member of Antifa or a white supremacist chanting "White Power" as he plows his car into a crowd of people is of no great concern to the one who is being oppressed. What difference does it make when one is afraid to walk down their own street or to speak an opinion that may have been deemed "unpopular" for fear of getting hit across the head with a bike lock, or getting a face full of cement-laced mace, or having their business burned down to the ground?

Although the KKK is no longer burning crosses in people's yards, their ideology is still alive and well. David Duke, the founder and former Grand Wizard of the Louisiana Knights of the Ku Klux Klan, who was denounced by former President George H. W. Bush as a neo-Nazi,[27] and who recently ran unsuccessfully for the U.S. Senate in 2016, endorsed 2020 Democrat presidential hopeful

Tulsi Gabbard.[28] She, of course, rejected his endorsement. But, the thought still stands that the mind that fuels such hate is still alive and well in this country. When that mindset dons a white hood or a black mask it threatens my family's security. Both groups' use violence and intimidation to achieve their end. Both groups threaten the stability of our country. Both groups, if allowed to move about unencumbered, naturally degrade our sense of what's right and wrong as a nation.

ONLY DEMOCRATS ARE MORALLY CORRECT, RIGHT?

Another effective tool used by liberals to spread a culture of poverty and a bankruptcy of values onto Main Street America is the use of guilt—specifically, guilt associated with what liberals consider to be right and wrong. It is puzzling to many, but liberals have a surprisingly effective technique of redefining morality for an entire culture. Just like that, with a twist of a word, a turn of a phrase, a bend in a concept, they're able to reinterpret long-standing American values.

It's so effective that it has been used to stop multibillion-dollar companies in their tracks. It's been effective in silencing those who see something wrong with the direction our country is moving but say nothing out of fear of being out of sync with this new morality.

Time and time again, we see liberals claiming the moral high ground. But it's their very idea of what morality is that has brought us to the doorsteps of a culture teetering on insolvency.

Consider Wayfair, a multi-billion dollar corporation that found itself in the crosshairs of liberal logic. Their employees took to the streets in protest over the online giant's sale of bunk beds and mattresses to a non-profit organization whose mission is getting migrant kids off of cold floors and into warm beds. The non-profit organization wanted to purchase beds for children and Wayfair is an on-line company that sells beds. Sounds easy enough.

However, liberals turned a simple business transaction into a referendum on "hate" and "intolerance." To the liberal, Wayfair selling beds to make the lives of migrant children more comfortable was equivalent to them agreeing with the policies of President Trump to secure our southern borders. Understanding how liberals have gone about redefining American values is pivotal in understanding how the culture of poverty is flooding Middle America.

First, redefining deeply held American values such as capitalism, for example, is not an easy task that happens overnight. It takes time. It takes raising up each new generation with a firm belief that they are the center of the universe. Liberals seem to have an overflow of this particular quality. Everything around them is defined based on how it makes "them" feel. Even their biological gender is not enough of a road block to ward off irrational "feelings."

Second, you must shift the conversation quickly away from the children who will be able to get off the floor and into a bed and once more place the spotlight back on you and how you feel. Third, you must have a very large megaphone to pound your virtue signaling into the hearts and minds of the American people—and here is where a complicit mainstream media comes in handy. Presto, just like that, the process of redefining American values begins.

Their sense of what's right and wrong is not up for discussion. If you disagree? Well, you're just wrong and must be silenced.

For instance, during the walkout, employees displayed disparaging signs with sayings like "WAYFAIR COMFY WITH CONCENTRATION CAMPS," "A CAGE IS NOT A HOME TO LOVE," and "PEOPLE

OVER PROFIT." These were just some of the virtue signaling that was done.

With annual sales over $6 billion in 2018, the $200,000 contract with Baptist Child and Family Services, a nonprofit government contractor that manages detention centers for migrants at the US-Mexico border, to purchase bedroom furniture represents a paltry 0.00003 percent of Wayfair's revenues, barely a drop in the bucket for the multibillion-dollar company, clearly suggesting that profiting off this one transaction was not their primary goal.

Perhaps the company's primary goal was as their mission statement suggests: "We partner with organizations that play a meaningful role in creating safe and comfortable living spaces because we believe that a secure home is not only a basic human need but also the foundation for well-being."[29]

Or, perhaps their primary goal was that of most US companies: to provide a quality product or service to their customers. Period.

Getting kids off cold concrete floors[30] and into a comfortable bed seems to meet their mission of providing a basic human need and well-being. It would seem that providing this care to the migrant children would trump all other needs.

Regrettably, it doesn't and it didn't. It would appear that only liberals possess the moral clarity to make sure we know that some things in life are more important than getting children off the floor. Namely, their own feelings. Or, as Madeline Howard, the twenty-nine-year-old project manager at the company who emceed the walkout event, said, "This is the first time I felt like I needed to hit the streets to make sure that I was proud of my company, that I was happy to work for them."[31]

By all means, let us all make sure Madeline is "proud" and "happy."

Which do you think matters more to the migrant children who are sleeping on cold concrete floors: well-rested Americans feeling good about themselves or having a bed to sleep in tonight themselves?

Even before their employees took to the street in protest and apparently in an effort to show good faith, Wayfair announced they would donate $100,000 to American Red Cross—half of what they were getting from the sale of the beds. They said they would do so "in their effort to help those in dire need of basic necessities at the border." But "as a retailer, it is standard practice to fulfill orders for all customers and we believe it is our business to sell to any customer who is acting within the laws of the countries within which we operate . . . This does not indicate support for the opinions or actions of the group or individuals who purchase from us." Although Wayfair did not go as far as outright apologizing and refunding the sale of the bed, the fact that a statement was needed at all reflects the impact liberal logic has had on redefining morality in this country.

In response, employees chided the company's effort on a Twitter page created just for the walkout, saying, "@Wayfair stated in an email today that they will be making a donation of $100k to the @RedCross. This is great news! And proof that Wayfair can & does do good. However, the Red Cross has nothing to do with these ICE-operated facilities."

No good deed goes unpunished. How did we get to where we are today? How did we get to a place where providing comfort to children is not our primary focus? How did we become a nation where the value of a human life takes second place to our political agendas? It starts with redefining our values and bullying the rest of us into silence.

REVISITING WHITE PRIVILEGE: POCAHONTAS

According to liberals, white privilege refers to the additional bene-fits or advantages people who identify as white receive beyond what is commonly experienced by non-white people who are under the same political, social, and economic umbrella. By this definition, one could presume that the ultimate disrespect would be a white person, who already enjoys these special rights just because of the color of their skin, pretending to be a non-white person in order to reap the few meager benefits that group receives. Benefits such as those that prohibit employers from discriminating based on race and national origin. Benefits that attempt to right some national wrongs. Benefits that tries to ensure all applicants, regardless of gender or race, have a fair opportunity in the hiring process and in competing for promotions, all in an effort to address past prac-tices of discrimination when white folks received not just some of the benefits, but all of the benefits. Now, enter Pocahontas.

Stuart Varney, a columnist for Fox Business, wrote, "Apply-ing for a job as a Harvard professor, Senator Elizabeth Warren claimed to be a Native American. Harvard eagerly accepted her claim—they could tick off two boxes to show diversity: female and minority."[32] The only evidence she had provided to prove her claim at the time was her "high cheekbones"![33]

According to liberals' definition of white privilege, Sen. War-ren is downright greedy. She's gluttonous, even. According to liberal logic, she doesn't only want the bountiful privileges and rights sprawled in front of her simply for being white, now she wants my privileges, your privileges, and everyone's little crumbs as well. Talk about white privilege.

Would Warren not qualify as the poster child of white privi-lege? Shouldn't the social justice warriors have a field day on this blatant infraction? Where are the virtue signalers when you need them? Surely, they've been triggered by this gross macroaggression of self-identity.

Alas, liberals are only concerned when conservatives supposedly break the rules. As we've seen over the past few years, liberals' strong need to keep the spotlight squarely focused on the false narrative that Conservatives are racists trumps their social-justice-virtue-signaling itch to make everyone's life miserable. This was seen in raw form when President Trump issued a classic roast at a 2017 ceremony honoring the Navajo Code Talkers, who were instrumental in helping U.S. Marines send coded messages in the Pacific Theater during WWII. In thanking them for their bravery and contribution to the country, President Trump paused just long enough to shine a spotlight on the elephant in the room. Namely, a sitting senator, who is clearly a white person and who callously identified herself on employment applications and on the registration card for the State Bar of Texas as American Indian for almost three decades.[34]

Many in mainstream media and the liberal left couldn't see the real story that was in front of them. That is, a siting U.S. Senator, who is white, with blonde hair and blue eyes had the unmitigated gall to self-identity as a class of people who were ravaged by scorn, hatred, and greed as a direct result of white people. That was the real story. Senator Warren directly benefited from opportunities she might not have otherwise received had she not identified as an American Indian. But, instead of focusing on this, mainstream media wrote one story after another about how offensive it was for President Trump to mention the name "Pocahontas" at the ceremony.

Pocahontas is not a racial slur. Pocahontas is a historical figure. Self-identifying as a Native American because you have "high-cheek bones" is a lie. That's the insult. But Sen. Warren, with the eager aid of the mainstream media has been given a pass because most "journalists" are liberal.

What white Americans have never fully understood and what black Americans have forgotten is that white society created the suburbs and the ghettos. White institutions created it, white institutions maintain it, and white society condoned it. (They still do.) But, it's in the ghettos where the culture of poverty first found its home.

The number one issue plaguing the black community is the pandemic fatherless rate. Curb this sickness and the black community would be well on its way to a full recovery. Unfortunately, victim-inducing narratives such as "white privilege," "white values," and "police brutality" lowers the bar of expectations in the black community. These victim-inducing narratives once adopted gives the black community permission to not succeed because the odds are against them anyway or because they feel like no one really expects them to succeed.

Disturbingly, this same lowering of the bar of expectation is being exported out of inner cities and onto Main Street America by using these exact same vehicles of "white privilege," "white values," and redefining American values.

Patriotism is our primary shield of defense. We must give people a sense of identity! What does it *mean* to be an American? Every individual responds to confidence, and this is not more true of any race than of the black race. Let them once understand that you are unselfishly interested in them, and you can lead them to any extent.[35] It's not just true for blacks, but for most people.

As a child, I remember standing up at the beginning of each new school day pledging my allegiance to the Flag of the United States. I remember being taught to think highly of my country. I grew up feeling as though I was a part of, not separate from, what made America great.

Understanding the remedy to our problem is patriotism, President Trump did just this with a renewed focus on American values. The 2019 Fourth of July Salute to America celebration packed the Lincoln Memorial site with thousands of America-loving patriots. It was a huge success met with the usual barrage of liberal media outlets' complaints.[36]

President Trump went toe-to-toe with NFL owners and their players who knelt during the national anthem. Again, he was met with the usual string of insults and cutting remarks by liberal media outlets.

The president, when making a case for American exceptionalism is called a dangerous isolationist.[37] Or his campaign slogan "Make America Great Again" was interpreted by *The New Yorker* as "Making America WHITE Again" because according to them "white men fear black men."[38]

Highlighting, championing, and defending respect toward our nation is the best way to reteach those values that propelled us into the status of the greatest country to ever exist. These same values will serve as a positive deposit against a bankrupt culture.

There was a time when I thought poverty was strictly measured in terms of dollars and cents. To me, poverty was poverty. There was no sliding scale to it. Yes, one person may have a little less or a little more money than another. But essentially, if you're poor, you're poor.

Until my dear uncle Herbert said to me that "city poor is much different from country poor," it had never entered my mind, having grown up very impoverished on a farm in southern Alabama, that there are measures of poverty that can't be counted in terms of money.

Clearly, we need real solutions and we need them now. How we get there isn't rocket science. It's quite simple. We just need to remember that a politician's perpetual vocation is a search for power. Perhaps it is because President Trump is not a career politician that he is doing more in his first term of president than most do in eight years. Instead of searching for more and more power, President Trump entered the White House with a bang. While the Democrat Party nips at his heals on every single turn with conjured up impeachable charges and daily resistance, President Trump has been busy securing our southern border, dealing a powerful blow to extremist groups by killing the ideological leader of ISIS—Abu Bakr al-Baghdadi, forcing North Korea to act sane, driving China to the negotiation table over trade deals and finding the magic wand that eluded President Obama for eight years to bring jobs back to our economy.

Politicians must be held accountable at the ballot box. It's essential in a democracy that the road to political power and decision-making be through the ballot box and through no other means.[39] But, when we're dealing with a Democrat Party that is without meaningful answers to our nation's problems and a complicit agenda-driven media we find ourselves on the brink of something ominous again.

Only speaking truth boldly will set us free.

6.

THE PATRIOTISM OF SLAVES

In my home office, across from where I'm sitting is a picture on my wall titled *History (1962)*. It's a black-and-white photo of three bathroom doors. One says "LADIES." The other reads "MEN." The last says "COLORED." At the bottom of the photograph, it says, "You cannot know where you are going, until you know where you have been."

This photo is a poignant reminder to me and to all who see it that America has come a long way since the days of separate restrooms. Yet to consider where we are in America now and where we still want to go, we must factor in our nation's past. America's past includes slavery. Slavery is not just a part of black history. It's America's history, as well.

Slavery was a dirty business. Even George Washington routinely remarked on the degrading effect slavery had on the master's character, which became arrogant and sensual from the habit of owning slaves and living without a measure of control.[1]

Frederick Douglass described the dehumanizing character of slavery, having an effect on both the slave and the one "owning" the slave. He remarked about the change in his once pleasant owner, who was not initially accustomed to owning anyone and who initially was sweet of spirit, but soon met with the debasing habit of slavery. "But, alas! this kind heart had but a short time to remain such. The fatal poison of irresponsible power was already in her hands . . . That cheerful eye, under the influence of slavery, soon became red with rage; that voice, made all of sweet accord, changed to one of harsh and horrid discord; and that angelic face gave place to that of a demon."[2]

History is replete with example after example of how the business of slavery debased all who came in contact with it—to a greater degree to the one who was owned, but the owner him- or herself did not escape completely unscathed. Slavery was a lewd and injurious business. Even the most pious and tender-hearted of people soon, under the influence of slavery, grew hearts as hard as stone. It was inevitable.

Though slavery had a corrupting influence on the one who owned the slaves, most assuredly slavery was thoroughly degrading to the slaves themselves. There is no equivocation on that fact. Too much is known today to allude even in the slightest way that for some of the "owned" slavery worked out well for them. I've read numerous accounts where the slave owner is said to have taken "good care" of his slaves . . . practically treating them like family. In reality, slaves were as much a part of the family of his "master's" house as my chocolate Labrador dog is to our family. Our dog is loved and well cared for. But, she is still a dog—*owned* and has no free will. She obeys my commands. Period.

George Fitzhugh, social theorist who published racial and slavery-based sociological theories, argued during the antebellum South that white women had not been robbed of the softness of their own sex in the slave south, as was the case with women in the North. Southern white women were considered the moral gatekeepers of society. So while her white husband found some advantage in the notion that black women could be easily debased, white women did not have to endure such advances and could instead "assume the high station for which nature designed her" to the task of humanizing the human race and blessing others.[3]

To the slave owner, it is abundantly clear that slavery was not just about free labor. Perhaps just as great of a motivation for many who owned slaves was the owner's access to uninhibited sexual relations with slave women. Even among some of the most pious men of those days you read about how they rationalized the dignity of the slave away, especially the slave woman whether she was being bred by the black male stud as Fredrick Douglass wrote about in his autobiography or "kept in a state of prostitution by white men who had little incentive to exercise self-control."[4]

Illicit sex with black women became such a problem in the antebellum South that many began to worry about "race mixing that would inevitably result in the disappearance of the 'pure' Caucasian."[5] The illicit act was so prevalent, some were concerned for "their white adolescent boys, who, some thought could never learn discipline or respect for Christian continence as long as they felt they could compel black women to sleep with them. This anxiety motivated a Louisiana planter to send his boys North to be educated. As he saw it 'there was no possibility of their being brought up in decency at home.'"[6] Slavery was about control, greed, power, dominance, free labor, and sex. It was sheer evil.

For the slaves, slavery not only was degrading, but it also bred hopelessness. Slaves had no hope for themselves, for their children, or for their children's children. Father, son, and grandson all plowed the same fields. There were no rising expectations among slaves. There was no self-determination among the owned. A life of crouching servility and obliging servitude is all they could see in their future.

Douglass again explained slavery as a form of mental darkness. There's no light, only darkness. He lamented over his own state of learning. The more he learned, the more he regretted learning. Learning left him feeling discontented and unhappy with no way to change his lot in life. He wrote about envying the ignorant slave. To him, education and slavery became strange and incompatible bedfellows.

The late author and urban sociologist Nathan Glazer posed the poignant question, "Why was American slavery the most awful the world has ever known?"

Without doubt, slavery in any form or location is evil. Yet, American slavery possessed a sort of heightened barbarity and cruelty that cannot be explained away and one that was not readily seen in other parts of the world.

Comparing slavery in Brazil and the United States, Glazer wrote that unlike the Brazilian slave, who knew that he was a man and that he differed in degree, not in kind, from his master, the American slave was totally ignorant of and completely cut off from his past and was offered absolutely no hope for the future. His children could be sold, his marriage wasn't recognized, his wife could be violated or sold, and he could also be subject, without redress, to frightful barbarities.[7] American slavery offered nothing more than utter hopelessness to the enslaved.

So why was American slavery worse than anywhere else in the world? In large part, because American slave owners mostly professed to be Christians—Protestants for the most part. We see the variances that take place in every religion. Some people are more devout than others. Some people are committed to a more rigid understanding of their faith than others. However, under a true consideration of Christianity there's no place in it that allows for a believer to own another person. There's no place in a true consideration of Christianity that allows for an earnest believer to behave in the debauched ways already outlined above. So, the only way an American so-called Christian, could own a slave and be in good standing with his faith was if the one he owned was *not* human. This distortion of truth is what allowed slavery to exist in a "Christian" nation for hundreds of years. White slave owners in America knew the difference between what was right and what was wrong. They rejected what they knew was true and instead adopted a reprobate mindset that created a form of slavery so barbaric and so universal that its effects are still felt today in the great disparities between the races and the lack of a strong lineage.

In the book of Genesis, everything was subjected to man's dominion. Everything except for another human being. Man was never designed to own another human being. This is why American slavery was exponentially more barbaric, more degrading, and more hopeless than slavery anywhere else in the world. Slaves before the American Revolution were utterly without hope. Theirs were a hopelessness that thoroughly saturated every single aspect of life leaving nothing for the one who was owned to hold onto for themselves—not even their own chastity.

Slavery as an institution, of course, was in existence well before the American Revolution. So, it's understandable that when the American Revolution began, slaves, above all others, claimed it as their own. It offered a flicker of hope. Thus, the American Revolution is littered with stories about the gallantry of slaves on the battlefield and at home.

The patriotism of slaves was a patriotism that produced hope, if only temporarily. But it was a hope that created opportunities for them for the first time to live above their predefined station in life. For the first time, they did not see themselves as victims. Their patriotism made them victors over their circumstances. They took possession of a freedom that was not their own and cloaked themselves with a hope not intended for them. This freedom they took hold of would not be the culmination of their fate. But from hopelessness to hope—a yearning was sparked.

Perhaps they resisted their reality and joined in the fight for independence for their posterity. Perhaps they fled the fields of their masters to fight in a war that would not liberate them so they could feel like men—to finally feel human.

One day they're witnesses to a black family being raffled off, one by one, in front of some tawdry tavern, and the next day, a black man, Peter Salem, wins the esteem of his white Minuteman unit and is presented to General George Washington not as a slave but as the *man* who had slain the officer leading the British detachment at Bunker Hill.[8]

Jehu Grant was a slave who fled his master's fields and served in the army for ten months. He said that the "songs of liberty . . . saluted my ear, thrilled through my heart." It was under the unremitting degradation of slavery that Grant petitioned for his postwar pension describing his decision to join the patriot cause:

> I was then grown to manhood, in the full vigor and strength of life, and heard much about the cruel and arbitrary things done by the British. Their ships lay within a few miles of my master's house, which stood near the shore, and I was confident that my master traded with them, and I suffered much from fear that I should be sent aboard a ship of war. This I disliked. But when I saw liberty poles and the people all engaged for the support of freedom, I could not but like and be pleased with such

things (God forgive me if I sinned in so feeling). And living on the borders of Rhode Island, where whole companies of colored people enlisted, it added to my fears and dread of being sold to the British. These considerations induced me to enlist into the American army, where I served faithful about ten months, when my master found and took me home.[9]

Grant was ecstatic for the opportunity to fight for freedom, even a freedom that was not his own and short lived, as his master eventually tracked him down and led him back into bondage.

This isn't something I pretend to fully understand. I cannot fully grasp the notion of black slaves fighting for their white master's freedom. It makes me sad. But I *can* understand their need for hope. These black slaves were intoxicated by the arousal of hope that must have whirled all around them.

Hope is a powerful stimulant. It can extract courage from among the most timid souls. It can inflame the tiniest flicker of optimism. It can embolden the smallest mustard seed of faith.

The hopelessness of slaves during the eighteenth century isn't that different from the hopelessness plaguing many black communities today. Inner cities are, in a way, a second form of slavery that was created and is being sustained by failed Democrat policies. Liberal policies that have created and sustained failing inner city schools. Liberal policies that have created and sustained a lack of jobs, low-expectations, and perilous political narratives. Producing for itself a culture that leaves most blacks walking into mainstream America having a very small grasp of the English language, owning no land, having little to no personal wealth, no significant business contacts, and sporting the well-known "mean-mug" look on their faces looking perpetually angry.

How are they expected to fit into corporate America? In all of their pseudo bravado, how are they to beat back feelings of inferiority to walk into a bank to request a small business loan?

I cannot imagine a bleaker, darker example of hopelessness, of feeling like you don't belong, than that of being a slave. However, even today many black Americans feel as though they don't belong to their nation of birth. They feel as if the *ideal* of America belongs to the white man and his posterity alone. It doesn't help that liberal politicians have used the stains of past slavery along with present day individual racism to help perpetuate a victimhood mentality in the black community.

Blacks are reminded daily by white liberals that they don't belong. They're told routinely that they're victims of a system that doesn't care for them because of the color of their skin. They're told they can't achieve much because the odds are against them. They're told by white liberals that only *they* can rescue them from the futility of their lives.

These victimhood-inducing narratives have consecrated perpetual voters to the Democrat Party. But even more disastrous is that these failed liberal narratives breed hopelessness. And hopelessness has bred low expectations within the black community. Why reach and strain for the next rung on the ladder of success if the odds are against you? It's as if the white man has greased that next rung on the ladder.

In spite of all this, the good news is that I believe an ethnic exodus is brewing. An awakening is occurring. A series of migrations off the Democrat plantation and into our American birthright is coming to fruition by more and more blacks, our Jewish brothers and sisters who vote overwhelmingly Democrat, and the Hispanic community, as well.

Those who feel disenfranchised from the American Dream need to take a lesson from the black slaves who looked over into the white man's world and grabbed up some of that hope for themselves, even a hope many said didn't belong to them. They *made* it their own.

It's like being in a dark room and then you see a flicker of light. It's not a constant light. But that flicker was a spark of hope to black slaves that allowed them—many for the first time—to dare to hope.

Patriotism breeds hope. Clinging to ideals that are higher than oneself raises the bar of expectation. Just like hopelessness breeds low expectations, patriotism, a sense of ownership, and a sense of governing one's own life breed hope. And hope produces opportunities to carve out a life for oneself.

America's Founding Fathers didn't always live up to the ideals of the Constitution. In fact, they're on record as failing miserably. Yet they raised the bar and stretched to attain a better self—to be a better person and to create a better world. So much of what we contend with today in the black community is the constant lowering, not raising, of the bar of expectations.

American history is imperfect. The issues we've grappled with have not always been literally black and white; there are some gray areas. We didn't always take the most direct route to get to where we are today. But we made it here, to where we are now. And where we are isn't where we need to be or want to be. But in order to continue to move forward, we must participate in the process with *hope* and courage. Otherwise, we're left to the flawed imagination of imperfect men. Or we're left to be exploited by politicians who want our vote but have no power and often no desire to bring about the changes they promise.

To the black community: We are *not* victims. We are victors. We are the recipients of a great inheritance, an inheritance we, for the most part, didn't sacrifice to receive. Many came before us and paid the ultimate sacrifice so that we can receive this inheritance. Many of those who came before us did not leave behind land or great wealth for us. But what they had they gave: hope.

THE BLACK AMERICAN AND THE US CONSTITUTION

President Obama proclaimed during his farewell speech that "Our Constitution is a remarkable, beautiful gift. But it's really just a piece of parchment. It has no power on its own. We, the people, give it power. We, the people, give it meaning—with our participation, and with the choices that we make and the alliances that we forge. Whether or not we stand up for our freedoms. Whether or not we respect and enforce the rule of law."[10]

The president was merely paraphrasing James Madison, who said the Constitution is "a mere parchment barrier"[11] if the branches of government refuse to exercise their checks and balances on each other's power. He wasn't remarking on the transient nature of the document, as if its authors intended for it to be changed with the blowing of the wind. Instead, he was calling on the three federal branches of government to compel the others to operate within the bounds of their power. To be checks and balances on each other to ensure that each branch of government stays within the fences of our clearly defined Constitution.

President Obama's words sound pretty. Therein lies the problem with the Obama administration. Therein lies the problem with those who tend to sit high and look down low at the rest of us—be it politicians, bureaucrats, Hollywood elites, the UN, billionaire George Soros, and the like. This level of arrogance over a document that has stood for over 230 years is why Obama could come before the American people and say with such self-assurance, "I have a phone and a pen," referencing his intent to bypass the Constitution all together, to bypass Congress and enact whatever laws his little heart desires.

Why? Because if the Constitution is a living, breathing document as most liberals claim, then it can be changed to accommodate the personal whims of the one holding the pen.

Please note: Our Constitution and historical precedents afford this level of executive powers to exist. Presidents before Obama weren't shy in exercising these powers and those who come after him will surely exercise the same privilege. However, it's the arrogance of Obama to proclaim such a privilege out loud that shocked so many and stirred up a flurry of debates on our ability to rewrite the whole document on a whim if it pleased us to do so.

Yet the Founding Fathers knew that while times change, truths do not—certainly not the truths on which they were basing this new government. Our second president, John Adams, noted the truth that "Our Constitution is made only for a moral and religious people. It is wholly inadequate for the governing of any other kind."[12] Meaning, our Constitution is only able to govern people who know the difference between what is morally right and what is wrong. People who know the difference between up from down, good from bad, left from right and a boy from a girl. It's wholly inadequate, completely incapable, of governing over any other kind of people.

This reality should alarm each of us. We're now living in a society where you don't even have to be black to be black anymore. Let us not forget Rachel Dolezal. Talk about making it up as we go.

America is the greatest country that has ever existed not because you and I are so keenly special. America is the greatest country that has ever existed because it was founded on the greatest political document ever written: the US Constitution.

America doesn't exist apart from the Constitution. And my storied life as a poor black girl from the Deep South using the established systems of our nation to pull myself out of dire poverty doesn't exist apart from a capital market system—a system that can only truly exist under the rules of engagement found within our Constitution.

We all need the established protections under the US Constitution, none more than minorities and the poor. I surely lacked pedigree, wealth, and influence as a young black woman. But the US Constitution is a warm blanket on a cold night. It shelters and defends. It guides and provides redresses and property rights so the wealthy cannot expropriate our land; it provides a promise of a presumption that we're innocent first and must have the ability to face our accusers. It gives us the promise that we can defend ourselves. There is no greater deterrent to a return of the days of the KKK than the knowledge that a black man might be armed.

We, especially in the black community, cannot afford to have random leaders make up rules of engagement as they go. It doesn't work that way, and history confirms it doesn't work out well for the average citizen.

If we undo the Constitution, we undo America. Many tyrants know this to be true. This is why would-be tyrants pay protestors and collude with politicians and other would-be tyrants to create chaos and disorder. To make themselves ungovernable.

The greatest way to undo America is to create a society of chaos and disorder. The Constitution isn't capable of governing unconscionable people.

Here's a note to every freedom-loving American: If you want to undo America, create a society where you can basically make up morality as you go. Create a society where everything is relative. Create a society where what has always been considered "bad" is now "good," and where those things considered "good" in the past now become "bad." See how that works for you.

A SLAVE'S HOPE

My family and I recently had the opportunity to visit President Washington's Mount Vernon plantation home. There were many nostalgic moments as we moved throughout the plantation. Paramount among them was our visit to the slave cemetery on the estate. The short, somber walk from President and Martha Washington's tomb to the final resting place of the slaves was surreal—its backdrop both muted and dreamlike at the same time. There were no ornate statues. No historian was needed to tell their stories.

My family and I weren't prepared for our hearts' responses. Comprehending the significance of the site, my ten-year-old daughter started to cry. She simply couldn't understand why people would own other people. It didn't take long before my heart, too, started to overflow. My son and husband stood by strong, embracing both of us.

At one time Washington had over three hundred slaves on his property. Unlike the president's tomb, there was no headstone to tell their stories. No long line of visitors was waiting to take a glance. But we knew we were standing on sacred ground.

After a few minutes passed, we spoke about the evils of slavery and the utter hopelessness it imposed on those resting beneath us. Then I was reminded of Jehu Grant and Peter Salem. For most slaves, they held out no hope for themselves. Their hope was for *someday*. If they held on, someday. If they endured, *then* someday. If they just persevered, someday, maybe, their children's children's children would be free.

Perhaps fighting for a nation to be free when they themselves were slaves was their down payment for securing a place for me. Perhaps they weren't so naïve to think white slave owners would suddenly get a dose of true religion, repent of their wayward ways, and allow slavery to quietly come to an end. Perhaps Peter Salem's joining in to fight alongside Washington was his attempt to build up some collateral that could be drawn upon by me some day. Perhaps he knew that someday the tides would change and his posterity would be free and that we would use the collateral he had earned with his blood to purchase a place in America. Perhaps . . .

Today, we know that we are their children's children's children. We are no longer victims. We are both free and equal.

Now we have an obligation to live well.

7.

THE BLACK HARBINGER OF AMERICA'S FUTURE

D
o not be deceived by the title. This book is not just for black people. It's for every American who sees the subtle— and the increasingly not-so-subtle—redefining of basic American truths—truths that are foundational to the freedom that's necessary for successful living.

A redefining of basic American values has taken place in our country. This shift in values may feel as though it happened all of a sudden. But, it did not. This redefining of values has been a work in progress for some time now mostly brought about by the continued implementation of failed liberal public policies. Specifically, failed liberal policies that were first perfected in black communities. Liberal policies that have not only *not* helped black communities but have made many of them worse.

Truth exists. When we live according to what is true, we generally prosper. But when we live according to false narratives, revisionist history, and scare tactics, we set ourselves up for failure.

For a long time now, many in black America have, by their votes, given liberalism a chance to deliver on its promises. Liberal politicians have come to our communities, spoken in our churches, dined at our potlucks, and made promises to those who needed to hear someone give them a reason to hope for the future.

The problem is that having been given that chance, lo these many years, the liberal answers from the liberal politicians have not helped our communities. Many are, in fact, worse than they were fifty years ago.

As a black person I know this to be true. I've watched from a front row seat as these misbegotten liberal policies have been introduced to and perfected in many black communities. These policies have decimated neighborhoods, destabilized the family structure, slaughtered whole generations, and victimized those left standing.

What we're witnessing in the black community today is a dire warning shot across the bow of America's future. The cancer that plagues black communities spreads every time another liberal is put in office. If we don't heed this warning shot, we have no one to blame but ourselves for the legacy we leave our children and grandchildren. The good news is that we *can* heed this warning... but we must act now. If we don't act, the decay we see in black communities will continue to spread to the broader American community.

As a harbinger of things to come, these failed liberal policies, though first perfected in the black community, are now spilling over into the larger American community. And sadly, I predict the results will be the same on a national scale. Failed policies, failed promises, and failed "progress."

How has this decay been allowed to happen? In a nutshell, white liberals!

White liberals[1] have perfected the strategy of destabilizing the black community. Once perfected, that strategy is now serving as a microcosm of a much larger and more far-reaching strategy. The decay that has been allowed to take place for decades in black America is spilling out onto the streets of America at large—promising the same catastrophic results.

Being a part of the black community has afforded me an up-close and personal opportunity to see the ill effects of policies instituted by mostly white liberal bureaucrats and politicians with the sad support of black enablers who continue to support policies and legislation that harm, not help, their constituencies. I can look at the black community and see the devastating outcomes liberal policies have had on a population so rich in flavor, with a depth of character and fortitude rivaled by none.

When black communities are destabilized, the sad results are predictable. Brokenness begets brokenness: broken marriages, broken homes, and broken children who grow up to be broken adults. Broken words, broken hearts, broken promises are the legacy experienced by so many Americans today. The spilling-out effect of this brokenness is hurting us all—and like a cancer, it spreads to the larger American family.

I hurt for all who are reaping the consequences of what past policians and presidential adminstrations have allowed to occur. In many regards, America today is an amalgamation of one failed liberal policy after another. This is particularly true in the black community. As a black American woman, I see clearly that our predominately black communities are on life support. We are dying a slow, tedious, and shameful death that's been mostly self-inflicted. But also fanned on by white liberals who use our lack of resources to their advantage to win elections. This is just one more reason why Donald Trump's arrival into the office of president was perfect timing. I do not know if America could have withstood yet another run-of-the-mill politician—be them liberal or not.

There is no greater way to unleash potential in a community than by bringing jobs back to those communities and doing away with restrictive regulations that make it nearly impossible for businesses to thrive. President Trump's economic policies have ushered in record low unemployment numbers across every ethnicity.

For example, the 2019 State of Women-Owned Businesses Report,[2] commissioned by American Express, reported that women-owned businesses fuel the economy and now represent 42 percent of all businesses in America today—nearly 13 million—employing over 9 million workers and generating revenue of $1.9 trillion. Across all ethnicities, 1,817 new businesses were started per day between 2018 and 2019.

Compare this to women of color, who are leading in almost every category. "Women of color represent 39 percent of the total female population in the U.S. but account for 89 percent of the net new women-owned businesses per day (1,625) over the past year." As of 2019, women of color account for 50 percent of all women-owned businesses—6.4 million—employing over 2 million people and generating a little more than $422 billion in revenue. Between 2018 and 2019, businesses owned by black women specifically represented the highest rate of growth over all women. We started 42 percent of net new businesses, which is three times our share of the female population (14 percent).

Interestingly, over half of all women-owned businesses are concentrated in three industries. One of which is called "Other services" such as hair and nail salons that accounted for 22 percent of the women-owned businesses (2.8 million firms).

In 2015, I saw a story about Isis Brantley who was arrested and jailed.[3] No, she didn't assault anyone, nor was she a political dissident. Her crime was she likes to braid hair and pass on her knowledge to other people. Isis has been braiding hair since 1979. For most black women, natural hair care is more about a cultural rite of passage as it is about having a cute hair style. But, in 1997 Isis was dragged out of her shop, in front of her customers, and handcuffed. She had previously been found guilty of braiding hair without a cosmetology license. A license that would have cost her $25,000 to comply and transform her natural hair care business into a barber college.

Speaking about the burdensome licensing regulations imposed on workers making them pay thousands of dollars to complete months—and years, even—of training President Trump remarked that he was surprised to learn, "nationally, the average training for cosmetologists is 11 times longer than the training for emergency medical technicians, and sometimes training costs $20,000 for a cosmetology license. So it takes a tremendous amount of time. And we have great respect for cosmetologists, but there's something probably a little bit wrong with that."[4]

Prior to President Trump, this sort of overregulating of businesses presented barriers to business ownership for many black women who earn a living for their families by braiding hair. This threat has spanned across the United States from New Jersey to Nevada.[5] Over regulation is a pervasive problem in this country. A problem that landed in the crosshairs of President Trump when he took office. Trump's drive to unshackle our economy from the bondage of over regulations became the roadmap for Republican state legislators who followed the president's lead and started aggressively rolling back foolish regulations such as those stifling hair-braiding. These braiding salons, that overwhelmingly impact black-owned businesses, are just one of many industries Republican lawmakers are working to deregulate further.[6]

It is vitally important for all communities, especially black communities, to begin voting in their *own* best interest. Whether you have a particular affinity towards President Trump or not should not be the main issue that you vote on. The litmus test we should all use to evaluate any political candidate is whether or not our lives have improved under their leadership. To do anything other is to resign ourselves to the same old political stalemates: Regurgitate the same empty promises you made last year and at the same time find ways to discredit the opposition.

We saw this latter strategy once again when former Vice President Joe Biden threw his hat into the already crowded 2020 Democrat presidential primary and pushed forward the manipulative narrative that President Trump believes racists are "very fine people" too. But for those who watched the full clip[7] of President Trump's remarks directly after a white supremacist drove his car into a crowd of protestors in Charlottesville killing Heather Heyer we saw the president take great pains to exclude white supremacists from his list of "very fine people."

He said, "We condemn in the strongest possible terms this egregious display of hatred, bigotry, and violence on many sides, on many sides. It's been going on for a long time in our country. Not Donald Trump, not Barack Obama. This has been going on for a long, long time. It has no place in America. What is vital now is a swift restoration of law and order and the protection of innocent lives. No citizen should ever fear for their safety and security in our society. And no child should ever be afraid to go outside and play or be with their parents and have a good time."

He went on to say, "I want to salute the great work of the state and local police in Virginia. Incredible people, law enforcement, incredible people. And also the National Guard. They've really been working smart and working hard. They've been doing a terrific job. Federal authorities are also providing tremendous support to the governor; he thanked me for that. And we are here to provide whatever other assistance is needed. We are ready, willing and able."[8]

The president did not say white supremacists are very fine people too. In fact, he made these statements before all of the information was in. He didn't know David Duke was there. He didn't know a "white supremacist" ran his car into a crowd. All of these particulars would come out later on in the day. But here he stood before a nation pleading that we return to order. Pleading that we do our part to heal our nation by loving one another. His comments were completely appropriate. But why should we allow facts to get in the way of a good narrative? Right?

Biden arrogantly relied on the belief that most Americans are truly bottom basement dwellers who wouldn't bother to investigate the truth of his claims. Like many liberal Democrats who aspire to the presidency, there was no mention of bringing good jobs back to America and our black communities in Biden's video. Democrats have made no mention of President Trump's stellar efforts to halt the wave of illegal aliens flooding our southern border and taking jobs our own citizens could fill. There's no moderate Democrat who has been brave enough to step forward and openly reject the dangerous tug to turn our nation into a socialist society. No mention of denouncing rising anti-Semitism. No mention of the innumerable threats posed by North Korea, Iran, China, Russia, Turkey, Syria, ISIS, unfair trade agreements, and so forth. Nothing said about the millions of black babies ripped from their mothers' bodies. No answer for the failure of inner-city schools entrusted with educating our next generation. No answer for the violence in our black neighborhoods. Silence about the drug epidemic taking our children captive. Sex trafficking? No answer there, either. Instead, Biden weaponized the sordid history of our nation in an attempt to win an election. Period.

White liberals running for office have come to rely on the black vote "gatekeepers" as a way to secure the large black voting bloc. Just speak in black churches with Al Sharpton or Jesse Jackson at your side and watch your poll numbers rise among black voters. When will we ever learn to turn away from this crass manipulation by the Left?

Civil rights pioneer Bayard Rustin said it best: "The notion of the undifferentiated black community is the intellectual creation of both whites—liberals as well as racists to whom all Negroes are the same—and of certain small groups of blacks who illegitimately claim to speak for the majority."[9] His words are not *just* relegated to black folks. They aptly apply to anyone willing to be manipulated. Replace "black" with "gay," "white," "poor," or "women."

White liberals have perfected and weaponized their monolithic view of the black community and extracted the maximum amount of misunderstanding and the optimum level of chaos and rebellion to achieve their ultimate goal of power, control, influence, wealth, and any combination thereof.

Not satisfied with exercising this control *just* in the black community, white liberals are now using their manipulative tactics to bring the most powerful nation in the world to a grinding halt. Liberals' ability to weaponize disaffected groups—whether blacks, the poor, or well-meaning social justice warriors—to see the state as a benevolent nanny allows them to gain wide sympathy and maintain the kind of disruption that makes it nearly impossible to govern, to the point where otherwise intelligent and reasonable people can justify abolishing ICE, creating sanctuary cities and states, not funding a border wall for their own security , and even impeaching a duly elected president.

Some may assert that liberal politicians are acting from good motives. And perhaps some are. But many are not. And to those who are, I have to say: Show us the results of your promises. Come take a walk with me through the cities governed by your liberal policies. We can start in Chicago, Baltimore, Detroit, DC . . . you chose. Show me the results of the liberal policies enacted from the liberal leadership of these and other cities with a large minority population.

It's a tragedy when good intentions and humane ideologies are weaponized against our own people. The need to direct one's own community is a basic necessity for a democracy to work. However, when politicians twist our values that "all men are created equal" to espouse open borders or policies that weaken our national security, we are all made worse. Or when our belief in the value of voting is redefined to extend to convicted rapists, terrorists, and murderers we are all made worse.[10] Or when our desire to see everyone thrive financially is warped into my subsidizing every human choice by paying higher taxes to cover free education, free healthcare, and a "moral" wage—we are all made worse.

A question I often ask is "How many inner cities are governed by Republicans?" To date, I've found *none*. Yet Democrats come before the American people offering free education, free healthcare, a mandatory living wage, and one social program after another. These types of programs, often launched *first* in black communities, rarely begin with a clear purpose, are not understood, are not explained fully, and bring about social losses that need not have occurred.[11] To repeat, let's take a walk through liberally governed cities and see how the minority communities are faring.

As a general rule, politicians sell what their constituents will buy. Liberal politicians are selling free stuff: free college, free healthcare, guaranteed jobs, guaranteed wages, unlimited and free abortions, universal childcare, and on and on. Specifically, they're selling one government program after another that promises to solve all of our problems. There is a major conundrum in seeking salvation from our problems by looking to the government to solve them. What has clearly been established within the black community and now awaits the rest of the American community are the inadequacies baked into every new program supposedly designed to alleviate our woes.

Then, when a government program fails, we're often told it's because we didn't allocate enough "resources" (i.e., money and government bureaucrats) to address the issue. Somehow we think if only we earmark more money, if only we do a better job identifying the problem, if only we create more governmental committees, if only we hire more competent people, if only we muster our full resources of intelligence, then we will fix the problem this time around. But this perspective takes little account of the fundamental political nature of social welfare measures—spawned in the first place to maintain a political leadership and then continuously adapted to a changing political environment.[12]

These government programs often have no intention of solving real problems. Politicians' promises frequently have nothing to do with their constituents. It's all about gaining, maintaining, and expanding their leadership into more and more areas of our life. We're handing over our freedom to live lives according to the dictates of government caretakers who are primarily concerned about the next election cycle. Seriously consider this statement— don't pass over it too quickly. Understanding it is foundational to us becoming aware of the real ruse.

If more government programs were the key, every black family would be living the high life. But we're not! Government programs have now been created to pay for our phones, our rent, our food, our clothing, our internet service, and our daycare bills. You name it, there's a strong chance there's a government program to cover the cost. Yet many in the black community live on in despair.

If life in the black community has taught us anything, it's that government programs are based on maintaining political power—not solving issues central to the community. Hence, we see Democrats voted into office overwhelmingly year after year, continuously improving their own lot in life while the community they represent endures rising crime rates, subpar education, violence, and high unemployment. Regardless of how likable and animated Alexandria Ocasio-Cortez's social welfare measures seem to be, they're designed first to insert and maintain political leadership and by extension political power, dependency, and control.

Oddly, their solution to failing programs seems to be initiating more programs—and turning even farther to the Left. In all fairness, the Left is experiencing the radicalization of their own strategies to herd people. Liberal ideas once deliberately financed and incubated by an adoring Democrat Party have now turned into a hard-core Left-leaning opposition party within the party itself, threatening its very existence. A moderate Democrat is almost unheard of in the media. Moderates have been hijacked by the media-popular hard progressive Left. These hard-core progressives, who are left of the Left, are now running for president on the Democrat ticket and enjoy a significant prominence in the media spotlight. These hardcore liberals are also setting the agenda for the overall party—namely, the Green New Deal;

universal healthcare; eliminating private insurance; giving felons, rapists, and terrorists the right to vote; open borders; gun control; late-term and full-term abortion on demand; legalization of drugs; and more. These are all moral values that promise to leave not just black America but all of America (save the elite Leftists in power) broke, broken, and bruised.

OPEN BORDERS

Consider the hard Left's desire for open borders. How does that help Americans, black or white? Yes, some of the Left will argue that it's not open borders they want. They would spout about morality and how America is, after all, a land of immigrants. That's partially true, but how is it moral and how is America made better with the unvetted and overwhelming flood of illegal aliens crossing our borders every day? Caravan after caravan assembled, fed, transported, and instructed on what exactly to say to breach our immigration laws. How is your family, around your dinner table, made better? You're not. None of these things improve the quality of our American civilization.

It's not racist to demand that an immigrant lay down their flag of origin and pick up the American flag as their own. President Theodore Roosevelt said it best:

> We should insist that if the immigrant who comes here in good faith becomes an American and assimilates himself to us, he shall be treated on an exact equality with everyone else, for it is an outrage to discriminate against any such man because of creed, or birthplace, or origin. But this is predicated upon the person's becoming in every facet an American, and nothing but an American

. . . There can be no divided allegiance here. Any man who says he is an American, but something else also, isn't an American at all. We have room for but one flag, the American flag . . . We have room for but one language here, and that is the English language . . . and we have room for but one sole loyalty and that is a loyalty to the American people.[13]

Was the Rough Rider a racist?

THE LEFT'S WAR ON THE BLACK FAMILY

Consider the black family who were told they would be better off accepting government-sponsored housing. A program that has proven to destabilize the black family as it disincentivizes marriage and discourages the black father from living in the home. How does that help us? We now know this subtly liberal policy encouraged by our government is, in part, responsible for the utter destabilization of the black family.

In 1960, before President Lyndon Johnson's liberal War on Poverty program and anti-marriage initiative was instituted, two out of three black children (67 percent) lived with two parents. In 1991, a little more than one in three (36 percent) lived with two parents.[14] In 2018, two out of five (40 percent) black children lived with both parents.[15] Compare this to 75 percent of white children living with both parents in 2018.

In the late 1800s, on average 70 percent to 80 percent of black families had two parents in the household.[16] Interestingly, during 1890 to 1940, a slightly higher percentage of black couples were married than white couples—this during times of great oppression of the black family relative to today. In 1890 and 1940, blacks were just coming out of slavery and were squarely in the midst of the Jim Crow era. If ever the black race was oppressed, it was during this time. Right? So why would it have been more prevalent to see an intact family during the 1890s than it is today?

Furthermore, "In 1925, 85 percent of black households in New York City were two-parent."[17] Today, only 26 percent of black households in New York City are married couples.[18] What happened?

White liberal policies are what happened. Blacks overcame the savagery of slavery. We got through the dehumanizing Jim Crow era. But white liberal policies have proven to be unscalable. White liberal policies have proven to be the black community's kryptonite.

Married-couple families declined from 78 percent of all black families in 1950 to 48 percent in 1991[19] to 27 percent in 2013. The number of black families maintained by women with no husband present has more than doubled.[20] High rates of marital separation and divorce as well as a larger proportion of never-married women with children are plaguing the black community. President Lyndon Johnson's liberal programs proved to be a cataclysmic failure for the black family.

Speaking to the insidious nature of liberal policies, professor Walter Williams said it best: "The welfare state has done to black Americans what slavery couldn't do, what Jim Crow couldn't do, what the harshest racism couldn't do. And that is to destroy the black family."[21] Famed economist Thomas Sowell concurs: "The black family, which had survived centuries of racism and discrimination, began rapidly disintegrating in the liberal welfare state that subsidized unwed pregnancy and changed welfare from an emergency rescue to a way of life."[22]

Now couple these statistics with the awareness that we're committing genocide on our own people via abortion and you have a complete recipe for disaster. It bears repeating that for every 1,000 black babies born, 477 are murdered in their mother's womb—that's a 32 percent kill rate.[23] Lynching has nothing on Planned Parenthood! This is black genocide by our own volition. Since its inception, abortion has killed over 18 million[24] black people in the United States—that's over a third of the black population today (46.5 million).[25] How have we allowed this to happen? I will never march with Black Lives Matter until all black lives start to matter to us. How many potential black doctors have we murdered? How many potential black presidents have we murdered? How many black lives were snuffed out by the "choice" of their own mother? But Chelsea Clinton says abortion on demand has contributed a $3 trillion economic boon to our society[26] and is the "Christian"[27] thing to do. She's a Clinton. She must know. Right? To top it off, racist Margaret Sanger, who is the founder of Planned Parenthood and who had eliminating the "undesirables" as an objective in her eugenics plan, is celebrated by these liberal politicians. Stunning . . . and sad.

What's amazing to so many of us is that the failing liberal mantras continue to persuade Americans, despite simple common sense. Will we never learn?

Border walls that once defined a nation's sovereignty have now become immoral[28] even though liberal politicians often live behind walled estates themselves. Motherhood was once an emblem of sainthood for women. Now we have a movement called "Shout Your Abortion." Infanticide was once considered beastly. Now elected officials are lauding its legitimacy *in some cases.*[29] Innocent until proven guilty once separated our nation from every tyrannical regime on the planet. It has now been replaced by the #MeToo[30] movement. Preserving a child's innocence was once our nation's highest aim. Now an eleven-year-old boy dancing provocatively before a huddle of gay men is not to be questioned.[31] Even younger children are encouraged to hear drag queens read stories to them. All of it is sheer madness! Values we once considered "common sense" have now been replaced with sheer idiocy!

Once we looked to the mainstream media to inform us. Now we've grown leery of fake news. Life, liberty, and the pursuit of every person's understanding of happiness was once considered an *unalienable* right. Now Americans murder more than 1 million babies in utero. Where are their unalienable rights? Once we believed that "We the People" formed our government and that our elected officials worked for us. Now we have seen their blatant extravagance and their ease in weaponizing the federal government against us—IRS scandals, Operation Fast and Furious, Benghazi, the FISA court, the Steele dossier used as opposition research and paid for by Hillary Clinton's campaign, used as a primary source by the FBI to get warrants to spy on then-candidate Trump's presidential campaign. All this followed by three and a half years of the Mueller investigation, the impeachment hoax committed by "shifty" Adam Schiff, and so on.

The spread of decay from black America to the broader American community has turned into a race between liberal politicians and American values that were defined by our forefathers and that worked in creating safe, stable homes to nurture the next generation. Who will win this race? Is all hope lost?

No, I don't believe so. An intelligent and politically informed community is the Achilles' heel of the Democrat Party. Conversely, an intellectually incompetent society that cannot discern manipulation is democracy's vulnerable spot. We must move quickly.

The black community *must* become a foreshadowing of good things to come, not evil. We must be able to learn from the lessons of the past. What once made our black families—and thus our black communities—strong? We must regain those values. We must insist that these values are held by those we elect to office to represent us. What liberals have done to the black community awaits the rest of America. The challenge of the next half century is whether or not we have the wisdom to do what's right for America first.

For better or for worse, our generation has been appointed by history to either lead America toward global assimilation that promises to doom us all, or into a new age of excellence once more.

Time is marching on. We must decide now.

8.

YES, RACISM EXISTS. WHAT DO WE DO ABOUT IT?

Does racism *still* exist in America?
Absolutely yes! Should we quietly live alongside it as some acceptable amount of gray areas in life?
Emphatically no!

But perhaps we should ask ourselves, are there *degrees* of racism? And is all racism the same? Should we fight with reckless abandon at the slightest whiff of it? Should we criticize without any recognition of just how far we've come in combatting racism? Can we consider the epic changes that have been made in the past decades, both politically and culturally—changes that reflect the efforts of an entire nation to do better?

Or should we just throw the baby out with the bathwater? Just because racism hasn't been completely extinguished, are our efforts to eradicate it null and void? Should we fight against existing racism with rhetoric reminiscent of December 31, 1862—one day before the Emancipation Proclamation freed more than 3 million slaves? Or as if it's 1963—one year before the Civil Rights

Act was enacted? Or should we fight as if it's Monday, November 3, 2008—the day before an entire nation, *our* nation, elected our first black president? These dates—and more—reflect huge steps our nation has taken to combat racism. Are we not to acknowledge how far we've come? Or are we content to pretend that little has changed and our nation is still as fundamentally racist as many on the Left would have us believe?

I maintain that there are degrees of racism and that all acts of racism should not draw down the exact same amount of energy and resources.

Because of the varying degrees of racism, I believe I have a couple of obligations. First, I have an obligation to now live in a manner that honors the sacrifices of those who came before me and who I believe suffered *real* and *systemic* racism. After all, there's no better solution to remedying racism than a life lived well.

Second, I believe I have an obligation to speak today in such a manner that honors the efforts of a nation that has worked hard to right the wrongs that were visited upon people like me because of the color of our skin. America has done so much to right her wrongs. So when we speak about racism that still exists today, we must do so with a panoramic view of the whole story—the past and the present.

Just as we must see racism by degrees, so must we view its remedies by degrees. We must see the degrees of racism in order to attack it with the precision of a scalpel-wielding surgeon and with the veracity of a fire-breathing Southern Baptist preacher. Our strike must become surgical and accurate, not the blundering and erratic blows thrown into thin air we often see on the nightly news—declaring *that's* racist, *this* is racist. In today's culture, almost everything has become a potential act of racism. We're all growing sick and tired of it.

I must confess, I often mull over the creation of some new word to describe the racism we experience today—a word that would accurately reflect the degrees of racism, a word that would distinguish between the *real* and *methodically* administered physical, emotional, soul-wrenching, and hopelessness-inducing racism our slave ancestors endured versus what we routinely call "racism" today.

In comparison to my ancestors, I simply can't embrace the concept of racism fully. I believe the word "racism" should be used and viewed while looking through a lens of reverence toward those who truly lived under its full weight.

I do not know what *real* and all-encompassing racism feels like. Neither, I suspect, do most blacks today. Racism, yes, but not the racism that severs families, that takes forty whip lashes to the back, or that endures the hot sun picking cotton from dawn till dusk, lucky to have Sunday off if the master sees fit. That kind of racism I do not know.

Have I been called the vile N-word before? Unfortunately, yes, only once, but I'll never forget it. I was only eleven years old at the time.

My stringy-haired white classmate wanted something I had, and apparently I wasn't obliging her fast enough. So, in her anger, she hurled the heinous N-word at me.

I remember quickly assessing my options. One, I could punch her in the throat, commence to dragging her across the classroom, and in all likelihood receive some leniency from our paddle-toting assistant principal, Mrs. Stallworth. Or, I reasoned as much as an eleven-year-old child can, I could tell our teacher, who just so happened to be black. I immediately selected option 2, thinking it would inflict the greatest punishment upon my arrogant little white classmate.

I decided I would tell it flatly. No need for dramatics on my part as uttering the revolting word itself would be all the melodrama I would need . . . or so I thought. But to my astonishment, I got a completely different response from our teacher than the one I anticipated.

Instead of jumping down this little white girl's throat, my black teacher asked me to define the despicable N-word. I remember feeling as if time slowed as I replayed in my mind what was happening. This was not going as I had planned. I slipped into some sort of lethargic stupor and fell into a trance broken only by our teacher's insistence that I go look up the word. With my pale, thin classmate still standing by, I remember walking over to the book-lined wall, slowly pulling out the dictionary, and looking up the loathsome word. How did this turn into *me* doing extra classwork instead of her?

There it was! I found the word. My sage of a teacher asked me to do the unthinkable. She demanded I read it out loud.

"A drunkard. Someone who's belligerent. An ignorant person," I remember reading.

To which she then inquired, "Is that you?"

"No!" I snapped back.

"Then okay. She's not talking about you," she snorted and glibly walked away.

"What?!" I remember screaming in my head. I looked at my haughty classmate. She just smirked and walked off. "She won," I whispered. I was sure she thought the same.

All these years later, I still remember this event like it was yesterday. I can remember the room with the little red paper flowers that decorated the walls. I can see my fellow classmates talking in the background and the soft, petite face of our teacher.

Today I realize I was the decisive "winner" in that little triad. My white classmate didn't receive the tongue lashing I had hoped for. But my dear teacher gave me so much more instead. She was teaching me how to reason well. She was teaching me how to be ruled by an informed mind rather than by my unruly emotions. How I wish I could remember her name. I would contact her and let her know how thankful I am that she took the time to teach a lesson that has traveled across many years with me.

Now I don't advise a white person to use that vile word today and think that I or any other black person will always take the high road and just walk away. However, it's a lesson I believe we all should learn. I can't control the words that will come out of another person's mouth, but I can control myself. I can't control what another person will think of me. But I can rein in my own thoughts about who I am, who I want to be, and how I choose to see the world around me. More and more, I'm realizing that racism has little to do with *me* and more to do with the hate that consumes another person's life. It's an exhilarating realization.

Unlike our enslaved forefathers, the words and the actions of a few hate-filled people don't have sway over who I am and who I will become. This is not to say acts of racism are to be tolerated. But it is to declare that having a proper perspective is key.

My own little babies often retort when someone says something not so nice to them, "You are what you say someone else is." I was not the N-word. My classmate was the belligerent one that day. She tried to demean me, but demeaned herself in the process. No one can truly demean a man or woman or child who knows who they are.

My little white classmate's words were vile, but they were never followed up with lashes on my back or any real threat of violence, as they were my ancestors. They were words. Hateful words. Despicable words. Words I myself have never felt comfortable uttering. But unlike for the slaves whose blood runs through my veins, those words didn't present a genuine threat of danger to me. No burning crosses would be in my yard that night. They were just words, words my wise teacher so aptly taught me to elect to ignore since it wasn't remotely a fair description of me—an option slaves or those living under Jim Crow laws did not have.

Yes, I've experienced some sleight-of-hand manipulations, dismissive glances, and innuendos one *could* attribute to the color of my skin. Yes, I believe there have been times I've been treated unfairly. Yes, I have felt people's attempt to marginalize me. Yet in spite of it all, I must confess I do not know and cannot know what *real* and *systemic* racism feels like, despite my impoverished deep South beginnings. I don't believe anyone in today's culture knows about a type of racism that envelops every single aspect of your life—where you live, what you eat, who you bear children with, or if you'll be able to keep those children or not.

Neither you nor I know what it feels like to be bred as a business strategy only to have our little ones snatched out of our hands and sold to the highest bidder. Neither you nor I know the struggle of striving to be accepted as a full human being, much less as a fellow citizen. I don't know the shame of picking up my dinner from the back door of a restaurant because I'm not allowed to enter through the front door. I don't know the humiliation of drinking out of the dirty water fountain labeled "colored" or taking my son into the "colored" restroom.

I have never been spat on or cursed out solely for the color of my skin. I have never had to guess the number of jelly beans in a jar to be eligible to vote, notwithstanding my master's degree and the white registrar's GED.[1] I have never been hosed down, billy-clubbed across the head, or attacked by trained dogs simply because I walked across a bridge in Selma, Alabama.[2] I've never been aroused from my sleep to see men covered in white sheets, a cross burning in my front yard, and my neighbor calling out for my black son. I've never been denied employment, a college education, financial credit, or a house in a good neighborhood solely because I've been deemed the "wrong" color. And yet, all this and more was done to my ancestors with the full approval of a complicit government.

By the grace of God, I will never hear any rendition of these words often attributed to Harriet Tubman urging me on, "If you hear the dogs, keep going. If you see the torches in the woods, keep going. If there's shouting after you, keep going. Don't ever stop. Keep going. If you want a taste of freedom, keep going."

Now that, to me, is *real* and *systemic* racism. Racism may feel different to you today than it does to me. I won't attempt to tell you how you feel. But how much of the above have you had to endure? All of the aforementioned is the epitome of *real* oppression and happened at the hands of fellow Americans, churchgoers even.

Right now some older readers with black skin are remembering that in their youth they *did* experience the awfulness of segregation—the "colored" restrooms and dirty drinking fountains, the back doors to business establishments, the move to the back of the bus. I acknowledge the sins you endured, but the truth is we as a nation have moved beyond those days. The extent to which we experience racism today, while real, is far from what we experienced a century ago or even a half a century ago. For that, we must also acknowledge the many white fellow Americans who dedicated their lives, their families, and their wealth to bring about the changes we've seen. And what's interesting is that, by and large, the black men and women who lived through the deprivations immediately following the emancipation of slaves and through the horrors of Jim Crow voted overwhelmingly Republican—Fredrick Douglass, Booker T. Washington, Dr. Martin Luther King Jr., and my paternal grandparents, to name a few.

My lack of being able to completely identify with racism as experienced by slaves and those living under the Jim Crow south does not, in any way, exonerate acts of racism committed today. It does, however, force me to ask: Do all acts of racism require the exact same amount of my time and effort? We only have twenty-four hours in a day. How can I be effective at truly getting at the root and not just pull off the leaves of hate?

We must learn to distinguish between real and systemic racism versus mere ignorant chatter. I fully recognize that the one indulging in ignorant chatter could also be the one making policies in Congress, sitting in the chief of police's chair, or heading up many of the Fortune 500 companies. The significant difference today is that our nation has afforded us the ability to root these ignoramuses out of office, such as law enforcement officers exposed for racist social media postings,[3] or Netflix firing their chief communications officer for using the N-word,[4] or Florida Secretary of State Mike Ertel being forced to resign after a blackface photo was revealed,[5] or a CEO being fired after he sent out a racist email to employees.[6]

"Does racism exist today?" isn't the right question to ask if we truly want to understand and resolve this form of hate. Of course racism exists, because I exist and you exist.

Nonetheless, when the question gets asked, there's no shortage of "victims" who rush in with their emotion-driven affirmative responses. Toppling Confederate statues does absolutely nothing to end real acts of racism. Holding public congressional hearings during a presidential election year to discuss the practicality of commissioning a study to examine handing out reparations is a ruse. It's all foolishness served on a platter by manipulative people whose sole mission is to create a distraction from their true agenda of simply garnering political power.

However, if the point of asking the question is to understand why many blacks, especially those living in urban areas, are languishing in what I've coined a "second form of slavery," then the better question to ask is, "Does *systemic* racism exist today?" Not blanket, garden-variety racism, but systemic, institutional racism.

Are inequality, intolerance, bigotry, and injustice the four pillars holding up the structure of our government, businesses, and law enforcement units? It most certainly was at one point in our country. But is it today?

We must seek to know if racism is so intertwined and woven into the very fabric of our country or an organization that it has embedded itself into every crevice, that it cannot be extracted without destroying the institution itself. Now *that* would make it institutional or systemic racism—and unacceptable!

Jim Crow laws are the perfect example of systemic racism. Slavery was systemic racism. Blockbusting and redlining residential neighborhoods that either overinflated prices of homes sold to blacks or barred blacks altogether from securing home loans were supported by the government making them systemic. Literacy tests administered by the state for the express purpose of disqualifying blacks and others from voting was most certainly systemic racism.

Systemic racism under these oppressive ideological and government-sanctioned institutions was completely intertwined into the fabric of everyday life, specifically in the South, but in the North as well. Systemic racism permeated every pore of the

Jim Crow South and through the institution of slavery itself. One would not have been able to separate the two—inequality from the government, intolerance from business practices, or injustice from law enforcement. Racism was complete. It was total.

On the other hand, if you ask, "Does *individual* racism exist?" the answer becomes a bellowing yes! Individuals can and do have personal prejudices. Individuals can have racist beliefs or assumptions about others who don't look like them, talk like them, or have the same pedigree as them.

One of my earliest memories of racism—perhaps today's culture would label it microaggression—was of my dear grandmother and me at the local corner store. One of my white classmates was behind the counter, as it was her parents' store. We were probably in the third or fourth grade at the time. Watching the exchange between my grandmother and this classmate made a deep impression on my young mind and heart that remains to this day.

If you know anything about the South, you know it's rooted in proper decorum. "Yes ma'am," "no ma'am," "please," and "thank you" are staples in any conversation. But on this day, I saw for the first time a kid my age speak to my grandmother with utter disdain. Speaking to her in such a manner I would have never thought to do to any adult. "What!" "Huh!" and "Yeah" seemed to punctuate each of her sentences. This, along with her frequent sideways glances, thrown at my precious grandmother showing her utter contempt.

Up to this point, I don't recall ever feeling the weight of racism or contempt arising merely from the color of my skin. I don't recall anyone in my family even discussing racism. But somehow, in watching this exchange between my most beloved grandmother and this insolent white classmate of mine, I connected the dots. I couldn't believe the arrogance I was witnessing from her.

My wise grandmother, all the while, did not challenge the clear disrespect. Instead, she bowed her head low when speaking to my young classmate, showing great deference.

I . . . . was . . . . shocked! I would have never gotten away with such blatant disrespect. We walked out of that shop never speaking a word about it. But I learned that day that we are not all equals in the minds of some. That thought was duly noted in my schema.

Even today, when I return to that same place each summer with my own little ones in tow, that experience that happened almost four decades ago rushes to the forefront of my mind about the low opinion some white people around those parts have toward the color of my skin. They don't know me. They can't tell you what I believe. They have never sat down to understand how I think. So they can't possibly have animosity toward me, the person. Their animosity is singularly toward the color of my skin.

That experience was a *real* experience. I still have emotions tied to that event. However, it would be racist of me to judge a whole group of white people by my interaction with this one person, or with two or twenty-two people. It would be ignorant of me to not see just how far we've come as a nation since then and in that little town even from the days of my own youth.

No! I will not exonerate hate. But now what? Should I wallow in it? Should I be victimized by it again and again? No! I elect to move forward.

To some, racism is racism. Hate is hate. Intolerance is intolerance. To them there are no differences in size, amount, degree, or nature. It is what it is. As is often the case, however, we tend to grow up in both years and experiences. Life has a way of forcing us to see the varying shades in life. Not everything is so black and white.

Unfortunately, this isn't the response of many in our country today—for both blacks and whites. I was shocked when Michelle

Obama declared openly during her husband's 2008 presidential primary campaign in Wisconsin that "For the first time in my adult life, I am really proud of my country because it feels like hope is making a comeback."[7]

How could someone who graduated from both Princeton and Harvard Law School feel so alienated from her country?[8] How could someone who won a job at a high-paying Chicago law firm and was in some way the beneficiary of affirmative action—another measure our country took to right her wrongs—feel for the first time proud of her country?

Over the past few years there have been times in our country when if you closed your eyes and just listened to the rhetoric you would think we were back under Jim Crow days. One would think we were fighting against white sheets and crosses being erected in our front yards. If you were awakening from a 160-year cryosleep you would think we were still breeding slaves.

But we're not! We're nowhere close to those times. Any attempt to equate today's times with slavery exceeds being intellectually dishonest. For the first black First Lady to muse that this is her first time ever being proud of her country is disingenuous at best.

OVERPLAYING THE RACE CARD

Let's face it. Some things that we "feel" are racist simply aren't. It's just people judging what we're putting out into the world for them to judge—our behavior, our attitudes, our choices, or our affiliations.

Yes, people profile. I profile, too. If you've lived past one day you've collected prejudices, preferences, and preconceived ideas and notions about certain people. One ethnicity of people, invariably, has partial thoughts about another ethnicity. However, not all responses we may receive from another person are born out of racism. Sometimes, maybe even the majority of the time, others' reactions toward us are generated by our behaviors. Perhaps they're responding to our choices and not the color of our skin. We must consider that everything we experience may not be about race.

For instance, if I, a black woman, see a young black man walking toward me in the twilight hours of the day with his pants sagging, looking a little "thuggish," guess what? In all likelihood, I'm crossing the street.

Likewise, if I, a black woman from the Deep South, see a young white man with a shaved head, tatted out, and carrying a Confederate flag walking toward me in the twilight hours of the day, guess what? In all likelihood, I'm crossing the street.

It's the same kind of thinking that keeps me from taking a shortcut through a back alley in the middle of the night near Times Square, or taking a quick jog through Central Park after midnight. Some may call it fear. I call it taking an active role to preserve my own life.

The fact is, I've lived beyond a day and have collected experiences, data, and background on certain characteristics, behaviors, and situations. In the above two examples, I'm not profiling their color. I'm profiling their behavior and their choices in life at the point they're presented to me. To say or do anything other is sheer ignorance. It's not tolerance to train ourselves and our young people to not observe and respond to others' choices.

It's not racist to judge behaviors. It's racist to judge me based on the color of my skin. It's racist to judge me based on some preconceived ideas about all black folks. This distinction has gotten blurred in today's rhetoric. It is in my *own* best interest to judge what people put in front of me to judge—their lifestyle, their choices, their attitudes, and their affiliations are all fair game.

It's not racist to judge a lifestyle associated with shenanigans. It's racist to take my experiences with a particular group of people or my preferences of being with those who look more like me or to even take those cues I've picked up along the way from those around me and then to apply those thoughts or experiences to describe a person I've never met.

My young classmate who called me the odious N-word undoubtedly learned directly from her parents to have contempt for those who share my melanic shade of color. But now what? Am I to teach my children to chase down every single person who offends them? No! It's my greatest desire to teach my children to reason well, to live an honorable and disciplined life, to choose love first and to choose to see the good, while not being naïve about the existence of evil.

Perhaps the greatest tragedy is that in overusing or misusing the word "racism" or "racist," we're ultimately cheapening the word. And this is done to our own peril.

Racism exists. Acts of discrimination and intolerance happen.

However, I earnestly believe most of what we label as racism today isn't racism at all, however. In my experience, most perceived acts of racism aren't intentional acts overflowing from a heart laden with bigotry. Perhaps it's carelessness. Perhaps it's ignorance. Perhaps it's born out of a need felt by some white people to push back against the narrative that they're inherently evil.

How do we expect white people to behave as we see a rise in some of the hateful rhetoric and distorted narratives that have instigated a nation to walk down streets shouting "Hands up, don't shoot,"[9] or to kneel during the national anthem,[10] or to create the false assertion of "white privilege," or to topple Confederate statues,[11] or to create "safe spaces"[12] as sanctuaries for blacks only, or to ban all white people from college campuses during a

"Day of Absence"[13] because we feel we need a break from Caucasian influences?

What do we expect from white people? To take it on the chin like good soliders? To just roll over and play dead as they and their children are marginalized and excoriated? Do we expect them to see it as their turn to be enslaved?

No! I don't know many black people who would idly stand by for a "no black people day." What we should expect from this reverse discrimination is greater pushback, greater resistance, greater acts of wanton racism, and perhaps the most tragic of all, the loss of a nation's heart to rid itself of all hate. I am saddened at the thought of seeing a callousing of the heart specifically among white conservatives, who have traditionally been the greatest champion of liberty for all people.

Nevertheless, there are those rare occasions when the color of my skin *is* the primary determinant of my worth in the minds of some who deem themselves superior. To a racist, all they will ever see is the color of my skin.

It is in response to these rare occasions that the word "racist" has a pivotal role to play in our society. Used judiciously and sparingly, labeling another's actions as racist has the ability to effectively push back against behaviors we, as a nation, have deemed intolerable, unsafe, and unwanted. The word itself shines a brilliant spotlight on attitudes we have come to disdain in this country.

It is unfair, even a dereliction of duty often committed by mainstream media, to call President Trump's supporters racist. The headline for the San Luis Obispo's Tribune read, "If you support Donald Trump, then you have to be OK with racism."[14] The Daily Beast led with the headline, "Trump is a Racist. If You Still Support Him, So Are You."[15] The Miami Herald ran with, "No, it's not the economy, stupid. Trump supporters fear a black and brown America."[16] Really? I support President Trump. Am I a racist? Am I OK with racism? Am I afraid of a diverse America?

The reaction the word "racist" elicits is exhibit number one on just how far our nation has actually come in righting the wrongs committed against blacks specifically. You see the veracity of this when the word "racist" is uttered in any setting. It causes others to stop, look, and listen. It compels the accused to recoil and retrace their steps and ask, "What exactly did I just do?" That's the power of this one word.

Off the backs of those who came before us, blacks today have inherited a powerful tool that can assail and beat back *real* acts of racism. We inherited not only the word "racist" but the heart of a whole nation that gives the word its power. And this above all else is precious and deserves to be protected.

When I, a black woman, stand and decry the unacceptable behavior of another as racism, I want people to take notice. I want to be heard. I want to elicit a response from my fellow Americans that causes them to come along side me and say, "Never again!"

But with white liberals overusing the word to influence elections because they can't effectively argue the merit of an issue is weakening a very powerful tool to push back against real acts of racism. Black people, especially, need to wake up to this reality.

Today we see mainly white liberals using the word "racist" as a punctuation mark to close out a thought. We are a country in danger of being exhausted at the very mention of the word. We are at risk of exasperating an entire nation. I must admit my own knee-jerk reaction whenever I hear someone use the word is a long, slow eye roll. This should not be the case.

Believe it or not, it's not uncommon to see white liberals grandstanding as they explain to me, a black woman, what real racism looks like and exactly how I should feel about it. It's also not uncommon to see them assign the word "racist" to explain what they don't understand or what they don't agree with.

Instead of debating the merit of an issue, we see one white liberal pundit or politician or activist after another weaponize the word "racist" for his or her own benefit to intimidate, to mislead for raw political power, or because they simply don't know enough about the issue to argue the merits. This should be unacceptable.

These people are not modern-day Quakers looking to sniff out and abolish racism. They're scammers looking to exploit and often fit in with the chorus of other "cool kids" who are using the word.

We primarily see white liberals explain almost every single issue we are contending with in this nation through the prism of racism, and thus they're cheapening the word in the process. This should alarm every black person. We, as a nation, are all growing tired of the overuse or misuse of the word. It's losing its potency and relevance in our nation.

GET INFORMED

Though he was a mere child during the preparation for the Civil War and during the war itself, Booker T. Washington observed, "I have never been able to understand how the slaves throughout the South, completely ignorant as were the masses so far as books or newspapers were concerned, were able to keep themselves so accurately and completely informed about the great National questions that were agitating the country."[17]

He recalled hearing late-night whispered discussions of his mother and other slaves on the plantation. He remarked on how they understood the situation. Even slaves on his far-off plantation, miles from any railroad or large city or daily newspaper, knew that the primary issue of the war was slavery. "Even the most ignorant members of my race on the remote plantations felt in their hearts, with a certainty that admitted of no doubt, that the freedom of the slaves would be the one great result of the war."[18] Though they were slaves, they knew their common fate was tied to the fate of the nation.

Compare Booker T. Washington's understanding of his time to today's. First, there seems to be little to no consideration that we're all on this boat called America together, and that if my side goes down, your side goes down as well. Second, it's not uncommon to hear a black person admit they don't vote in either the primary or general elections. Such an admission no longer warrants the raise of an eyebrow. Strings are generally not tied together linking voting to one's fate as it most certainly was during the days of slavery. I wouldn't be surprised if slaves in the backwoods of Alabama were more informed on the pressing issues of their times compared to their descendants today. We choose the priorities of our life. For some of us, we've erroneously prioritized scrolling our Facebook page higher than choosing to get and stay informed on our nation's most pressing issues. And yet, as Fredrick Douglass overheard his master tell his wife when she was caught teaching young Douglass how to read, "[Learning] would forever unfit him to be a slave."[19] These words are stenciled on the walls of my heart, as well as over my office door. It remains as apropos today as it did when it was first declared. I surmise there's nothing that threatens America's greatness more than an undereducated population. We're not in danger of being *un*educated. Americans know a lot. But we are *under*educated on those precepts that have and will continue to sustain our dominance as a nation, such as the rule of law; the dignity of work; the sanctity of life; the preeminence of faith, family, and country; and the belief that the motto "In God We Trust" reigns supreme, not the government.

From the idealistic to the pragmatic, according to one survey, only 16 percent of Americans can correctly identity the five freedoms protected under the First Amendment: freedom of religion, freedom of speech, freedom of the press, freedom of assembly, and freedom to petition.[20] All of these are the values that bind us together and make us unique compared to every other nation that has come before us. They propel us to victory in every situation.

In spite of this, according to a YouGov-administered survey measuring patriotism, nearly half of Americans believe we are a racist country.[21] It doesn't help that universities "have become ground zero for political intolerance. Egged on by leftist administrators and professors, radical students howl like wounded animals when exposed to any views outside the left-wing narrative."[22] One of those narratives being, "America is a racist country." In this same study, roughly 40 percent believe America doesn't have a history to be proud of. Given what we know about world history, it seems almost impossible that so many Americans could be so misguided and naive.

As a nation, we're grappling with our identity in many ways.

So where do we go from here? There are those who would have us believe our nation's glass is half full of racists. I see it quite differently. I worry our nation won't survive if we can't discuss real and important issues both rigorously and sensibly. I also worry we'll never truly extinguish racism if we label everything we disagree with as racist.

9.

THE IMPORTANCE OF
THE BLACK VOTE

"Black people don't expect much" was the man's reply, which cut through the air like a hot knife through butter. It both shook and irritated me to the core, causing me to turn around in my chair like a boxer dazed from an aptly planted punch. Spoken so openly and succinctly, it caught me off guard. I feared a bitter truth had just been spoken.

While waiting in the green room to go on national TV, I struck up a conversation with an older liberal Jewish white man I've come to know and thoroughly enjoy debating. In the midst of our conversation he looked at me squarely and inquired, "Do you know what the problem is with black people?" To which I sarcastically replied with a smirk, "Oh, older white Jewish man, please tell me the problem with black people." He replied pointedly, "Black people don't expect much."

You could hear a rat pee on cotton. There was complete silence in the room. All I could do was turn around and let his words roll over in my mind, while I remained silent until it was time for me to go on air. I was rendered speechless, which is not an easy feat to accomplish.

Later, I shared this story with many of my black friends. They too let out a sigh of exasperation that someone would say such a thing. Our knee-jerk reaction was to rebuff the assertion, perhaps because we felt a stitch of shame or maybe because it came from the lips of a white man. Or perhaps we recoiled at his words because we're all too aware of the lack of transparency in the political class oftentimes making it difficult to know exactly what it is we should expect. This opacity surrounding how decisions are made and how to bring real change into our community has the ability to beat down a whole class of people—especially as economic dominion by a corrupt group saps all hope of real change.

Yet I suspect we each know there's *some* truth in this man's statement. My Jewish friend hit a sore spot. He wasn't rude. He wasn't condescending. He was *blunt*. Black people don't expect much, which is not to be confused with wanting much. We want a great deal. But because we don't expect much or demand much or believe we deserve much better, politicians and powerbrokers don't do much to help our crumbling communities—offering only their verbal promises and assurances to keep our votes in their column.

"Believe," like the word "expect," is a verb. It's an action word. To really believe in something causes a change to occur in our life, no matter how great or small that change may be. To truly believe in something or to truly expect something compels us to change our posture—we adjust ourselves from kicking back comfortably in our recliners to sitting on the edge of our seat. Most people have a tendency to utter these words in haste with no intention to follow them up with concrete actions or a tangible shift in behavior.

The problem with the black community is that we truly don't expect much from our political class or from ourselves. It's evident in how we vote. It's evident in the conditions we allow our children to grow up in. You say you expect more. Great! I expect more, too, and I can prove it by how I vote.

I've also shared my Jewish friend's assertion with several high-ranking white politicians at the state and federal level just to see what their response would be. They didn't flinch as though I was introducing a new thought to them. One even cried, "Yeah that's true," adding his own two cents to take the thought even further.

In the black community we often lament about hanging our dirty laundry out for everyone to see. We have this tendency to believe that if we don't acknowledge something, no one will notice it. What we fail to realize is that our dirty laundry is walking up and down the street every day. Everyone knows we habitually vote in large blocs for a political party that has given us very little in return for our blind loyalty. Al Sharpton doesn't even bother to hide his arrogance as he stands in front of the black community as a proud gatekeeper of our vote, as if we can't think for ourselves. Everyone knows our streets are some of the most dangerous streets in America. Everyone knows our children are crumbling under the weight of poor schools. Everyone knows we are the number one consumers of abortions.

More and more of our dirty laundry is getting off school buses every afternoon at three o'clock with their pants sagging to their knees. Our dirty laundry is often the loudest and proudest in the room. Everyone sees it.

So, to some degree, my Jewish friend was correct. How else can we explain black parents raising their precious babies in trash-lined neighborhoods swarming with rats, maggots, and used drug paraphernalia, flanked only by the stale stench of sweat and urine hanging in the air? How else can we explain six Baltimore schools not having a single student test proficient in math and English?[1] One may say, "That's not acceptable! No one living under those conditions believes it's acceptable." Yet despite these inhumane and utterly unacceptable conditions, the people are still there. They continue to live amid the horrid conditions that remain as intractable as cancer that metastasizes within the hidden folds of the brain. In short, they settle for the status quo. They don't expect much. Unbelievably, they've found a way to be content in their state.

An ample amount of the blame can be placed at the doorsteps of administrators, teachers, politicians, crooked unions, corrupt powerbrokers, the white man, the milkman, and so many others. But how much of the blame should be placed at the doorsteps of the parents? Or more specifically, at the doorsteps of black parents who should vote for true change but don't bother?

I understand how low self-esteem can dash the greatest of hopes. I understand that low expectations can trump even the best of intentions. But we don't live in a totalitarian country. We're not completely powerless. Yes, it will take much time, considerable courage, and herculean efforts to turn around our devastated communities, but to decide to do so is well within our power. We must believe it's possible for us to become our own solution. Despair, the sibling of low expectations, isn't an option. We have the next generation directly behind us to consider.

One of the many beauties of not living in a totalitarian society is that we get to decide who our elected officials will be. This is no small fact. It's the most essential of points. Politics and the conditions of most urban areas are one and the same. Change the politics, and you change the conditions.

If voters will change what they expect from their politicians and it's reflected in how they vote, the politics will change, followed by a change in living conditions. Even if we must hover over every single ballot box to ensure the results, the effort is well worth it. Even if we must become a perpetual thorn in the side of our elected officials to investigate and prosecute fraudulent government officials and their powerbrokers, we must become the thorniest of thorns.

There's a straight line leading from how we vote to how we live. The two are connected at the hip. This is one of the great disconnects in the black community. However, blacks are not the only ones suffering from this lack of understanding. As the false promises of socialism threaten to take hold in this country, one could easily argue that this disconnect is shared with many Americans. How we vote matters! And it has nothing to do with how much money you have in the bank. A person with $100 in the bank has the same voting power as the person with $1 million in the bank—one person equals one vote.

If we're truly distraught over our children not being able to read or write proficiently, it's *we* who determine who should sit on the board of education. If crime is rising and our police department is slow to respond, it's within our direct control as to who resides in the mayor's office and appoints our chief of police. As voters we shape our local, state, and federal government. *We* decide who will get the privilege of representing us. If our streets are overrun with rodents that have made their home in the flood of trash teeming in our streets, it's up to us to elect board of commissioners who will appoint responsible city managers. No one else is better suited for the job of changing our communities than us. And part of our responsibility is to vote for men and women who will commit to and follow through with effecting the changes we seek.

The common denominator in each decision to improve my own life is *me*—the voter. *We* choose. *We* establish. *We* elect the politicians, local and otherwise, who will see to our trash being picked up and who will strategize to ensure crime moves out and thriving businesses (and jobs) move into our neighborhoods. This isn't rocket science. But it does demand that we begin to expect more for ourselves and our little ones. Black parents have the greatest vested interest in making sure their children can thrive in their predominately black neighborhoods.

Some will decry that this is just a pipe dream. These naysayers would have fit in perfectly with the bluecoats who cried the same when our Founders spoke about creating a constitutional republic. Some will respond with, "But you don't understand . . ." Oh yes, I do! I understand completely.

Change must start somewhere. We've grown accustomed to waiting to be saved from without, waiting on someone from somewhere to swoop down and rescue us. Perhaps if we wait long enough someone from somewhere will miraculously pop up. Maybe. But in the meantime, our children are growing up under horrendous circumstances in many urban areas.

When asked about the water crisis in Flint, Michigan—just up the road from Detroit and from where 2020 Democrat Presidential hopeful Marianne Williamson lives, she rightly observed, "What happened in Flint would not have happened in Grosse Pointe."[2]

She is correct. Her analysis is both astute and relevant. She's not saying it would never happen in Grosse Pointe because 87 percent of its residents are white. She's not saying it would never happen in Grosse Pointe because white people love their children more than black people. She's saying it's because of the difference in expectations among the residents of those two communities. The expectations of those living in the affluent suburb that boasts a poverty rate as low as 5.6 percent, where 70 percent of the residents are married, and the median home value is over $300,000 are to have their trash picked up every Monday and Thursday morning. If not, you better believe it will be a short political career for the mayor and other irresponsible officeholders.

THE POWER OF THE BLACK VOTE

Winning less than 85 percent of the usual 88 percent to 90 percent of the black vote could prove fatal to any Democrat running for president. And the Democrats know it. This is why every four years Democrats come grinning in our faces talking about all they're going to do this time around.

With the exception of Bill Clinton, who faced a formidable Ross Perot as a viable third party candidate, no other Democrat has ever won the presidency since the days of President Kennedy without garnering at least 85 percent of the black vote.

Our black vote matters. In fact, it's imperative. For more than fifty years, the black vote has safely rested in the back pockets of the Democrat Party. We have been their yellow brick road to the oval office—their insurance policy to getting into 1600 Pennsylvania Avenue.

We have served the Democrat Party faithfully. We have been their most loyal subjects. It's high time we *expect* more. It's time they stop winning our vote and start to earn it.

WHAT DO WE HAVE TO LOSE?

During the 2016 election, Donald Trump narrowly won and lost eleven states. Trump won Michigan, Wisconsin, Pennsylvania, Florida, North Carolina, and Arizona with the slimmest of margins. Of greater interest, however, are the states often thought of as liberal bastions—New Hampshire, Minnesota, Nevada, Maine, and Colorado—where Trump lost by similarly razor-thin margins.

What does all of this mean? I believe it means President Trump will pick up these eleven states on November 3, 2020—he will solidify the states he won in 2016 and he will pick up electoral wins in those states he narrowly lost. Looking to future elections, President Trump has laid the ground work for all conservative presidential candidates coming behind him. This is no easy feat.

In addition to maintaining a strong economy, the path to solidifying and picking up additional wins for any candidate decidedly runs through the black community. This isn't just my opinion. It's backed by facts.

Specifically, in Maryland, where President Trump lost by 25 percentage points, the black population is as high as 33 percent. To his credit, President Trump, through a series of tweets, has shined a national spotlight on the unbearable living conditions of blacks in Baltimore City, putting it in his crosshairs.[3] Or consider Nevada, where he lost by a paltry 2 percentage points, but the state has a black population of 12 percent. Virginia, where he lost by only 5 percentage points, possesses a black population of 21 percent. Try as they may, liberals cannot nullify the policies and the national conversations that are being had that positively impact the black community.

President Trump threw down the gauntlet to the Democrats. He has shown that it's possible for conservative candidates to make inroads in the black community. The Republican Party, as usual, is light years behind. But Trump is showing them how to fight for the black vote.

A rational mind may try to muddle or distract from the conversation, but it can't deny the significant impact of prison reform through the First Step Act, record low black unemployment, the lowest black youth unemployment level in history, forgiveness of the hurricane loans given to historically black colleges, $1 billion in childcare for underserved populations, and the job-producing Opportunity Zones that specifically target black communities. These things matter.

Blacks care about securing our southern border. Blacks care about the gentrification of their neighborhoods not only as affluent people move in and force them out, but as illegal aliens compete for their jobs at cheaper wages. Blacks care about sanctuary cities that create more favorable laws for Hispanics than for the black men and women who live there.

We have not seen a president fight harder for the black community since the days of Abraham Lincoln. What in the hellfire and damnation do we have to lose by voting for candidates like President Trump, who show an active willingness to address the issues plaguing our communities? We have nothing to lose and everything to gain.

Future Democrat office seekers will need younger black voters to flip critical states that helped elect Trump in key states like Pennsylvania, Michigan, Ohio, and Wisconsin. Black folks aren't stupid. Democrats are going to be woefully surprised as they begin to see more and more blacks come off the Democrat plantation. Hopefully, the positive efforts of President Trump will not be made in vain and will be seen at the ballot box for generations to come. Hopefully future Republicans will learn from his success in the black community and take a lesson from his playbook.

For instance, we can look to North Carolina's 2019 special election as a microcosm of what we may expect in future presidential elections and certainly serving as a bellwether of Trump's impact on the black community. Right out of the gate, political pundits started their prognostications about Democrats taking over a US House of Representatives seat that's been held by a Republican since 1963. In typical Republican fashion, they started hedging their bets.

Not surprisingly, to me at least, the Democrat candidate struggled in areas that are predominately black. Even more, the Republican candidate in this election was able to flip two counties that vote overwhelmingly Democrat—Richmond County, with a black population of 31 percent, and Cumberland County, with a black population of 36 percent. The Republican candidate nearly flipped a county with a Native American population of 39 percent and a black population of 24 percent. His winning strategy was simple. He tied himself to President Trump. Period.

What may appear to some as a series of erratic tweets from the president was really a well-timed assault on the conventional wisdom that Democrats *own* the black vote. President Trump is making one of the most pivotal assertions that no one owns our vote exclusively. We are free in every sense of the word to choose for ourselves.

THE HISTORY OF THE BLACK VOTE

It's not uncommon to see people scoff at the idea of blacks leaving the Democrat Party, not because something viable is being offered by the party but because they don't know history—specifically black history.

Blacks haven't always voted for the Democrat Party in such a predictable pattern—voting at rates as high as 95 percent for one party. This seems unthinkable to me, downright illogical. How can a race of people as diverse as a box of chocolates vote in such a unanimous pattern and it be left undisputed for so long?

The answer is an age-old one: There's power in numbers. Since the days leading up to, during, and immediately following the Civil War, blacks knew we, as a bloc, shared a common fate in this country. We were our brothers' keepers. We haven't always offered such blind allegiance to the Democrat Party. There was a time we voted for what was in *our* best interest.

There was a time blacks voted the dreaded R-word. That's right, we once voted overwhelmingly Republican and for good reasons that were all in *our* best interest.

After all, the Republican Party was started by abolitionists Amos Tuck and our greatest champion, President Abraham Lincoln. Meanwhile, Democrats strongly opposed giving any rights to blacks at the time and for more than a century thereafter. From the Emancipation Proclamation in 1863 that freed the slaves to the 1964 Civil Rights Act, which abolished Jim Crow laws, it was the Democrat Party that actively and with great gusto impeded the lives of blacks. Democrats permitted no blacks to attend conventions in any official capacity until 1924.[4] Interestingly, the Democrat Party today would have us to believe that the original Democrats who held so much sway over our country to enforce Jim Crow laws for more than a century after the emancipation of slaves, suddenly got religion and became the sweet lover of minorities we see today. Implausible.

We voted Republican during the days following emancipation and through the Democrats' Jim Crow law days because it was in *our* best interest to do so. Period.

Then the tide began to turn. President Franklin D. Roosevelt, a Democrat, understood the hopelessness left in the wake of the Great Depression and infused capital, work programs, food stamps, and other government assistance to ease that hopelessness. Blacks, already living below the bottom rung of life, would have been the Depression's foremost victims and Roosevelt's foremost benefactors.

Thus, black voters began to vote Democrat. Not en masse yet. But we were voting in *our* best interest, and at that time, it was the Democrat Party who saw the nation's need and was providing help.

During the long days of Presidents John F. Kennedy and Lyndon B. Johnson, the national conversations and tempers were sweltering. These two Democrats turned the national conversation to the topic of equality for blacks. While the emancipation of slaves gave black people freedom, the passage of the Civil Rights Act put us on the path to equality. Although President Johnson worked to introduce the bill, it was the Republican Party that gave him the votes needed to pass the measure so it could be signed into law. But history only tells of the president who was in office when the bill was signed. As such, many people do not know that it was the Republican Party who ensured the passage of the Civil Rights Act—not Democrats.

Whether we like or dislike their remedies to dispense equality isn't of great importance at this time. We can debate (and I have in other chapters) if Johnson's War on Poverty actually helped the black community or not. However, the primary point is it was the party with the "D" in front of its name—the Democrat Party—that was discussing the elephant in the room. Someone was finally shining a national spotlight on the immoral and hopeless, the malicious and vile, and the open and institutionalized forms of racism that had gripped the nation by the throat for more than a century after slaves were liberated. The common perception at this time—and perhaps rightfully so—was that Democrats were fighting for parity among the races. The reigning idea was that it was Democrats who recognized the uphill battle of bringing to par a race of people who had been wrung dry of ambition, lacking familial connections and order for more than three hundred years. Again, we voted in *our* best interest as a group.

Today, more than half a century since the 1964 Civil Rights Act, another seismic shift is taking place within the black community—or at least it should be, as we ask ourselves, "What anchors us today in the back pockets of the Democrat Party?"

One of my favorite pastimes is taking my children into our local Apple Store for their computer programming classes and, while there, engaging affluent white women thoroughly saturated in liberal logic in a discussion about political realities from the mindset of a black woman who wants the best for her children. This is only second to me having long discussions with black people about our community and what needs to happen. In both cases, it often seems like an uphill battle—and again, this is often because of expectations: low expectations in the latter discussions and out-of-touch expectations in the former discussions.

It's immeasurably less tricky to speak with liberal white women and black millennials on these hot-potato topics than to speak to older, more seasoned black adults—not as many land mines to tiptoe around. Perhaps the older adults feel as though they've invested too much now to just up and leave the party completely. I'm unsure.

However, my conversations with millennials and liberal moms are not calmer discussions; sensitivities always seem to run high at first. However, I find those conversations more fluid and more straightforward. They're not without the usual emotional flare-ups, but the conversations are able to move forward in spite of those outbreaks.

I also find that black millennials are able to quickly connect the dots between what's occurring within the Democrat Party and how it's impacting their own personal lives. Young black millennials seem to have less loyalty to the party supported by their parents and grandparents. Perhaps this is because of the little rebels in them that seek to challenge the stated norms. Or perhaps it's because they're not as strongly connected to the experiences older black folks can remember not too many decades ago. Instead, they've grown up relatively privileged, watching politicians make promise after promise and keeping none of them. Yes, social welfare spending has increased substantially over the years. But their lives have not dramatically improved past the hood where they live or beyond the financial ceiling they've hit.

The civil rights movement came and is now history . . . and history always moves forward. Lincoln, a Republican, freed the slaves. Yet blacks eventually (and for good reasons) started voting Democrat. As time and policies change, so should how we vote change to reflect what's in *our* best interest. Voting Democrat is no longer in *our* best interest.

To the eventual peril of the Democrat Party, an unrest is growing within the black community. Black voters are waking up, in part due to President Donald Trump's awareness of their true needs.

Unlike most Republicans, President Trump showed his disdain for the seemingly conventional wisdom that the black vote is securely resting in the Democrats' back pocket. He directly challenged the notion that the black vote is *owned*, sealed, and stamped Democrat. For many on the Left this is a dangerous lesson for black folks to learn so late in the game when every vote matters and their radical agenda depends on wooing the Hispanic vote while still banking on the uncontested black vote.

President Trump showed like no other Republican before him that every *legal* American vote truly matters. He went after the patriot vote, the veteran vote, the legal Hispanic votes, taxpayer votes, law enforcement votes, blue collar votes, rich votes, poor votes, and specifically black votes. Anyone who's not talking to every community, specifically the black community, is running a fool's race.

What is the Democrat Party offering the black community except more of the same: crime-ridden neighborhoods, shooting gallery communities, higher taxes, more social welfare, and unfettered access to abortions?

President Trump made a case for the black community and meeting our needs in the process. What do we have to lose besides the rats and rodents?

Universal healthcare, free education, the Green New Deal, taking away private insurance, guaranteed minimum wage, and pandering to the Hispanic community is all that the Democrat Party is offering the American people. Calling for more sanctuary cities, abolishing ICE, and decriminalizing border crossing not only left an unwelcome taste in the mouth of many moderates and independent voters, but it also showed a seismic shift in the priorities of the Democrat Party.

Black people are not number one on Democrats' list of priorities. We never were, in my opinion. But at least they showed a valiant effort to pander to us every four years. Today, while our communities are crumbling, Representative Robert Francis (Beto) O'Rourke spoke broken Spanish at the debates,[5] while other Democrats promised to make the whole of America a sanctuary for illegal aliens, causing blacks to stop and finally ask, "What has our loyalty to the Democrat Party gotten us?" Perhaps it's time we begin to expect more.

Albert Einstein asserted, "A new type of thinking is essential if mankind is to survive and move to higher levels." In other words, we can't solve our problems with the same thinking we used when we created them. Perhaps it's time for something new. Everything is at stake. We have everything to lose.

In all probability, the strain on the black community cannot weather another generation unabated—corruption in our urban areas is too great, bureaucracies are too powerful, and the culture of despair and dependency is too widespread.

Our solution to the many and overwhelming problems that plague our communities start with *us*. It doesn't end there. But it does start there. *We* are the solution we've been looking for.

It's time we begin to *expect* more.

10.

SOCIALISM IS SLAVERY

Having once been set free from slavery, it's disappointing to see so many in the black community lured into the economic slavery known as socialism. Young whites, too, are being seduced by this failing utopian fantasy.

We don't own humans outright any longer. Instead, we make them dependent by modifying their self-determination. Socialism is simply another form of slavery.

As far back as 1965, Daniel Patrick Moynihan, the late Democrat senator from New York, noted, "Slavery in all its forms sharply lowered the need for achievement in slaves . . . Negroes in bondage, stripped of their African heritage, and were placed in a completely dependent role. All of their rewards came, not from individual initiative and enterprise, but from absolute obedience—a situation that severely depresses the need for achievement among all peoples."[1]

How does this differ from what we're experiencing in America today? Even the most basic understanding of what it means to be an American is rapidly evolving. Currently, our nation is even debating whether illegal aliens are Americans, too. Thus we in the black community are being stripped not of our African heritage this time but of our American heritage.

Once more, we're being promised the essentials of life, not as a reward for our efforts but simply because we exist. We're being conditioned, almost groomed, for dependency as more and more of life's options are being reinterpreted as a "human right."

But what is socialism? Several have opined on the topic, yet ambiguity and vagueness still exist for many. So, what is it exactly?

The *Oxford English Dictionary* defines it as "a political and economic theory of social organization which advocates that the means of production, distribution, and exchange should be owned or regulated by the community as a whole."

According to *Encyclopedia Britannica*, socialism "calls for public rather than private ownership or control of property and natural resources . . . everything that people produce is in some sense a social product, and everyone who contributes to the production of a good is entitled to a share in it."

Sounds harmless enough, doesn't it?

Then there's *Cambridge Dictionary*'s definition of socialism as "any economic or political system based on government ownership and control of important businesses and methods of production." At least this definition dispels the pretense that "We the People" have direct control over something. One may declare that if it's government-owned and government-controlled then it's owned and controlled by "We the People"—theorizing that the government merely represents us.

But how does socialism play out in real life? We need only to consider recent events in Venezuela. As I write this, zoo animals are missing because starving Venezuelans are stealing them for food.[2] So how does a country with the world's largest oil reserves, who willingly voted for socialism and where the people supposedly now own all of the wealth, are reduced to dumpster diving and filleting zoo animals to survive? How many of these desperate people feel they have direct control over the resources of their country that's now managed at gunpoint by a handful of elite politicians?

Unfortunately, there's no need to go abroad to look for examples of government fraud and corruption. Looking at our own political landscape should quickly rid us of such silly notions. If one thing is evident, "We the People" don't have control over much of our government. This sad realization was crystalized as we watched the unfolding of the Operation Fast and Furious scandal, the Benghazi scandal, the IRS scandal, the Russia hoax to undermine a presidency, FISA abuses, former FBI Director James Comey leaking classified information to reporters, the Clinton email scandal, the Ukrainian scandal, and the list goes on.

I once heard a young lady who had lived under the rule of socialism define it as "the political and economic notion that the government and public office is way more efficient and intelligent to control the economy than the average person." She went on to explain how socialism manifested itself in a handful of elites having the ability to expropriate businesses, then take those seized businesses and putting them in the hands of others they deemed more worthy to run it for the "good of the people." She discussed price controls, quotas, government subsidies, and the haughty criminalization of certain activities the elites deemed weren't in the public's best interest and threatened their control over the masses. All of it was done, she explained, for the common good of the group under the auspices of the majority. Individualism is routinely violated for the supposed common good of the group—a common good, she explained, that never materialized.

Today, we're confronted with a new word, a kinder sounding word that we're repeatedly told isn't the exact same as socialism. They call it "democratic socialism," and like socialism of old, it promises to solve all of our problems and to smooth out all our inequalities. Almost everything is free or subsidized or guaranteed under this new word. What could possibly go wrong?

One difference under this new type of socialism (that we're told isn't really socialism at all) is a shift from the nationalization of the means of production—the factories, raw materials, tools, land, trucks, banks, and so on. Recognizing that socialism is "intellectually bankrupt after more than a century of seeing one after another of its arguments for socializing the means of production demolished,"[3] now the Bernie Sanderses and Elizabeth Warrens of the world "seek to socialize the results of production"—in short, to redistribute wealth created by those who own the factories or work at the jobs through the vehicle of taxation.

Adding the word "democratic" to the word "socialism" doesn't change the fact that it's still socialism. Hamas was elected by a "democratic" government despite the fact that Hamas calls for the destruction of Israel on a daily basis and the eradication of all Jews in their official charter. Thus proving that simply adding the word "democratic" to another word, like "government" or "socialism," doesn't make the motives or the results any more pleasant.

The results of a democratic socialist society are no different from a plain old socialist society. Sure, adding the word "democratic" may make people feel better about the idea of "mob rule" or "elite control," but the outcomes are the same—wanton lack, long bread lines as we see in Venezuela, or a disincentive to work as we see in many European countries where the government provides great numbers of subsidies.

Being a descendant of slaves and the recipient of their hard-fought freedoms, I have no intention of becoming a slave today in any form of the word, even if the slavery being offered today isn't one of gross physical labor, just mental submission.

I remember watching a video of President Ronald Reagan saying, "The most terrifying words in the English language are 'I'm from the government and I'm here to help.'" The government's first duty is to protect the people, not run their lives. Our government should be about the business of protecting our southern border, assisting our president in deporting criminal illegal aliens, ending the sanctuary some states are giving to illegal aliens, and protecting "We the People." Instead, much of the Democrat Party is set on telling us which cars to drive, the temperature our thermostat should be set on, and whether or not we should be allowed to eat meat.

This cradle-to-grave legislation pushed by the likes of Bernie Sanders, Elizabeth Warren, Joe Biden, Cory Booker, and the rest of the ultra-liberal Left is nothing new. There have always been men (and women) desiring complete control over other peoples' lives. What they are offering is not what our Founding Fathers had envisioned.

Our best bet for freedom remains a capitalist market system. Those who are hurt the most under a socialist market system are typically minorities and the poor. I recall the words of some friends whose families fled Poland as they talked about the overbearing control of the government and the restricted freedoms of the people. I remember friends from Italy discussing how you can't get anything done in Italy unless you're willing to bribe bureaucrats or are connected to the inner circles of government. Both scenarios tend to hurt minorities who don't have that kind of connection, clout, or pedigree and the poor who lack the means to bribe their way into influence.

Socialism simply substitutes the judgment of the individual with the judgment of a few arrogant elites—not so dissimilar to slave owners. Under socialism we're supposed to assume that the bureaucrats and the elites know which bread, which donut, which health insurance, which neighborhood, which job, which shirts and pants we want and at what price. Instead of millions of individuals making millions of individual decisions about what we want, these arrogant few will decide what we should have and what we should pay for it—all done under the auspices of what's "good for the group."

I look at this issue personally. With my extremely limited background, how could I ever have made my way out of my poverty-ridden circumstances unless I had the freedom to choose my way out? In hailing from one of the poorest areas of the Deep South, where we had no running water or insulation in the house and all of us slept in one large room, what chance would I have to be the first in my family to finish college? Our family had no power to influence, no elite networks on which to rely.

Routinely, when I tell my story of moving out and up from the backwoods of Alabama, I make the point that what I've been able to achieve could only have happened in America under a capitalist market society. Prayer, personal fortitude, much sweat, many tears, and a market system that has clearly defined rules of engagement is what brought me out of a desperate situation.

As a child, I was too young to fully realize the despair surrounding my upbringing. Because of my ignorance, I thoroughly enjoyed my childhood. As an adult, however, and now looking at those who remain trapped within the limited wingspan of my birthplace, I see that it was most certainly one of despair.

It was the opportunities inherent in capitalism that brought me out—that and keeping my nose clean, not having children out of wedlock, going to college and graduating, finding relevant internship programs to enhance my skills, landing my first paying job, keeping that job for four years, having good credit, maintaining that good credit, marrying an amazing man who is also a responsible person, staying married, raising our family, and on and on. None of these things happened by chance. Nothing fell out of the sky and landed in my lap. I sacrificed. I worked hard. I prayed a lot and cried even more! But I also followed some basic rules of life.

Living under a market system that allowed me the unhindered freedom as a woman, a poor person, and a minority to engage in it and that, more times than not, rewarded such choices is the reason I made it out of a despairing start in the world. As I often told my little cousins, who were coming up in life behind me: If I can make it, so can you. Then I would give them the steps and tell them exactly what they had to do. I've discovered that knowing what to do isn't the hard part. Disciplining yourself to do what you know you must do is the test.

Today our American values and principles—the very ones that helped me move up in life—are being redefined or negated altogether. Contempt for the systems that created these values and principles—individualism, personal choice, personal responsibility—are all being redefined through the prism of the "common good." Or as Michelle Obama explained in a 2008 campaign speech for her husband, "The truth is, in order to get things like universal health care and a revamped education system, then someone is going to have to give up a piece of their pie so that someone else can have more."[4] After all, it's for the common good of the group. I wonder if she still feels the same about giving up a piece of her pie after purchasing a $15 million mansion in Martha's Vineyard.[5]

Or as Bernie Sanders squawked, "A lot of people in the country would be delighted to pay more in taxes if they had comprehensive health care as a human right."[6] He sounded so sure of himself in the interview. It seemed like a foregone conclusion in his mind that Americans would willingly, even cheerfully, be taxed at 70 percent, as estimated by some, in order to cover his inglorious Economic Bill of Rights. If I give the government upwards of 70 percent of my earned income, how am I going to pursue my own idea of happiness on the 30 percent that's left over? Isn't "pursuit of happiness" one of the foundational principles in our country?

Journalist Jemele Hill lectured us in an *Atlantic* article titled "It's Time for Black Athletes to Leave White Colleges."[7] She says black athletes should attend historically black colleges and universities in order to draw donor money and attention to black schools. She rants about white colleges attracting the best black players for the use of black labor to make white folks rich—a throwback to slavery, she claims.

She narrows her focus, calling specifically on tier 1 black athletes to fall on the sword for the "good of the group." First, she advocates for a sort of isolation on the part of the player based on the color of their skin. Second, she recommends that they actively work against their own best interest. It's a socialist mindset.

Hill lists several reasons why it's more advantageous for a black athlete to attend a predominately white college. She goes on to suggest that they should be willing to take one for the collective good of the team, work against their own best interests, and attend predominately black colleges instead.

She gives two reasons black athletes should be okay with falling on the sword, and both reasons circle around the fact that at black colleges there's a bunch of black folks there. That's just not a compelling enough reason as evidence by top-tier black athletes continuing to attend predominately white schools. What Hill is advocating is a form of segregation. It amazes me when I see black people actively advocating for any form of segregation. It's as if they did not get the message that segregation did not work out well for us when it was tried during the Jim Crow era. These black athletes seem to get it and that's a good thing. To adhere to Hill's flawed logic is, again, to work against their own best interest.

It becomes apparent that to Hill there is nothing of greater value than the color of my skin. Apparently her logic—or lack thereof—isn't very compelling to tier 1 black athletes either as they continue to do what's in their best interest.

These young black athletes, many of whom come from disadvantaged backgrounds, have made themselves marketable. They've made themselves unique. Through blood, sweat, tears, and sacrifice they've moved from simply being just another black kid with a basketball and a dream to something much more. They've increased their marketability. Similar to how a doctor who specializes in neurosurgery increases his worth by honing his skills, these young athletes have increased their worth, so much so that colleges are willing to roll out the red carpet. These young black players should be applauded, not shamed and harangued. This is a capitalist market system operating at its finest.

Socialism depends on arrogance. To the true believer, it doesn't seem to matter that socialism has failed in every other society where it's been tried. The arrogance of those pushing socialism in its various forms says, "This time will be different, because this time *we're* doing it."

Socialism isn't a shining example of humility. Socialism tries to claim the moral high ground, but in reality it's very snooty.

Though it has failed in modern history and in our own hemi-sphere in Venezuela, liberal progressive Democrats continue to promise that this time will be different because they are here and they will do it better. "It has never worked, but we are here now, so don't worry," they tell us.

I'm not surprised by the calls for socialism by those who will be the leaders of it. They will be the ones who get the overwhelm-ing majority of the benefits: the power, wealth, and control. Of course they want socialism.

What's astonishing is how willing some people are to give socialism a clean slate. Not the leaders of socialism—I completely understand why they want socialism—but the people, the citi-zens, the everyday Janes and Johns. When it comes to the sub-ject of socialism, these people have an extraordinary ability to stick their fingers in their ears and go "La-la-la" until the subject is changed. They want nothing to do with facts, logic, and his-tory. They pretend we have no history of how socialism has failed before. They gloss over the blaring examples of what socialism has done to Venezuela and elsewhere. I'm convinced that the only way a nation brings socialism to its shores is because of a willful and selective amnesia on the part of the citizens.

Not all citizens are willing to give socialism a clean slate, of course. There are many, particularly among conservatives, who may be enticed by the idea of free college for their pending high school graduate. But they are not willing to pretend facts don't exist. They don't stick their fingers in their ears to distract from hearing how socialism has impacted Venezuelans. Liberals are targeting them, dangling the promise of their child going to col-lege for free, but there are many conservatives who are not willing to trade their freedom for the bondage of socialism.

I'm not buying it. To be placed in a dependent role is a throwback to every form of tyranny that has ever existed. Dependency lowers the need to achieve. If I give you everything, why work for it? Rewards should come from individual initiative and enterprise, not from slavish obedience. Frederick Douglass wrote glowingly about the first time he worked with the hope of reward. His new master, Mrs. Lucretia, was sending him to Baltimore. She charged him to go down to the creek and wash off the layers of plantation encrustations. To boot, she was giving him a pair of trousers. For a child who had all but gone naked his entire life on the plantation, he said, "The thought of owning a pair of trousers was great indeed!" He went "in earnest" to complete the job because he was working for a reward for the very first time.[8]

A quote commonly attributed to Thomas Jefferson warns that "Democracy will cease to exist when you take away from those who are willing to work and give to those who would not." For a black woman from the backwoods of Alabama the prospect of such is chilling.

IF MONEY COULD SOLVE OUR PROBLEMS

If ever there was a true believer that politics and adequate government funding could resolve the systemic problems in the black community (in any community), it was President Lyndon B. Johnson. A crude, oftentimes crass, vulgarian completely obsessed with his image, LBJ was a contradictory individual—both a documented racist and a civil rights champion at the same time.

Johnson's utopian society was premised on the rationale that government had within its grasp the ability to solve the depressing cycles of ignorance, lack, disparities, inequalities, and past wrongs. All that was missing was the presidential will to get it done.

Well, he had the political will and the serendipitous series of unfortunate events—the assassinations of President John F. Kennedy and Dr. Martin Luther King Jr.—to garner the sympathies and votes needed to pass transformative bills into law that directly impacted black communities, namely the 1964 Civil Rights Act, the 1965 Voting Rights Act, and the 1968 Fair Housing Act. He also lifted racist immigration restrictions and forced FBI director J. Edgar Hoover to turn his attention to crushing the KKK. At that time in history, Johnson did the most of any president to move blacks toward equality since Abraham Lincoln.

But like most liberal presidents, he lacked the basic understanding that people aren't widgets. They are complex. They don't all respond the same way. They don't all see things through the same lens.

The reality that people are not widgets has always been a difficult concept for liberals to grasp, not just today, but always, as evidenced by LBJ's experience as a teacher of Mexican American children in Cotulla, Texas. About 75 percent of the residents at the time were Mexican Americans who only spoke Spanish. Diverse economic opportunities were sparse in this dry and treeless land. Most lived in hovels and were too preoccupied with survival to concern themselves with moving up in life. But that didn't distract LBJ. His students were poor, often coming to class hungry. They needed him. They needed his solutions. Whether they knew it or not was of no great concern to Johnson.

Within three months of his arrival, he had introduced a torrent of activities to spur on a competitive spirit that he believed was lacking but necessary if these poor kids stood a chance in succeeding. So he instituted spelldowns, public speaking tournaments, volleyball, baseball, and track events. He even paid for most of the equipment and doubled as the debate coach, the soft-ball coach, the volleyball coach, the song leader, and, in his spare time, the assistant janitor.[9]

So committed to changing their lives according to his diag-nosis of the problem, Johnson soon banned Spanish from being spoken on school property, including the playground. If anyone was caught violating this cardinal rule, they were sent to his office and punished. In Doris Kearns Goodwin's book *Lyndon John-son and the American Dream*, she writes, "It was true, of course, that knowledge of English would be necessary to break out of the confinements of Cotulla poverty. But his approach contained no awareness that his pupils' own cultural traditions and language might constitute an independent source of strength and fulfill-ment."[10]

There was no awareness of diversity of strength, of courage, of dreams apart from what *he* believed were the universal desires of everyone. Sounds familiar—universal healthcare, universal education, guaranteed government jobs, guaranteed minimum income, universal childcare, even now a universal universe with Democrats wanting to decriminalize crossing illegally into the US.[11] From the days of LBJ to today, Democrats have not changed. They remain the judge, jury, and prosecutor over what ails Amer-ica and what the solutions must be.

To believe in the power of socialism is to believe in the same-ness of all people. This is perhaps the most serious sin of socialism and those who espouse it.

Maybe in the 1920s, the idea of America having more than one American Dream was just too absurd. Surely, today, we real-ize the diversity in the American Dream, the diversity in what it means to each individual and in how to achieve it. The American

Dream isn't one size fits all. America has proven to be resilient enough to withstand this diversity and to thrive.

During his nine months at the school, Johnson never broke away from his usual pattern of assessing the patient, prescribing the medicine, and administering it, too. From beginning to end, he believed he knew what their chief problem was and its remedy. All that was needed was someone with the willpower to manage the prescribed dosage. Surely, the children benefited from Johnson's efforts. But Johnson, like most politicians today, "never seemed aware . . . that the benefactor might destroy his recipient's capacity to grow and find expression on his own."[12] The year LBJ left Cotulla, all his programs ended.

Why the need to give away so much free stuff—universal this and universal that? Is it to make our lives better? Is it because one political party cares so much more about people than the other? Or is it for control?

LBJ once said, "I wanted power to give things to people—all sorts of things to all sorts of people, especially the poor and the blacks." Never the anonymous donor, LBJ expected a high price to be paid for his benevolence—"gratitude, affection, a trust manifested by the willingness to let him decide what was best for them."[13]

Unnervingly, there are people among us willing to make this trade. They're willing to trade their individualism and their personal choices for the things the government promises them. I've heard several of my own black friends voice their support for a system like socialism that promises to cure all our national ills despite the fact that history shows such trade-offs hurt minorities and poor people the most.

Every socialist promise has a trapdoor. Every government handout has a string attached. This has been shown over and over again throughout history.

With today's rise of democratic socialist advocates and their benevolent agendas, it appears that a lack of motivation to throw money at every single problem isn't our issue, nor is a willing culture that would allow a handful of elites to control their lives. Despite our ever ballooning national debt, one politician after another incessantly campaigns before an obliging audience to spend even more money to remedy our struggles and to soothe our troubled minds. More and more promises are made that will surely engulf the culture under the control of a centralized government that will bleed money until nothing is left and nobody has anything.

THE POWER OF POLITICS

It's important to keep in mind that when we're talking about politics, we're really talking about power. Despite a politician's best intentions and the doe-eyed optimism of their constituents, government programs are almost always designed first to gain power, maintain power, extend power, or any combination thereof. Rarely are their chief purposes to resolve issues.

In that regard, socialism demands blind trust. We must trust that the few arrogant elites who obtain tremendous power and control over our lives have our best interest in mind more than we ourselves have. We're required to believe they want us to succeed more than we ourselves want to succeed. But remember the trade-off. Under socialism, we trade personal choices and individualism for the "common good" as defined by the few.

Even LBJ ran into this problem when concessions were made to the newly minted Fair Housing Act that weakened HUD's enforcement powers to punish discriminatory landlords and real estate agents—essentially, making the transformative law moot in many regards. However, the dog and pony show of the strong (namely, LBJ) caring for the weak (i.e., blacks) was triumph enough in the political arena,[14] so any concessions made were deemed acceptable.

The lack of purity in politicians' intentions and their knee-jerk reaction to ceaselessly create government programs are significant hurdles any genuine effort to solve issues would have to overcome. But they're not our only issues, and in my opinion, they're not our greatest hurdles.

Under liberal ideology, all differences must be quelled. All variances must be cured. Discrepancies are to be remedied. Disparities, in any form, should spark anger and resentment and therefore must be banished.

For most liberals, the medicine to cure such national aliments is the redistribution of wealth and opportunities via one government program after another. Now, this proposition might sound appealing to bleeding-heart liberals and to those who generally find themselves on the bottom rung financially. This was certainly LBJ's soothing antidote to the thoroughly saturated lack that flooded most black communities in the 1950s.

It remains the antidote today. One of the most recent forms of this redistribution is in what's proposed as "reparations" for the offenses of past slavery. It's another program designed to throw money at problems that are not rooted in finances alone.

Already, nearly 70 percent of black college students receive some sort of need-based financial assistance, compared to 40 percent of white students.[15] Surprisingly, 41 percent of blacks alone receive some sort of government aid.[16] Yet despite all of this financial assistance, blacks still languish in underfunded schools while living in dilapidated shooting-gallery neighborhoods with high fatherless rates and epidemic HIV levels and winning the prize of being the number one consumers of abortions, which have murdered whole generations of black people.

Clearly, if more money could resolve our issues, we would all be golden. But the money currently being thrown at our problems in an attempt to resolve them or at least absolve our nation of its sins isn't working. So how, exactly, will it help to give additional payments to blacks to "repair" the consequences of our enslaved history?

According to the Episcopal bishop of the Diocese of Maryland, Eugene Taylor Sutton, reparations will allow white people to look black people in the eyes. He remarked that our white brothers and sisters need reparations for their souls.

How very deep! But not really, nor is it biblically accurate in my opinion. What our soul needs is to be transformed by the renewing of our mind through the reading of God's Word, not white folks throwing money at black folks to absolve a wrong they themselves did not commit. This is a fact I believe a clergyman should be more aware of. With such rhetoric, how are we as a nation supposed to have rigorous discussions on how to remedy real inequalities? It's not exactly a conversation starter.

A QUESTION OF IDENTITY

So, if money isn't the solution, what do we do with the mess we've inherited as a nation? What is our national responsibility for past wrongs? Where does the guilt lie? When is enough finally enough?

I believe one answer is for each of us to find our God-given identity and root our lives in that identity. I believe this is a yearning for many in the black community. We want a sense of who we are, a heritage. I know I long to have a heritage that extends beyond my grandparents.

I think I realized the universal quest for identity by other black people when the movie *Black Panther* was released. I knew that I had such a yearning.

The reaction of blacks across America was astonishing to many white people. Even I didn't expect some of the shows of frivolity and madness, either. Much of the response from otherwise sane black people was ridiculous, such as donning similar African-styled apparel worn by those living in the fictitious country of Wakanda and performing ceremonial rituals and screaming "Wakanda forever!" The crossed-arms Wakanda salute became a symbol for black pride for international soccer players, basketball stars, the packed arena of the Apollo Theater in Harlem, and Sachia Vickery, a US tennis player who gave the Wakanda salute after she won at the 2018 Indian Wells Masters tournament. They all are seemingly unfazed by the fact that Wakanda is not a real place. It's all a myth. It would have been comical except I knew what they were seeking—not attention so much as identity.

Wakanda, as reflected in the movie, is an isolated, technologically advanced country that is home to brilliant black men and strong black women, a land rooted in respect, oneness, and strong familial connections. It's the heritage black Americans crave but were robbed of by white Americans. The problem is that even though we weren't collectively robbed of this heritage by white people who are living today, black Americans are still without a strong heritage as a direct result of the actions of white people.

It's such an evil legacy we have *all* inherited. On the one hand, I can't fault my fellow white brothers and sisters today for something they personally had absolutely nothing to do with. Most of them would abhor such behavior had they lived during those times. They would, no doubt in my mind, have been abolitionists. Yet, on the other hand, the effects of more than two hundred years of slavery and nearly one hundred years more of oppression under Jim Crow laws has had a devastating impact on the black community that's still seen today.

Off the backs of enslaved and oppressed black people, whites prospered and accumulated great wealth. That's a fact that must be acknowledged even today.

I recently took my beloved younger brother, Tyrone, and his two little ones along with my own family to the historical Cliveden mansion in Philadelphia. Here the prominent family of Benjamin Chew lived a lavish life of wealth, influence, high fashion, and privilege. Chew rose to the position of chief justice of the Province of Pennsylvania before the American Revolutionary War. After a period of political exile during the war in which his mansion was commandeered, he came back to Philadelphia and was reappointed to the Pennsylvania bench as the president of the High Court of Errors and Appeals.[17] He was highly connected to William Penn and his family, settling property disputes on behalf of the Penn family between Pennsylvania and Maryland (1751) and Pennsylvania and Connecticut (1754).

Benjamin Chew's life was one of great privilege afforded off the backs of other people, namely his slaves. Nine of his many properties were plantations. Although he was a prominent man in his own right, the greatest portion of his family's wealth came from owning other people. Two generations removed, his grandson Henry Banning Chew would marry another plantation owner in Maryland and continue the family tradition of owning other people and accumulating great wealth from the free labor of others.

Today, how do we compensate for uncompensated wages? How do we offer reimbursements for time stolen, hopes dashed, children trafficked, innocence sullied, and family connections unsympathetically raffled off to the highest bidder? Are reparations the answer?

Bruce Schulman, author of *Lyndon B. Johnson and American Liberalism*, writes,

On the very day he signed the Voting Rights Act, LBJ warned that people "must be able to use those rights in their personal pursuit of happiness." The nation still had to address the "wounds and the weaknesses, the outward walls and inward scars" that continued to prey on victims of discrimination. "For centuries of oppression and hatred," Johnson asserted, "have already taken their painful toll. It can be seen throughout our land in men without skills, in children without fathers, in families that are imprisoned in slums and in poverty."[18]

I understand this need for heritage and identity. I, too, want to feel significant, strong, and in control of my life. Though I would never wear one, I understand why black women wear T-shirts saying BLACK GIRL MAGIC. I understand why the motto "Black Lives Matter" quickly became more than a chant against police brutality to a rally cry over our place in this country. *I get it.*

Whites can't tell blacks to just "get over it." But neither can blacks continue to play the victim card and incessantly accuse whites today for the sins of their great-grandfathers.

If the constant roar is "whites are racists" and "blacks need to get over it," how in the world will we ever begin to address our root issues? We will simply pass this foolishness on to our children to contend with, as our Founding Fathers intentionally left the topic of slavery out of the Constitution and effectively handed the problem on to the next generation to figure it out.[19] And, here we all are. What a sad thought.

In order to find my identity as a black woman who is a descendant of slaves, I took to reading all sorts of books on all sorts of topics. I pieced together the stories of those who came before me and pierced through my own feelings of obscurity and insignificance, which could only be remedied by finding a strong identity, finding my place between the slaves before me and time, and then finding my place in America and embracing my country and the opportunities it provides.

IS SOCIALISM OUR PATH FORWARD?

In 1967 decorated Vietnam vet and Pentagon staffer Lieutenant Carlos Campbell of the US Navy spoke from a black man's viewpoint about discriminatory housing practices before the Senate Subcommittee on Housing and Urban Affairs and identified three vehicles that promise full participation in the American Dream given fair market conditions for all. Those vehicles were education, professional credibility, and financial integrity—each being necessary for obtaining full participation in the American Dream and each being rooted, to some degree, in self-determination, a process by which each person controls their own life.

Unfortunately, today we see a government all too willing to strip us of that control to chart our own lives. Believing they know best, we have a segment of our government more than willing to insert itself into the role of Supreme Being and play God to an obliging part of our country, who, sadly, appear to be growing in numbers.

Foundational in liberal ideology is the belief that the significant difference between blacks who suffer from lack and whites is privilege, privilege that they can pass out like candy at a Thanksgiving parade via one government program after another.

At the core of today's liberalism is the reckless common belief that we're all the same—we all share the exact same values and the exact same basic aspirations, and we all deserve the exact same opportunities. According to liberal logic, not only do we all deserve the same opportunities, we all *want* the exact same things.

Liberals have added to the freedom of religion and the freedom of speech the freedom from all want. But then again, who could ever offer freedom from all want except for someone or some entity who believes they are God?

Yet in most impoverished communities this is exactly the role government has obliged itself to take—the role of God. Today, liberals are extending their governmental benevolence to all Americans and becoming the forever doting, all-encompassing rewarder of those who are endlessly dependent on them.

Never mind the statistical fact that it's to the degradation of the black community that most black women are married to the government. He (the government) pays the rent. He buys the food. He covers the light bill, the gas bill, and incidentals. Under the Obama administration, he (the government) even provided broadband phone and internet service.[20]

Senator Bernie Sanders has used the term "human rights" to dream big for a democratic socialist—believing that if he becomes president he will have access to the federal government's piggy bank. Calling something a "human right" in today's society allows the federal government (elites) to leapfrog over states' rights and individual rights and the separation of powers.

Socialism and labeling a thing, *anything*, a "human right" go hand in hand. It has become the key to amass untold federal government control.

According to Sanders's website, "quality education is part of our basic human rights . . . Everyone has that right, not only those who can afford to buy it."[21] This mantra is now being interpreted in the minds of millions to mean that the federal government must now provide higher education for free to every single person in America. I have seen little to no conversation about the out-of-control cycle we're already in as a result of the government being involved in our higher education system. Universities raise the cost of tuition. The federal government rushes in to cover those costs with federal student loans. Universities raise the cost further. The federal government rushes in once more to cover those costs. The cycle is endless, and presently, universities have no real incentives to stop raising the cost of tuition.

Senator Sanders is determined to cover these costs by making the rich "Feel the Bern." He wants to offer free college education for all and forgive up to $1.6 trillion of student loans by taxing Wall Street. The plan calls for charging bankers 0.5 percent on stock trades, or 50 cents on every $100 of stock, as well as a 0.1 percent fee for bond trades. He believes this will generate roughly $2.4 trillion over a decade.

The slogan being used to help sell his plan to the American people is both emotional and compelling at first glance: "The American people bailed out Wall Street (in 2008 market crash). It's time for Wall Street to bail out the American people."[22]

It sounds good at first blush, and I will in no way try to defend Wall Street or the massive taxpayer bailouts executives received that covered their rear ends while Middle America was left to spiral out of control. However, similar to most liberal bailouts, this one also expands the reach of government without solving the initial problem. Government gets to come in and wave its magic wand, and all of our problems will magically disappear.

The problem with the sovereignty of the government, however, is twofold. First, the plan "doesn't match the complexity of the cost education problem," according to Joni E. Finney, director of the University of Pennsylvania's Institute for Research on Higher Education[24]—meaning that Sanders's plan is providing a

Band-Aid to the problem on the back end and never addresses the real issue impacting most students on the front end: the high price tag charged by universities. It's like trying to stop the bleeding of a severed artery by poking your thumb in it—it's ultimately going to fail big time.

Universities will simply do what they've always done, but now with reckless abandon. All debt will be paid. Whatever they charge will be covered. No more having to placate the excessive whining about the high cost of education from constituents. Wall Street's paying the bill. Score! Universities will raise the cost to educate and bleed the American people dry.

Second, I've often warned those who are easily enticed with the label of "free" attached to it that rarely are things ever truly free—this is even truer when dealing with the government. Someone always pays, and more often than not that someone is you and me, the taxpayers. Likewise, under Bernie's proposal, the government will tax financial institutions on all stock, bond, and derivatives transactions.

Every time someone buys or sells a financial instrument, Uncle Sam will levy a fee. But who's actually paying that fee? The bankers? Wall Street? Your accountant? Or is it you?

Similar to manufacturing companies passing on the cost of rising tariffs on imports, banks will simply pass the costs of doing business on to the consumer, the end user, the mutual fund owner, you and me. We will be paying the cost of Bernie's pipe dream, which does nothing to resolve the actual issue of rising education costs. Bernie's pipe dream will become a hidden tax on the American people. This additional tax levied on us will be unending as colleges ceaselessly raise the cost of tuition.

No aspect of LBJ's "Great Society aroused higher expectations in the Congress and the country than his War on Poverty;

none occasioned so much controversy and disappointment when it was put into effect."[24] LBJ soon realized that poverty couldn't be defined in terms of money alone. He realized there weren't enough social programs that could be created to address all our woes—something today's liberals would be wise to take note of.

Unfortunately, although one social program after another explodes in cost, making them almost untenable to survive, liberals remain undeterred. Seemingly blind to the moral cost of their policies and the lack of self-reliance they oftentimes inspire, they forge ahead. In fact, they appear to have no use for morality unless it's being used as a club over the heads of conservatives.

Lincoln freed the slaves. LBJ gave their descendants equality on paper. Trump has helped them realize that equality in real time. Now, Left leaning Democrats are offering slavery once more via socialism.

We clearly see a lack and a struggle in poor black communities. We see the disenfranchisement. We see a separate and very unequal school system, deplorable living conditions, and a lack of job opportunities inside and outside of black communities.

But this separate and not equal treatment isn't solely because of the color of our skin. It's not just a race issue. It's a political issue. It's a societal issue. It's a civility issue.

Time and time again, with one example after another, when the government steps in and attempts to play God, poor black communities suffer the most. The government has the ability to either incentivize or disincentivize a behavior. Since President Johnson's War on Poverty social programs, out-of-wedlock births in the black community have soared from 20 percent in 1960 to over 73 percent today. What we often see when the government steps in and provides financial assistance is that it takes away one of the greatest incentives of getting married: financial support.

So, as well intentioned as it may have been, Johnson's War on Poverty was another socialist program that disincentivized desirable behaviors among black people.

History appears to be repeating itself once more.

11.

A LESSON FROM THE JEWS: MOURN, FIGHT, MOVE ON

My story is the American story. Yes, I'm black, but, I'm an American, too. People who share my melanic shading fought for the liberation of this nation right alongside General George Washington. We built the roads. We picked the cotton and tobacco. By the sweat of our brow, we helped turn this nation into an economic giant rivaled by none. America is just as much my country as it is my European brothers' and sisters'. I need not ask for permission to occupy this space. I'm not a second-class citizen. America isn't a temporary stop on my way to someplace else.

Nevertheless, I'm not blind, deaf, or stupid. I can walk and chew gum at the same time. I can both acknowledge my ancestral rights to this land and yet recognize our shortcomings, our failings, our evils and wrongs as a nation.

One tragic result of America's failings is that by and large the black community has been robbed of one of our most basic human rights: the right to a lineage.

My Romanian friends have a lineage. My Uzbek friends have a lineage. My Italian friends have deep roots. They can trace their family tree back across many generations. They know which side of the family their crooked nose came from. They know from whom their children got their artistic inclinations. They take courage from the stories about how their great-great-grandfather overcame insurmountable odds to rebuild his life here in America, and of Mema's personal strength and fearlessness. They have stories and a proud history—a valuable legacy to be passed down from generation to generation.

It was their birthright to inherit this depth. It is their legacy to now pass down to their children's children. It's not their fault that I don't have such richness, color, or depth to my own story. The sting is still there, though. I feel the void.

Most of us in the black community don't have such a legacy. For most, our family history doesn't have the depth, richness, or the color of the immigrants who came to settle America by choice, not by enslavement.

This lack of a lineage—a legacy—leaves a sting. At least it does for me, and I believe it does for many of us descended from slaves.

I want to know who I am. I want my children to know who they are. I want them to have a legacy as enriching as my Italian, Asian, or Western European friends.

Once, while attending a girlfriend's annual Big Italian Pizza Party, I was debating whether or not I would take a DNA test. One woman chided, "I would never take one of those tests. I don't want to know any more about my family." She meant well, but her words stung. She doesn't need to look to a test to learn her family's history. *I do.*

Lineage is our allotted portion of history, family traditions, and background. It wasn't until recently that I realized that lineage isn't just personal; it's national as well. It's not just about me and my stories, me and my losses. Intertwined in my personal story is our national story. Understanding this truth forces one to look outward and not perpetually inward.

The impact of having a national and personal lineage became crystal clear for me on my first trip to Israel.

We spent thirteen-hour days traveling the length and breadth of Israel. First, we traveled up the Mediterranean coastline from Tel Aviv to Haifa's underground Rambam hospital. Then we trekked across the width of the country to Tiberias, climbed up the steep and narrow roads to the top of the Golan Heights, and hiked up the well-fortified red mountain of Masada in the south. Later we floated in the Dead Sea and culminated our tour at the Wailing Wall.

Above all, the greatest impression made on me during my nine days in Israel came from the stories I heard from two ethnic Jews. There was a point in time that they, too, were lost. A severing of their lineage, in part, had taken place. Knowing this piqued my interest and caused me to listen intently to their stories.

They, along with many others, made *aliyah* (a returning to the homeland for Jews) and immigrated back to Israel. Back to their home country, back to a lineage that was told to them in stories while sojourning in strange lands, and back to a culture fortified by ancient Jewish traditions.

Foremost was Tzvi Khaute,[1] who introduced himself as an Indian Jew from the lost Tribe of Manasseh. An untrained ear may gloss over this monumental proclamation, but most will readily pick up on the significance of any Jew knowing which tribe he comes from. The phrase "Ten Lost Tribes of Israel" doesn't exist for nothing. It's rare to know which tribe one comes from.

Nevertheless, there he was, speaking with such boldness that his strong accent soon dissipated and we understood him fully. We were all on this journey together, and he was leading the way.

As a child, Tzvi grew up in the small Indian village of Churachandpur near the Burmese border. He radiated with pride as he spoke about his Jewish traditions as they were practiced in India. In fact, he confessed that there was a time his people didn't even know they were Jews until a Muslim man came to their village, saw them practicing their traditions, like observing Shabbat, and declared to them, "You're a Jew!" To which they responded, "What's a Jew?"

They were simply practicing centuries-old traditions that had been passed down from one generation to the next. In fact, Tzvi grew up listening to and practicing traditions that had been preserved for more than twenty-seven centuries. Ponder that lineage! Twenty-seven hundred years ago, the Bnei Menashe—as they knew themselves—had been exiled from Israel by the Assyrian Empire. And yet, all those centuries later, their heritage, traditions, culture, and identity had been preserved, kept unspoiled and handed down to a little Jewish Indian boy named Tzvi.

It was because of this inheritance bestowed upon Tzvi that he came to know he was only sojourning temporarily in India. He spoke about feeling separate from the rest of the country in India—politically, socially, and ethnically. He hadn't lost his identity, despite his circumstances.

How many times in our own political discourse have we had people stand up and declare something to be un-American? How many times have people come to the microphone to proclaim that our desire to protect our borders, to know who is coming into our country, and to know how they intend to provide for themselves isn't in keeping with what it means to be an American? How many times have we been told that it goes against American values to demand accountability from our leaders to pass responsible immigration laws that favor American citizens first, or to pass laws requiring voter identification? How many times has it been stated that a border wall between us and our southern neighbor is immoral?

I recently went to the southern border wall of our nation. There I had the opportunity to spend time with moms who live on the border. I will forever be changed by that experience. Throughout our country, we get to haggle over words such as "migrants" or "illegal aliens," "invasion" or "caravan." But those living alongside the border have no time for such useless rhetoric.

Those border moms sleep with AR-15s next to them. These border moms I met are the first line of defense. It's not fearmongering if the fear is real.

I spoke with some of the seven thousand military personnel President Trump initially sent down to secure our borders. Each person I spoke with said, "This is exactly where we should be." If we can send people to secure the borders of South Korea, surely we can send people to secure our own borders.

We're fighting a different battle today; it's a battle for our identity as a nation. There are deliberate efforts to redefine who and what America is.

Today it's a border wall; tomorrow it will be something new. But when we hear these decrees about what it means to be an American, we must realize that this is the redefinition effort crafted by the Left.

Once America was defined as the land of the free and the home of the brave. Today, we're often told America is arrogant.

Once America was defined as having clearly marked boundaries and secure borders. Today, we're told that to hold staunchly to the idea of established borders and boundaries is immoral.

Once Americans were defined as citizens of America. Today, holding to such a belief is considered racist. To those who are determined to redefine America, everyone and anyone is an American. Eight of the ten presidential contenders raised their hand during a 2019 debate when asked if they support the decriminalization of border crossings. All of them support giving illegal aliens sanctuary from those laws that impose certain penalties for being in America illegally.

In 1933, our government passed into law the Buy American Act, requiring our government to prefer US made products in its purchases.[2] We all danced wildly in the 1980s to the chorus in Bruce Springsteen's "Born in the U.S.A." There was a time we could sing "I'm proud to be an American" without death glares tossed our way. Today such rhetoric is considered phobic.

Why? Simply because in allowing America to be redefined, we're surrendering our sense of lineage. When our children are offered a revisionist history of their nation, we're capitulating to the redefiners. When our founding fathers are no longer heroes but racist white men, we're giving up a precious (and sometimes flawed) history—but, our history nonetheless.

Unlike Tzvi, somehow we've emancipated ourselves from the blood that was spilled by those who came before us. Somehow we've allowed others to make us feel bad about our success as a nation, a success that was purchased, in large part, by the sweat of our ancestors—both black and white.

We know we have a lineage because it's in books and it's been memorialized in shrines, statues, and museums. But we've forgotten who we are. As such, less-than-honest people have easily manipulated and deceived us to neglect our own rich national heritage. We've lost the yearning to revere those who came before us. The passion to pass our national lineage on to the next generation has waned. Our statues are being dismantled, portraits of our founders are being removed from classrooms, and history texts are being rewritten to conform to this revision of our identity. Those of us who refuse to accept the redefining of our nation are subject to name-calling and harassment.

When we've lost our identity as a nation, our elected officials can chant #MeToo when it benefits their side and then wink at congressional slush funds used to silence legitimate victims.[3] When we've forgotten who we are, people can unfairly lambaste our president with false allegations but then criticize our motives as phobic when we question a sitting member of Congress's irrational fixation against the nation of Israel.

When we've forgotten who we are, we allow such egregious malpractice against truth to take place that it becomes patriotic when people kneel during our national anthem. It's considered protected free speech when they burn our flag.

I remember pledging my allegiance to the American flag when I was a child. So many of us pledged our loyalty and fidelity to this banner that symbolizes something so much bigger than our individual selves.

To all Americans, specifically black Americans, the flag bellows, "You belong!" It represents freedom not just to the white man, but to the black man as well. Whites weren't the only ones caught up in the raptures of freedom during the American Revolution. Black slaves willingly fought for the liberty of this land, charging into battle behind a Betsy Ross flag.

The Bald Eagle Protection Act of 1940 protects the bald eagle from being mistreated and provides criminal penalties if violated; the American flag should be treated the same way. This flag is draped over American soldiers' caskets—over the caskets of both black and white soldiers who have fallen. It oftentimes leads the way into battle. It may not be synonymous with patriotism for some, but it's universally recognized as such by many. I am one of those who consider it as such. If liberals can ban certain speech on Facebook and Twitter as harmful, we should be able to ban the burning of our beloved flag as illegitimate speech as well—and blacks should lead the way.

Why? Because America is our identity. Blacks have a stake in American history. We helped build this country into what it is. To degrade the flag that represents it is to do further damage to our already limited sense of heritage. For better or worse, however you may feel about this country, this is our home. It's where our black ancestors scratched out a life for themselves and are buried. It works against our own best interests to degrade this country.

What has sowing seeds of disrespect gotten us as a nation? As a black community? Are we any better off or even more divided? If we can run behind the flag into battle, we can rally behind the flag and protect it from desecration, especially from desecration by those who have often sacrificed next to nothing to create the society that allows us to live with such liberties. President Johnson was on point when he declared, "Faith builds, cynicism destroys; do and dare, strive and succeed."[4] That is how you achieve anything.

The Muslim man knew Tzvi's people were Jews by the traditions, culture, and rituals they practiced as handed down to them through their lineage. That raises the question: How would a stranger identify us? What could he look at and say, "Aww, you're an American!"

Perhaps standing for the national anthem? Or learning about our Founding Fathers—pulling from their stories, rather than toppling their statues and hiding their portraits? America, with all of her twists and turns, is my and every American's lineage.

In part, I act a certain way because I'm an American. In part, I walk into a room with a certain demeanor about me because I'm an American. Injustice doesn't sit well with me because I've been spoon-fed a healthy diet of life, liberty, and every man and woman being created in the image of their Maker.

Tzvi spoke to us about fighting for and claiming what is rightfully his by birth. He's a Jew from the tribe of Bnei Menashe. Upon the creation of the state of Israel, his tribe began their struggle to reclaim their land. He said, "The first official letter was sent in the name of the Bnei Menashe to, then prime minister, Golda Meir in 1974. We wrote, 'we are Jewish. We want to come back home.' But, we received no answer."

In fact, they wrote every year until the mid-1990s, when their letters were no longer put to the side as they had been in previous years. Tzvi said, "When Michael Freund, chairman and founder of Shavei Israel, was working with the Israeli government and by happenstance came across one of their many letters. Michael asked, 'What is this about?' to which the person in the office said, 'It's nothing. We get a letter from them every year.'"

In 2006, the first official *aliyah* of members of the Bnei Menashe community took place, in accordance with the Jewish Law of Return. This took place some thirty years after the first letter was sent requesting permission to return home. He boasted about not using the words "immigrate to Israel" to define their return. Israel was always theirs. They had been isolated from the larger Jewish community for centuries because of the Assyrian army, but they were not colonizing an unknown land. By their lineage, the land was always theirs, and they came to reclaim it.

Listening to Tzvi made it apparent to me what must happen when we've lost our identity. *We must fight to get it back.* We must be relentless in taking back what is rightfully ours.

Contrary to some current thought, America doesn't belong to the world, and America is not borderless. America belongs to her citizens. America is defined by her borders. She is not just an idea. America is a real and tangible place located in North America, bordered on the west by the Pacific Ocean and to the east by the Atlantic Ocean. Along the northern border is Canada, and along the southern border is Mexico. America is more than a vision. She is more than an awareness that can be bottled up and transported around the world. America is our home. She is not a melting pot of ideas or nationalities. We have our own identity, and there is no greater time in our history than now to proclaim this and to draw a line in the sand. Our culture is being redefined down to its lowest common denominator.

We are not a land of immigrants only. Contrary to popular belief, when people come to this country they are to pick up the American mantle as well. We are not a land of Iranian immigrants alone. We are not pockets of Mexican immigrants only. We are not little islands of African immigrants over here and Chinese immigrants over there. When we come to this country, we come to a land that has its own identity, its own culture. We are a land of citizens who have come from different parts of the world and have now assimilated into the American culture.

When you know who you are, your fight becomes your conviction—that's what I learned from Tzvi. Your fight to reclaim your identity becomes more than a passing fad. You're not so easily manipulated. You stand tall and continue to fight.

None of this is to say America hasn't wronged people across the globe in her quest for more. More power. More riches. More land. More control. Nor am I saying America is perfect or that we need to pretend wrongs have not been committed. Believe me, as the posterity of slaves, I can vouch to America's wrongs and their lingering impact. But, as David Safafa, an Ethiopian Israeli I met while in Israel, declared, "I will criticize my country. But, I will do so with love."

Many are running around our nation today willing to cut off their noses to spite their faces and despite the irreparable damage it will cause to themselves and then to their own posterity. They are angry with our nation and, in some cases, perhaps with good reason. However, many of the complaints we hear about America are from people who are woefully underinformed, and when challenged their responses are riddled with anger and little logic. When change is called for, we must find better ways to remedy our problems instead of redefining America down to just open land, open borders, and anyone can come as they please. We are a land of rules. We are a land with a defined culture all on its own. We are a land with a language of its own. We are a land with defined borders. We are a land of citizens with a government sworn to protect the interest of her citizens first and foremost. All of these things are being redefined.

While Tzvi's story reaffirmed my determination to fight for our national identity, David Safafa's story created a sense of hope that, although my personal identity has been severed, I'm still a whole person. Inside this skin of mine, I have one chance to live an extraordinary life. I'm not a victim. I can be no one other than who I'm determined to be. I will not spend my life in unrighteous anger, nor will I harbor feelings of inferiority.

David's story caused me to tear up. As he spoke, I couldn't help but see the parallels between our two nations. The similarities between black people and our problems and solutions here in America and his there in his black Ethiopian community are striking.

They are some of the most beautiful people. Distinct complexions. Beautiful eyes. Warm smiles. Yet I walked out of the room after listening to David's story with a lump in my throat. I couldn't shake the thought, *Now, what do we do? Now, what must be done to move black folks up the ladder of life? What's next?*

David was born in Gondar, Ethiopia. He made *aliyah* when he was ten years old and thus grew up in Israel. Today, he holds a bachelor's degree in business management and economics, as well as a law degree, and he's currently completing his academic master's degree in law at the Hebrew University of Jerusalem. David owns his own law firm in Jerusalem. He's married to a beautiful wife who recently gave birth to their first child—a son. By any measure of the word, David is thriving in life.

Even so, he shared how his story isn't the typical story of the roughly 150,000 Ethiopian Israelis living in Israel. David is the first Ethiopian Israeli to graduate with his law degree from the University of Haifa. From appearances, I would judge David to be no more than thirty-five at the most, so it's a telling statistic for him to be the first at anything in Israel in this day and age.

He spoke about the fight to reclaim their lineage when the first Ethiopians tried to migrate back to Israel in 1985. They attempted this feat by foot. It was called Operation Moses, and the plan was to walk from Ethiopia to Israel via Sudan. Roughly four thousand died along the way. The Israeli Defense Force airlifted about eight thousand to Israel. Then in 1991, Operation Solomon brought roughly fifteen thousand Ethiopian Jews to Israel.

Unlike Tzvi's community, the Ethiopian community didn't receive land from the Israeli government upon their return. One of the first things you notice while walking through Jerusalem is how segmented it is. There's the Jewish quarter, the Armenian quarter, the Arab Israeli quarter, the Christian quarter, and on and on. Every group, including Tzvi's community, has a portion of land on which to further cultivate their heritage, support each other, and nurture the next generation—all except the Ethiopian Jew.

One can begin to see where the problem lies as you listen to the two ethnic Jews' journey. Whereas 92 percent of the Indian Jews who came to Israel had a college education, Ethiopian Israelis came to Israel grossly undereducated. In addition to having little to no education and receiving no land, Ethiopian Jews also had a language barrier and cultural disparities in how men interact with women, and they had no wealth.

As I sat and listened to David, the parallel of the American black man just forty years removed from slavery was deafening. For those blacks coming out of slavery not knowing the language, having no wealth, no land, no education, and no associations of considerable value, yet being expected to compete with their white counterparts from such a place of deficit, mirrored what David spoke about as his people's experience of coming out of Ethiopia and integrating into Israeli culture.

David was speaking a narrative I know all too well. He spoke about the great poverty among Ethiopian Jews in Israel. According to David, 52 percent of Ethiopian Jews live below the poverty line, while 62 percent of Ethiopian children live below the poverty line. Ethiopian Israelis lag in employment, wages, and education, and they have protested what they call institutional discrimination. According to the Myers-JDC-Brookdale Institute, a government-sponsored think tank, as of 2013 only 27 percent of Ethiopian-Israeli students qualified to go to college, as opposed to 51 percent of all Israelis. The social standing of Ethiopian-Israelis has changed very little over the decades. David said, "Our history was severed. This places us at a great disadvantage. But, we are not victims. We can improve."

He focused on education as the most significant strategy to equalize the differences between black Ethiopian Jews and all others. He spoke about the community coming alongside parents and encouraging them to take an active role in their child's education—going to the school, talking to teachers, reviewing their child's homework—simple things that have a profound impact. He cited their work to encourage qualified Ethiopians to run for elected positions within the Israeli government. Today, there are three Ethiopian Israeli judges. In 2016 Avi Yitzhak became the first Ethiopian Israeli to attain the rank of colonel in the Israel Defense Forces,[5] and in 2013 the first Ethiopian-born Miss Israel was crowned.[6]

For some, I suppose it's profitable to keep the proverbial spotlight forever shining on our past sins as a nation and on every slight ever committed by anyone who doesn't look like you. Some people are just too sensitive. Others are legitimately wounded that our nation committed such shocking crimes as buying and selling human beings. Still, there are some who are tired of being made to feel bad for something they didn't do and would have never done. They say, "Move on already." I agree with the latter two groups.

It's past time to acknowledge, learn, and move on responsibly. In large part, we must be able to move onward and upward. We can't set our hair on fire every time we sniff out racism.

And yet, in all of this, I come back to the sense of loss in the black community that we who have lost our sense of lineage feel. I lost something that was my right to inherit. I lost a significant portion of my identity, and I will never get it back. To tell me to get over it is callous. To ask me to consider what our nation has done to right her wrongs toward me and those who have come before me is more than reasonable. America today is not the same America of the 1600s. Nor is she the same as she was during the Jim Crow era. We must be able to recognize our nation's growth and accept it.

Otherwise, we will spend so much of our lives weeping over the past that we miss out on what's in front of us and what's available to us today. We can't change the past. Slavery happened. Jim Crow laws existed. Let's ask what is needed to move forward.

America, as a whole, has lost something of worth as a result of slavery. Blacks have lost the link to their lineage. America has forever ceded the moral high ground in the eyes of many. We must all have a moment to grieve our losses.

But then it's time to rebuild. If any nation understands this, it would be the Jewish nation of Israel. The black community must look around and create a lineage from what may not be ours from birth. Americans must learn to fight to keep what is ours by birth—and then we must all move on.

America's fate is the fate of the black community and vice versa. Our fortunes are tied together. If my side of the boat goes down, yours goes down as well. If any segment of America loses its national or personal identity, it is a loss for us all.

Israel didn't create racism, nor did America. However, we can't pretend it doesn't exist or that it doesn't impede or cause challenges in many lives. At the exact same time, we can't pretend that racism is all that we see.

We must find a way to recognize our losses and mourn them, and then to move past them.

12.

MY HOPE FOR THE BLACK COMMUNITY

We in the black community are in survival mode—and barely that. I can't imagine things getting any worse for us. So much damage to the root of who we are has already been done. And yet I believe there still may be some room to fall further if we don't wake up and abandon the failing liberal agenda in favor of conservative principles that can give us a fighting chance.

The conservative principles I talk about aren't new. They extend far into the past but are still effective in today's world and are valuable for tomorrow's world, too. These principles extend beyond any present leadership in our country. They go beyond President Trump. They extend beyond the Republican Party. Learning these principles and applying them in our daily lives— and our political lives—is and always has been far and away in our own best interest. But embracing these successful principles means throwing off the shackles of the false principles of white liberalism.

For many black Americans this will mean answering some basic and deadly serious questions about who we are. Are we strong enough to endure the charge of not being "black enough" if we don't vote a certain predictable way?

Too many of us have been eager to prove just how black we are, just how *down* we are with our own people by going with the liberal crowd. But in asking the crucial question of who I really am, I've learned that my identity isn't determined entirely by the color of my skin. Contrary to what some believe, I'm much more than my skin color—and so are you.

I am a child of God. I am who He created me to be—a mother, a daughter, a wife, a sister, a niece, and a friend. And I am an American—and in that order. And isn't that what we've wanted all along, to be judged by the content of our character and not the color of our skin?

Proverbs 23:7 (NKJV) says, "For as he thinks in his heart, so *is* he." Where our mind goes, the rest of our being will follow. Much of our battle for identity is fought and decided in the mind. "Who do you say you are?" is the most profound question we can ask ourselves. If our answer is that we're victims, or second class, or failures, we will act out of that perceived identity. On the other hand, if we declare that we're victors, first-class citizens, and successes, we'll act out of that perceived identity. Which identity do you think will have the happier and more productive life? Which identity are you? Are you a victim, or are you a victor? Which identity do you want for your children and grandchildren?

We're all individuals with one chance to live an extraordinary life. To know the reason for our being—our purpose, why we're here—makes life all the more worth living. For instance, a Christian might respond that her purpose is to spread the gospel message of Jesus Christ. A hippie might say that his purpose is to spread love and not hate. An agnostic might declare his resolve is to improve his mind. An environmentalist may well believe they're compelled to leave the planet better off than when they arrived. An activist at heart may be driven to resist the powers that be in whatever form that takes. What's most important, however, is what *you* say and do based on who *you* believe you are.

Throughout this book and in my public life, I speak and write of the black person in terms of the black community as a collective. And I certainly understand why black people coming out of slavery and moving through the Jim Crow era and beyond often spoke in terms of the collective. But we must also never forget we are first and foremost individuals, not part of a herd, and thus not required to react to life with a herd mentality. And we must do this knowing that for every black person there will come a time when they must consider what is in their own best interest separate and apart from the collective. In so doing, they will find they must leave the herd and consider what's best for all in the larger American community, despite color, gender, or socioeconomic status.

Sadly, the question of identity within the black community is one that too often goes unanswered, causing acute discontent. Sometimes we don't even know how to solve the question of identity, and so we simply muddle on, waking up each day and tossing a few prayers toward heaven, paying our bills, sending our kids off to school, picking up our to-do list, and passively hoping all goes well. Such a person is like a boat with no rudder. It will get nowhere except where the tides take it.

I heard one person moan that his purpose is "simply to survive"—a rudderless boat adrift, hoping for the best. We don't have to live like that. When we muster up the courage to ask ourselves the serious questions of life—when we gain a rudder—we find that our answers will chart the course of our lives and lead us to victor not victim status. This is true not just in our personal lives but in our political lives as well.

Our political and personal lives are inextricably intertwined. It's impossible to unravel or separate or know where one begins and the other ends. We're very much like a Penrose triangle, an optical illusion of a triangle with no beginning or end.

I've seen a tremendous amount of compartmentalized living and herd-like thinking among even the most well-intentioned people who, I suspect, haven't discovered what their identity is and how their identity affects all they do, including their politics. They don't see how their political stance matters and how their vote aligns with how they see themselves. Many of us follow the dance of kindness at the expense of truth. We see it most prominently displayed in politics, where the truth of a matter is rarely spoken for fear of not being politically correct, of not offending the herd, and of possibly losing political capital. But if we're going to have our identity grounded in truth, not in liberal fantasy, we're going to have to once and for all speak plainly as to where we stand on some bedrock principles. Chief among all principles is knowing the difference between what's right and what's wrong.

WHAT IS MORALLY AND FACTUALLY RIGHT?

Do black lives really matter? Are white people privileged? Are fetuses just a lump of indistinguishable cells, or are they human beings? Is homosexuality a moral issue or an issue of DNA? Are there really many genders, not just two? So many of life's questions have a political component, and when acted upon politically, it's important to discern and act on truth rather than on falsehood. It's more beneficial to move forward based on what is the better thing to do. But then we have to ask, "What is true?" What is false? What is the better thing to do? How does one set out to make such distinctions? And who does the distinguishing?

When my daughter started kindergarten several years ago, I came across a sheet of paper buried in a mound of paperwork that accompanied her home from her first day of school. It was a kindergarten welcome package.

Among the various sheets of paper informing me about the many policies and procedures I would be expected to follow throughout the school year, there was a formal letter introducing me to my daughter's guidance counselor. My first thought was, "Why does my five-year-old daughter need a guidance counselor?"

I remember having a guidance counselor when I was in high school. She guided me on whether I was going to take the ACT or the SAT. She helped me decide which classes to take, how many credits I needed to graduate, which college I would attend, and other matters where I truly needed her guidance.

So you can imagine my initial shock when I saw my daughter, at the ripe old age of five, now having her very own guidance counselor. I needed to know more, so I asked to see the guidance counselor's teaching objectives. Shortly thereafter, I received a list of thirty-five of what I considered the most ridiculous and inappropriate intrusions into my daughter's life.

Essentially, I was informed that the counselor acts as a second parent. Lesson number 5 on the list of thirty-five objectives announced that the counselor would lead my five-year-old daughter on a quest to distinguish between telling the truth and telling a lie.

The first of many questions that arose within my mind was, "Whose standard will the counselor use to determine what is true versus what is false?" Would she use our culture's standard of what is considered true? Would she use her own standard of truth? Or would she use some objective standard? For example, many in our nation believe President Trump to be a racist. Is this true or false? How would my five-year-old daughter's guidance counselor arrive at her conclusion? I personally believe this is a question best left to the parents to discuss with their children. However, we have numerous examples of teachers usurping parents and having this discussion with their students. Would she declare our president to be a racist because a USA Today opinion columnist does? Columnist Jonathan Zimmerman called on all schools and all teachers to "make sure our children do not behave like [President Trump], stating, "Schools are required to teach the skills and habits of democratic life: civility, tolerance and mutual respect. When the president breaches those norms, we have to call him out."[1] Furthermore, Zimmerman goes on to declare, "So far, most GOP politicians have kept quiet in the face of Trump's bigoted barrage. Our teachers can't—and shouldn't—do that." Is this the standard of "truth" my daughter's five-year old guidance counselor would use in distinguishing between what is true and what is not? After looking at all that President Trump has done to specifically help the black community, I believe there's enough concrete evidence to state he's not a racist.

Or should I be concerned if my black child's white counselor attends one of many white privilege conferences that have taken place across our nation? The conferences are based on the false premise "that the U.S. was started by white people for white people?"[2] If my child's counselor attends this event, should I be concerned about how she comes to her conclusions about what is true or not? One thing I've come to realize over many years is that what may be considered true by me may not be considered true by others. Likewise, what others consider true may be utterly false to me. Truths that used to be common sense are often now questioned or outright discarded. Common sense is no longer common in today's voyeuristic culture. A popular cultural trend today is asking, "What's your truth?"—as if there's no such thing as objective truth.

When I met with my daughter's counselor for the first time (and before removing my child from the public school system altogether), I instructed her that her job is not to parent my child. Both of my children have parents—a father and a mother. Both parents are highly active in our children's lives, and we will set the standard of morality in our home. Not the government. I politely but firmly reminded her of the educator's first job, which is to teach reading, writing, arithmetic; throw in some science, history, and social studies; and send my children back home to me. *We,* not the state, will parent them.

We can look around today and see numerous examples of grown people having a difficult time handling what would have been considered common knowledge just a few years ago. We see family members, neighbors, friends, and legislators all having a tough time distinguishing between right and wrong.

For instance, should people who identify with a gender that is in stark contrast to their anatomy be allowed to use the opposite sex's bathroom simply because they feel like it? Is this a good thing or a bad thing? Is the radical group Antifa really protecting our First Amendment by prohibiting certain speakers they deem inappropriate from speaking? Is this a good thing or a bad thing? The Oregon House of Representatives passed the Reproductive Health Equity Act,[3] which would allocate $10.2 million of taxpayer money for services related to contraception planning, including abortions. The governor of Oregon said she would readily sign this bill into law when it lands on her desk. Is this a good thing or a bad thing?

The answer to each of the above questions depends on whom you ask. The Democrats in the Oregon House of Representatives who passed the Reproductive Health Equity Act without any Republican votes, would undoubtedly proclaim it as a good thing. Those who support the activities of Antifa would decidedly say it's a good thing to deny speakers they disagree with participation in public debate. Former president Barack Obama, who strongly advocated for what he believed were equal rights for the LGBTQ community, would emphatically stand by the letter the Department of Education sent to public schools to allow transgender bathrooms.[4]

It's a legitimate quest for me as a parent to seek to understand whose standard my daughter's kindergarten guidance counselor was using to distinguish between what is true and what is false. What moral compass would she use to determine what is right and what is wrong? And clearly, discovering truth is not just a black issue. It's an issue for all of us. There is no black truth that is not also white truth and vice versa. We Americans are all intricately intertwined, just as our political life is by nature intertwined with our personal life. We share a common fate.

My concern is that I believe we within the black community often lack the ability to distinguish truth from manipulations of the truth. How do we consider what's true?

DETECTING TRUTH

One of the best methods I've employed to help me detect a lie comes from a story I once heard many years ago. It involves the techniques federal agents use in their efforts to identify counterfeit money.

One would think that federal agents spend hours upon hours studying all of the possible ways a counterfeit bill could be introduced into our monetary system. Perhaps it's counterintuitive, but as the story goes, in order to readily detect counterfeit currency, federal agents spend the bulk of their time studying the real thing. Instead of spending the bulk of their time studying every counterfeit bill they encounter, they spend their time studying real currency.

What a good analogy in discerning truth from fiction. If we become so familiar with truth, we will more easily discern untruth. We will no longer be fooled by counterfeit "truth."

It's not for me to delineate line by line what is true and what is not true. I've put in the work in my own life and in the lives of my family to help us quickly detect and call out a lie. It certainly starts out with knowing who you are as a person and why you're here. But it continues with understanding what's in your own best interest. And knowing what is true always works in our own best interest.

I suggest we all take the time to ask ourselves some questions and to revisit some old concepts that not too many years ago the majority of us would have considered to be common sense. Concepts such as it's not the color of a man's skin that defines him, but the content of his character. Or men in black masks showing up at Antifa rallies are really no different from those who wore white sheets targeting people they disagreed with, terrorizing the public, and usurping the law.

The fact is, truth is not as relative as the liberal mindset would have us believe. There *is* objective truth.

OBJECTIVITY OF TRUTH

Hopefully most of us would readily agree that there are objective truths in the world. For instance, almost everyone would agree that Newton's law of gravitation is an objective truth in that its truthfulness isn't dependent on our acceptance of it as being true. Its authority over our lives exists whether we believe in it or not. If you jump off a roof to try to defy the law of gravity, you are going to experience the sad result of not believing the objective truth about gravity.

Unfortunately, the voices of those who would argue that objective truths apply only to natural laws (such as the law of gravity) are increasing at an alarming rate in our society. They do not believe that the unwavering truths that exist in the natural order of creation have complementary moral and objective laws (truths) that are equally unfaltering and steadfast—whether we deem them so or not. These moral and objective truths aren't dependent on our feelings, our experiences, or the passing of time to be trustworthy. They are unwavering.

THE FOUR HORSEMEN

For years we've been bombarded with the messages of "tolerance," "relativity," "political correctness," and the latest one: "inclusivity." Almost all important issues of the day are judged, analyzed, dissected, and determined through the filters of these four horsemen. They have effectively replaced objectivity. Even devout Christians stop to consider if something is PC or not before proceeding—truth be damned.

These four horseman—with the cooperation of the media—make identity politics a reality. Categorizing people into little boxes is only made possible because these four horsemen make it possible by silencing or demeaning those of us who believe that objective truth still exists. They are the driving force behind every false narrative, such as white privilege, reparations, open borders, gender relativity, and much, much more.

Because of tolerance, we accept intolerable behaviors from groups of people deemed to be at a disadvantage. For instance, instead of speaking the truth about the tragic results of the high fatherless rates within black communities, it's easier to simply blame police brutality or drugs for the resulting epidemic of violence because, after all, blacks are simply disadvantaged. Even though we all know the statistics, we say nothing about the widespread epidemic of absentee fathers destroying one of the largest minority groups in our country.

Because of relativity, we've thrown out objective truths, such as "If speaking proper grammar is good for white folks, then it's good for black folks, too." We've embraced illogic instead, as seen with American University embracing the false logic that English as spoken in America is racist. The university is advocating that their professors grade students' papers based on effort rather than actual results. We've made allowances for poor-performing schools in black communities because of relativity, deeming certain things true only if they apply to this group of people but not to that group of people. We've allowed a skewing of the truth to apply to those we feel are disadvantaged, so much so that we now have universities pushing the idea that knowing how to write a complete sentence is supporting white supremacy. Or consider the College Board's initial rollout of a new grading system that gives SAT test takers an additional score based on the environment they grew up in.[5]

In the first half of 2019, the College Board added a "disadvantage" score—they called it the Environmental Context Dashboard—to SAT test. According to a *USA Today* article, "The College Board says the move aims to even the playing field so that striving students from low-income backgrounds get full consideration by college admissions officers, even if their overall scores aren't high as those of wealthier peers."[6]

This is just another liberal Band-Aid on a very real problem in disadvantaged areas. If liberals really want to help these disadvantaged children improve, then the solution is to make sure they understand how to conjugate verbs. If liberals truly want to help these students improve, then start by not telling them that English is racist. If the desire to improve the readiness of those living in disadvantaged areas is a real desire to see real change, then liberals should stop blocking school vouchers that allows parents to pull their students out of failing schools and place them into thriving environments regardless of their zip code. Personally, as a black woman who grew up in an extremely disadvantaged environment, skewing results of a test would not have helped me learn algebra or logic or improve my vocabulary. Only studying did that. Only a system that deems me worthy of knowing these vital skills does. Now that I no longer live in a disadvantaged state of being and have worked to give my own children a better start, are they now to be penalized because of my hard efforts? Illogical!

Because of political correctness, we've been prevented from speaking out forcibly against those who are brazen enough to assault a police officer. A year ago we saw mostly minorities throw buckets of water onto unsuspecting police officers. Instead of a nation rushing in immediately to condemn such behavior, we were initially paralyzed, not knowing if we should speak up or not. Instead, a majority of the media waited until they got a ground-swell of support condemning the bad behavior before deciding to speak up themselves.

In a recent study, 79 percent of those under the age of twenty-four think "political correctness is a problem in our country." Astonishingly, 61 percent of traditional liberals even believe we've gone too far in our PC culture.[7] Not surprisingly, 97 percent of devoted conservatives believe it's a problem.

Because of "inclusivity," we're now left with skinny eyebrows being deemed "problematic and cultural appropriation."[8] "God bless you" has been declared an anti-Islamic microaggression.[9] The New School, a private college in New York City, issued a guide titled "Common Examples of Microaggression in an Academic Setting," listing small chairs as a microaggression against over-weight people.[10] Securing our southern border is deemed racist. A Seattle-area councilman who was concerned that hosing down human-excrement-covered sidewalks might be racially insensi-tive as he makes the connection of when hoses were used against civil rights activists during the 1960s.[11] Believe it or not, the list could go on and on and on.

As standalone words, "tolerance," "relativity," "political cor-rectness," and "inclusivity" are pretty innocuous. But they don't stand alone. They have been weaponized in our culture to silence those who would speak the truth. And the truth is we Americans share more common ground with one another than we're led to believe. But, because of these four horsemen we don't talk plainly to one another and we don't speak truthfully. This has proven det-rimental to efforts to help the black community.

The constant pounding of these messages over time has had a penetrating effect on the minds, vocabulary, and behavior of an entire nation. These four horsemen have had an apocalyptic effect on our country, rendering us paralyzed at times when it comes to making even the simplest decisions. They have effectively brought to a slow crawl legislation protecting our southern border, issuing travel bans on would-be terrorists, stopping the dismemberment of little babies' bodies for profit, prohibiting drug injection sites, to not legalize marijuana, banning sanctuary cities, and more. By the way, none of these liberal policies helps the black community.

If you doubt the validity of this—if you doubt their power— walk out your front door wearing "Make America Great Again" paraphernalia, especially in communities where the four horsemen are worshipped. Or go to your local Starbucks and try to strike up a conversation—it probably won't go well for you. Even if we're led to do so and have the resolve to carry it out, it's hard to fight the constant parading of these messages through the media, academia, and even from the pulpits of some politically correct churches. The messages of tolerance, relativity, political correctness, and inclusivity have been quickly woven into the fabric of America.

In and of themselves, these four horsemen sound innocent, even idyllic. Why would anyone protest them? But as they take hold and even morph into new meanings, they become obstacles to objective truth. The sexualization and sterilization of children's bodies is an example. In what reality is the normalization of an eleven-year-old boy pretending to snort a line of ketamine and dancing in a wig and crop-top in front of a crowd of hooting adult men as they threw dollar bills at him sounds right?[12] But this is exactly what happened to Desmond Napoles, known as Desmond is Amazing, who is a "drag kid," fashion model, and global LGBTQ icon. This eleven-year-old child presents himself as a sexualized caricature of a woman, dressing in heels, makeup, flamboyant attire, and bright colored wigs and gyrating in a wild and suggestive manner before gay men as they throw money at him. How do we raise healthy, gender-secure children while enabling such inappropriate behavior under the banner of "inclusiveness" and "tolerance"?

With this in mind, allow me to challenge everyone to think long-term when confronted with any set of beliefs. Every choice we make and every ideology we espouse carries consequences that reach further into the future than today and touch generations to come.

At their root, each of these four horsemen implies that everyone has feelings and opinions and that everyone's feelings and opinions are equally valuable. Of course, everyone has feelings. But are they all equal? Are they all of the same value?

We see it on many college campuses where only one side is allowed to share their opinion, that side typically being the liberal Left side. College campuses have become minefields for comedians, and several very prominent ones have chosen to skip college campuses altogether. The legends Jerry Seinfeld and Chris Rock have stopped performing on college campuses, saying college kids can't take a joke. Bill Maher was protested at the very liberal University of California in Berkeley as he gave the commencement address because students were angry over his jokes about Muslims.[13] The documentary *No Safe Spaces* shows evidence of how conservative voices are being shut down on American campuses. Former Immigration and Customs Enforcement acting director Thomas Homan was escorted off the stage at the University of Pennsylvania after students started chanting "Abolish ICE." The liberal Left doesn't want to discuss ideas. They believe that only their side knows the truth. They've proven time and time again that they consider themselves to be correct, and everyone else is not only wrong but does not deserve to be heard. This is not American.

For decades the black community, especially in urban areas, has been allowed to live as though objective realities don't exist. We've gone virtually unchallenged about the epidemic fatherless rates among black men. We've gone unchallenged about the pervasive use of abortions as a birth control measure. Everyone in mainstream America has essentially turned their heads and looked the other way when we walk out into society with four shades of blue weave in our hair. We've made allowances for Ebonics to be spoken instead of clear English.

What is true cannot be subjective. Knowing proper English is good for all Americans. It can't be good for white folks to speak it but allowable if blacks don't. If I was in China, I would speak

Mandarin. If I was in Israel, I would speak Hebrew or Arabic. I'm not. I'm in America. And here, our official language is English. So, it doesn't behoove us to placate a language the majority in our society doesn't readily understand and associates with ignorance.

Most of us would wait in line at the bank for the teller who speaks in a manner we can all understand and exudes a certain level of intelligence. We would likely avoid the line for the bank teller we can't understand. Truth cannot be subjective. Either it is what it says it is or it's not. Like gravity, either truth exists or it doesn't. But if it does exist, we would be wise to order our lives accordingly or face peril.

Consider another instance of political correctness based on subjectivity—with potentially dangerous results. Back in April 2010, the White House announced President Obama's latest initiative of achieving political correctness with his plans to remove language such as "militant Islamic radicalism" from all documents outlining his national security strategy.[14] It appeared that in the mind of our former president, if we change the vocabulary we use to fight terrorism, if we start investing in Muslim businesses, if we support scientific research and combat polio in Muslim countries, we would be successful in changing the Muslim view of America. Presumably, they would stop chanting "Death to America" in countries like Iran.[15]

Somehow, in the mind of the Obama administration, this strategy would cause Muslims from around the world who are committed to jihad to suddenly rise up and cooperate with America.

Former president Obama's significant change in strategy didn't occur in a fishbowl. This shift in how we identify our enemies occurred while the Iranians, specifically, were not acting in good faith. At the time of Obama's decision, we had enough information to tread very lightly with Iran's president Mahmoud

Ahmadinejad, who in October 2005 stated Israel should be "wiped off the map."[16] Obama's politically correct decision was made on the heels of Ahmadinejad declaring in December 2009 that Israel could not do a "damn thing" to stop the Islamic state's nuclear program, a program that we in the West reportedly believed to be "aimed at developing an atomic bomb."[17] Obama's shift in strategy occurred in the face of Israeli prime minister Benjamin Netanyahu's statement in March 2010 that "a radical Iranian regime armed with nuclear weapons could bring an end to the era of nuclear peace the world has enjoyed for the last 65 years."[18]

Yet, in light of it all, there were those who were willing to rewrite reality and replace it with their own set of beliefs. Because of the four horsemen of tolerance, relativity, political correctness, and inclusivity, by and large the American people said nothing, though a few of us mumbled our disdain under our collective breath.

This isn't a call to take up arms or to be rude, disrespectful, or unnecessarily confrontational. Instead, I'm making a plea for us to seriously consider the world around us and the direction in which we are headed. It's a call to do more than just politely nod our heads in consent of a moral and objective truth. It's a call to take to the streets of public opinion with our firm belief that certain things are right and certain things are wrong. We must stop using the vocabulary of the Left and openly reject certain principles that don't line up with our core beliefs.

WHY ARE WE TALKING ABOUT THIS?

What's the point of this discussion? Why are moral and objective truths so important? Why can't we all just get along? Why can't we just allow people to live how they want to live? Why must we be so darn judgmental?

The answer is that moral and objective truths frame our view of the world and our view of humanity; they set up boundaries for man's imagination, and by truth, our steps are rightly ordered.

Consider this. During the July 7, 2016 Dallas shooting that claimed the lives of five police officers, twenty-five-year-old Micah Johnson did the unthinkable. He specifically set out to kill as many white police officers as he could as payback for what is perceived across our nation, among many, as racist police officers' targeting of black people.

After this happened, every fiber in my body shouted, "Finally! Surely now liberals, Democrats, and progressives alike will see the lunacy behind their incessant fanning of destructive narratives such as police brutality being the number one issue affecting black people."

Instead, I was stunned to see President Obama seemingly excusing the shooter stating, "I think it's very hard to untangle the motives of this shooter. By definition if you shoot people who pose no threat to you, you have a troubled mind."[19]

I was later left bewildered when my own friends and some family members, people I know to be otherwise of sound mind and body, express sympathy not for the slain police officers but for the murderer. They showed traces of appreciation and understanding for what he had done by explaining that they were trying to understand what must have driven him to such a point of desperation.

What? I couldn't believe it! How have we slipped so far into this moral abyss? Are we so morally bankrupt as a nation that we can no longer distinguish between what is good and what is evil? It was certainly clear to me that it was as a direct result of lies and false narratives that got those officers killed. There were no magnanimous reasons that led a killer to kill. He, too, at best was also manipulated right along with millions of others.

TRUTH FRAMES OUR VIEW OF THE WORLD

America could not have been founded and shaped to be the greatest country in the world without a framework of moral and objective truths—truths that don't change with the passing of time, experiences, or circumstances, truths that distinguish us from most nations. As Thomas Jefferson wrote, "When in the Course of human events, it becomes necessary for one people to dissolve the political bands which have connected them with another, and to assume among the powers of the earth, the separate and equal station to which the Laws of Nature and of Nature's God entitle them, . . . they should declare the causes which impel them to the separation."

Jefferson goes on to tell the world why they must separate from England: "We hold these truths to be self-evident, that all men are created equal, that they are endowed by their Creator with certain unalienable Rights, that among these are Life, Liberty and the pursuit of Happiness." Our very foundation as a nation is built upon these "self-evident" objective truths. Our Founding Fathers were compelled to risk their lives and their wealth for the pursuit of a truth that was objective and real.

Black Americans have been the beneficiaries of this moral and objective truth. Granted, not at first. I've taken great care to not minimize the evils of slavery or the hand our Founding Fathers played in perpetuating such an evil. Furthermore, I don't excuse those who perpetuated our sufferings during the Jim Crow era, nor do I overlook our modern day purveyors of racism—be it white supremacists or the Democrat Party.

But I'm not blind, nor do I suffer from amnesia. The words found in Thomas Jefferson's writings were used to eventually shame a nation into doing what was right. Those words served as judge and jury over the acts of a nation involved in such terror.

Those words have prevailed time and time again to make restitutions for what has been stolen. Those words and our lessons as a nation have allowed us to shine a beacon of light that has positively impacted the world.

TRUTH SHAPES OUR VIEW OF HUMANITY

Not only does a moral and objective truth shape our view of the world, it also frames our view and compassion toward humanity. It answers the questions "Am I my brother's keeper?" "Is all human life valuable?" "Can I do away with another's life if it inconveniences me?"

On April 18, 2010, a security camera captured Hugo Alfredo Tale-Yax's fatal stabbing after he thwarted a mugging. Within seconds after Hugo saved a woman being accosted, he was stabbed several times. He continued to chase after the assailant, but then collapsed from his injuries. What was more shocking than his untimely death, though, were the responses of would-be Good Samaritans who just walked by.

A minute after his collapse, "a potential Good Samaritan walks right by. And so does the next person and the one after that. A procession of more than 20 people seem to notice and yet fail to help. One man pulls out his cell phone, but instead of calling 911, he snaps a picture. Another man nudges Tale-Yax, rolls him over twice, seems to see blood, but then walks away. For nearly an hour and a half, Hugo lay there until someone finally called for help."[20]

Are we so desensitized to the needs of those around us that we could reason with ourselves to walk right past a person in such dire need? For all the preaching of inclusivity, tolerance, political correctness, and relativity, we've actually become weaker in our humanity.

We've not only just walked past Hugo in his time of need; we've walked past distressed neighborhoods. We've walked past the fatherless child. We've walked past the empty rhetoric of our national and local leaders who promise us the world and never deliver. We've walked right past the genocide in our own back-yard, while millions of unborn babies are murdered every single year. The four horsemen have caused us to grow cold in many ways and unwilling to get involved and make a difference.

This lack of response shown by mostly liberals who preach inclusivity, tolerance, political correctness, and relativity is the complete opposite of what we see coming from most conserva-tives, specifically President Trump.

The pro-life Center for Medical Progress went undercover to expose the many lies and greed of Planned Parenthood. In one of their many undercover footage a high-ranking Planned Parent-hood official was caught leisurely discussing the sale of aborted babies' body parts over a large salad and a glass of red wine to would-be purchasers.[21] This high-ranking official talked glow-ingly about harvesting fetal organs from aborted babies and joked about selling enough of them to purchase a new Ferrari someday soon. Compare this and many other examples that were caught in this expansive undercover operation to one of President Trump's first acts as president. President Trump began his presidency on January 20, 2017. Three days later, on January 23, 2017, he banned American foreign aid to health providers abroad who discuss abortion as a family-planning option.[22] He spoke often during the campaign trail about his opposition to abortion and promised to make this policy shift a top priority if elected. A liberal joked about killing babies and selling their body parts to the highest bidder. President Trump reinstated a policy to stop the funding of such killings. Who has grown cold to the value of a human life?

Because I'm the by-product of a rape, perhaps I'm more sensitive to certain stories. Perhaps they catch my attention more readily. However, I vividly remember the story of a ten-year-old girl who had become pregnant. Allegedly, she was raped by her stepfather. This poor little soul.

Although this happened in Mexico, I remember this story becoming a lightning rod on both sides of the abortion debate here in America. The young girl's home state allowed abortion in cases of rape during the first ninety days of pregnancy. But the ten-year-old girl was well into her seventeenth week of pregnancy—nearly six weeks past the limit.[23] The debate circled around protecting life at all stages without exception versus a woman's choice to do with her body as she pleases, even if that woman is a ten-year-old child.

How should we respond to the heinous situation the innocent ten-year-old child found herself in? Additionally, what should our response be to the innocent life she now carries? To some, these are hard questions. To some, this story is solely about the life of the ten-year-old soon-to-be mother.

Having been that innocent child in the womb of my mother, the answer is not so difficult for me. Life is life, and it deserves to be protected. The most heinous of wrongs had been committed against that precious little girl as it had been against my own mother when she conceived me at the age of eleven. But two wrongs don't make anything right.

My mother, like this little child, was wronged. Killing me or the unborn child in this little girl's womb does not correct the first wrong. It doesn't make the violence visited upon her go away.

This objective truth applies to both the ten-year-old child and the person she carried in her womb. Truth isn't reliant upon our choices. It is what it is. The protection of life, especially the life of the most vulnerable, is an age-old value passed down from civilization to civilization. It's not based on circumstances, our personal timetables, or our private opinions. Either life is worth saving or it's not.

The world may consider this predicament a sticky one to judge. But for those who believe in moral and objective truths, the choice is clear.

TRUTH ESTABLISHES BOUNDARIES

C. S. Lewis writes in *The Abolition of Man*, "When all that says 'It is good' is debunked, what says 'I want' remains."[24] Think about it. If we decide as a nation to no longer be encumbered by religious sanctions, inherited traditions, and established values, then we choose to be led by one of our most basic of human instincts—self!

If we're all governed by self and what makes us "happy," we will soon see a bunch of little *selves* running around doing whatever pleases them. Self seeks after that which answers the questions "What pleases me today?" "What satisfies me today?" "What makes me happy today?" We can each attest to how self can be a fickle little thing. The only constant about its egocentric nature is that it's constantly changing. Its temperament is dependent upon its mood, its environment, and its fertile but depraved imagination, all of it changing with the passing of time.

Picture a nation where the volatility of self is the new template used to determine what we will consider good and what we should value and esteem. Although this picture may be unsettling to some, the most disturbing unasked question is, "Who will decide these new values for us?" Whose *self* will set the new standard for us all?

My grandmother Hattie would often say to a household of six women, "There can only be one queen bee in this house" and

"There can only be one cook in the kitchen." There will always be the one person or the one entity who will set the rules everyone else must abide by.

This is one of the many tricks of the four horsemen. They promise greater self-rule. But in the end, a dictator rises to bring order to the chaos that would otherwise ensue if everyone starts doing what seems right in their *own* eyes. Everyone's opinion cannot be equally valid in the operation of a society. There must be one standard.

Now entering stage left is socialism. As we've discussed at length in chapter 10, socialism is yet another form of slavery. We can't own people outright any longer. So, instead we make them dependent.

New systems of belief are constantly being peddled through our school system, corporations, and government and in our homes. At face value, many of these new beliefs may appear harmless, idyllic even.

For centuries, one civilization arising from another civilization has given credence to the fact that certain behaviors merit our approval or disapproval and our reverence or our contempt. Today, in our modern times, we see a quickening in pace to abandon any religious sanctions, any inherited traditions, and any emotional appeals that would hinder one from doing whatsoever his or her little heart desires.

I shudder at the thought of the day when the last remaining moral value is removed and the floodgates of man's imagination are opened. Man fighting diligently against his own core would be comical if the effects weren't so tragic.

The truths in this chapter aren't just for philosophical discourse. They're not topics discussed by those who have too much time on their hands. They're not something to engage ourselves in just to pass the time away. Moral and objective truth is under assault. If the objective standard by which we order our lives collapses, whose standards will we then live by? Entering the stage after socialism is communism. Vladimir Lenin made it clear that the true goal of socialism is communism. He would know better than most of us.

In recent years, we had only a socialist minority trying to impose their opinions on the masses. Today, the reach of that minority has amassed a formidable size of the American population. When Bernie Sanders first came out during the 2016 election offering us socialism, most of us laughed. Today, we're no longer laughing as we see one Democrat officeholder and presidential contender after another try to out-socialist Bernie Sanders.

Black Americans especially stand to be hurt the most as we shift from a system where the rules of engagement are clearly marked to one where we make it up as we go. Therefore, black Americans must become watchful for their own interests. We must know what is true and what is false and then align our lives accordingly.

Sadly, too many have chosen to lay down what we know to be true for the sake of one or more of the four horsemen.

No, this is not a call to be rude, disrespectful, or unnecessarily confrontational. Instead, it's a call to seriously consider the world around us and the direction in which we are headed. The *Titanic* was a glorious ship. Built to last. Unsinkable. But when it sailed into iceberg territory, it was doomed to sink on April 15, 1912.

Today we are on board the *Titanic*. The date is April 14, the day before it sank, and the iceberg of socialism is ahead. What is true about it? What is false? Will we adjust our course or will we sail on, oblivious?

My hope for the black community is that we begin to remember who we once were.

13.

WE ARE VICTORS, NOT VICTIMS

Recently my family and I visited one of the stations along the Underground Railroad, where we had the somber opportunity to retrace the steps of escaping slaves.

A station was considered a safe house that would provide refuge to those fleeing slavery via the Underground Railroad. It was a journey fraught with ambiguity and rife with danger. Never was a step taken on sure ground.

Escaping slaves would stop at these various stations along their long and arduous journey to freedom. For me, my children, and my husband, it was truly a mind-blowing experience to follow in the steps of those whose history still streams through my veins and to consider their unspoken stories.

Imagine, if you can, stepping into the shoes of a runaway slave—if they were one of the lucky ones who had shoes. Imagine summoning up the courage to walk up the back stairs of one of those safe houses. To dare to knock on the door. To dare to stretch out your feeble arms. To dare to hope with bated breath. When the person on the other side of the door opens it, to force yourself to utter the password.

"A friend of a friend sent me."

Then, to hold your breath once more, hoping beyond hope that the person on the other side is truly a friend and will provide refuge. To pray to God, this isn't a trap that might result in your untimely death and the death of those huddled up outside by the shed waiting to see your fate. It was a daunting experience that was a reality for many who looked very much like me.

There you stand. Focus intense. Gaze locked. You could hear a pin drop. Every muscle in your body is stiffened and ready to run. *Dear God, let him respond with the refrain!*

"A friend of yours is a friend of mine."

While visiting the safe house, we were able to read some of the stories that William Still, an important organizer of the Underground Railroad, recorded of some of the escaped slaves. One of the stories Still recorded was that of Betsy, a female slave.

Not much is known about Betsy except that she had a baby boy. One day Betsy was sent to the field to work. She laid her baby boy down under an oak tree. Later on, her child almost died. We don't know what happened to the little boy or what precipitated her panic. What we know is that for Betsy, this incident, whatever it was, was reason enough to seek freedom. If not for herself, then for her posterity.

As we look at the culture around us today, various strategies are being used to elevate the real and not-so-real concerns in the black community to the forefront of our attention. Many of those strategies are being played out on our television and movie screens, in the classrooms, in homes, and on the streets all across our nation. Innocent lives are being lost, blood is being spilled, and an antagonistic spirit is brewing in hearts across university campuses, economic statuses, social ladders, race, and zip codes that promises a weaker, not stronger, America.

What the black community is fighting over today is quite the reverse of Betsy's fight. I can't help but compare the two struggles. As I do, what dawns on me is that Betsy was a slave whose entire environment told her she wasn't even human. I doubt even one black American today has started out in life with a similar judgment laid against them.

Betsy's environment told her she had no personal worth outside of what she could be sold for in the marketplace by her master. Her environment instructed her that at any moment her master could radically change her situation—could even separate her forever from her beloved child—and she would be able to do nothing about it. Yet something in Betsy said, "I want freedom. If not for myself, then for my little bundle."

Can you see it? Can you see her strive? Her environment was telling her one thing, but Betsy knew somewhere deep inside that she was more than her environment. Her environment didn't accurately reflect who she was. She could be better. She could do better—both for her and for her little boy.

I say to the black community: Your surroundings may be telling you one thing. Right where you stand there may be signs and graffiti walls that are trying to measure your worth. Your community may be telling you that you're less than others, that you're without privileges in this country. Your community may be telling you that you're a perpetual victim. There may be those who sit in high places repeating the mantra that you're a victim, you're a victim, you're a victim, and that it's someone else's fault for your situation, that you can't achieve because the odds are stacked against you.

And perhaps they are.

But consider for a moment, what would Betsy do? What would she and so many other slaves say if they could see what you and I see today? What would Betsy think about the opportunities black Americans have today, opportunities she could never dream of for herself or even for her son? Yet we have those opportunities!

We are not slaves! We're free! We are the inheritors of a great inheritance in this country, one our black forefathers and our enslaved great-great-grandmothers worked for—even slaved for.

Their efforts built this country. That's their inheritance to us, an inheritance, for the most part, we didn't sacrifice to receive. Many came before us and paid the ultimate sacrifice so that we can receive this inheritance. I submit that because of their sacrifice for us, you and I now have a debt that can only be repaid by living a life worthy of their sacrifice.

In the minds of some, only the white man has a debt to repay for slavery. I submit that every black person's debt is even greater. We are indebted to our slave ancestors for every sacrifice, for every scrap of energy they mustered up to hold on, for every time they swallowed hard and bore the pain, and for enduring so that we could come forth as their seed today.

They held on not for themselves—they held on for us! They deposited their tears, their sweat, their prayers, their blood, their hopes and dreams, believing we would make a generous withdrawal someday.

Are we withdrawing from their rich deposit? Would they be proud of us?

Some of us have never even considered the need to make a deposit ourselves for the generation coming up behind us. Some of us are so busy and consumed with ourselves that the thought has never entered our mind that the black community our children will inherit is nearing bankruptcy.

Again, imagine the hurdles Betsy had to overcome to dare to want more for herself. Consider the land mines she had to navigate to give her child a better future. Now compare it to what we have to do to carve out a better life for ourselves today.

We are victors, not victims. If Betsy can do it, you can do it. You can be more than your environment. Your children and grandchildren can prosper if you give them the right foundation now. Too many black parents are raising children who will inherit bitterness, resentment, and even hate for the circumstances of their birth. Such a waste! Our children deserve better—and our ancestors would be the first to agree. Will their pain count for nothing?

So how do we withdraw from the bountiful deposit of our ancestors?

To start with, as trite as it might sound to some, just believe.

Look for the doors of opportunity and then walk through them one by one. Run, if you have too. Hold your breath. Swallow hard. Bear down. Hope beyond hope. Go through every door that's placed in front of you. You are your own best chance for moving up and out of whatever situation you find yourself in today. If not you, then who else should come to your rescue? The white man? The policeman? The politician? *You* are your first line of defense. You are your best advocate. You are your best hope for a better life for your posterity.

The liberal Left can't rescue us. They have absolutely nothing to offer any of us. We can see how and where they've invested their energy and time and know they have nothing of value to give us. They're bankrupt of workable solutions. All they have to give is more slavery via more dependency, chaos, division, and ultimately socialism.

President Trump has reclaimed the spirt of the Republican Party. He has injected energy and hope. He has taught the

Republican Party how to take a stand and fight for what's right. Personally, I have never seen a politician—white or black—work so diligently to bring the black community up the ladder of economic mobility and face so much opposition in doing so.

The only time I remember seeing a white person in our little small community in my childhood was either around election time or when the insurance man came to collect premiums.

I will never forget it. I was so young. I walked into our little hilltop church, and there in the pulpit was a white man! I didn't understand what was going on. It shocked me. I had never seen a white man in our neighborhood before. I distinctly remember hearing him say something that rhymed and the black folks in my church got excited. It looked like they approved of him.

Years later, as adults living outside of Dallas, my husband and I decided to attend a predominately black church in one of the poorest areas of the city—hoping we would be a positive influence. Once more, I walked into church, and there was a white man in the pulpit. Of course at this point in life, I was no longer surprised by the appearance of a white person in a predominately black church. However, this church was overwhelmingly black, so to see a white man in the pulpit was out of the norm.

Once more, blacks in the congregation were muted in their response toward him at first. Then he said something that rhymed. Once more, I saw the congregation get excited. I overheard one say, "He's for us." I don't recall what he said any more than I recalled what the white man said in my youth. But what struck me was the response of black people.

I distinctly remember a rhyme being spoken and the atmosphere changed. Perhaps the black people appreciated the white speaker's attempt to identify with them. I have no idea. But suddenly he was one of us. Suddenly, the mood changed from skepticism to familiarity, all over a rhyme I wouldn't be able to recite back today.

Fast-forward decades later and not much has changed in the black community or with our interactions with our elected officials. They still come around every four years with a big grin and some promises in hand and do a little jig for us. Hillary Clinton came with hot sauce in her purse once.[1] It would be funny if it wasn't all so demeaning.

We must demand more from ourselves first. Then we must demand more from our elected officials. They give us the crumbs because for decades we've accepted crumbs.

We need a greater return on our investment. We've given Democrats the White House each and every time they've won it. We need a greater return because we have a significant debt that can only be repaid by a life that's lived well, a life that ceases being manipulated by Democrats' free handouts, which have destabilized our communities.

Another step forward for each of us is to learn our identity, followed closely by knowing our worth as individuals and the worth of our collective vote as a black community.

The parody we see in the Democrat Party has become so commonplace we don't even notice the twisting on its head of our Constitution or of our way of life. Securing our southern border wall has now become a vanity project according to several prominent Democrats who have refused to give President Trump the funding he needs to secure our border.[2] ICE rounding up illegal criminal aliens has now become a call to citizens to go on a hunger strike to "shut down" the agency.[3] Representative Rashida Tlaib called on citizens not to wait for Congress to do their job by passing responsible immigration laws. Instead, she encouraged them to "shut down" ICE by starving themselves. Protecting an individual's right to keep and bear arms has now allegedly become not what the Founding Fathers intended, according to Democrats in the Hawaii Senate.[4] The War on Drugs has become a push to legalize marijuana across our nation. Innocent until proven guilty has fallen to "just believe the woman" as Democrats rushed to cast off the restraints of the Sixth Amendment during the Supreme Court nomination hearings of Justice Brett Kavanaugh. And ultimately, if you don't like the election results, a duly elected president can now be targeted, maligned, and on the road to impeachment without any tangible evidence of a crime.

It should anger us all what the Democrat Party is doing to our nation and to the rule of law and order, and how they are squandering our inheritance. Democrats are like C's and D's on a report card—too many of them is never a good thing. Week after week we are blindsided so much that most of us feel numb to it all. Week after week, trying to digest the latest news is like trying to drink from a fire hydrant—it's next to impossible.

The jury is in, folks: We are a divided nation, and it spells trouble for all of us. Though I maintain that the black community is nearing bankruptcy, I'm also dubious that America can withstand these assaults much longer. Mark 3:27 says that a house cannot be overtaken until you bind the strong man. The strong man in America is our Constitution, our understanding of the difference between right and wrong. It is under assault from the Left, who call it a "living Constitution" to allow for any interpretation a liberal interpreter wants to give it.

In these dangerous times, we must demand more from ourselves and from those who claim to represent our best interest. We have a debt to repay for the many untold sacrifices that have been made on our behalf by an entire nation—both blacks and whites.

We must also redraw lines of civility among the races and our elected officials. We're now living in a culture where it's not good enough that we agree to disagree. I must now annihilate you. I must obliterate you. I must actively comb through your social media pages and find something, anything to denigrate you in such a way that there's no coming back for you.

We've forgotten that we are talking to fellow human beings— to mothers, fathers, sisters, and brothers. Being an American used to mean something more than it seems to mean today. There was a sense of decency. All of that has gone by the wayside in our effort to be right by any means necessary.

I've noticed three things about hate. First, hate is real. It's not unique to one particular color or one particular political party—we see it on the Left as well as on the Right. Its sole mission is to divide.

Second, hate can be profitable: More newspapers get sold, more people are likely to vote your way, and you can get more clicks on your website. The purveyor of hate has no real concern about the effects of division, just that he or she is dividing and that it's profitable. But when we're divided, we're weaker. We're all left more vulnerable.

Third, hate needs a willing host to survive. It must embody a physical human being in order to carry out its plans. Hate is not a bigot. It's impartial and will embody any willing vessel. We must not allow ourselves to be the vessel of hate.

We in the black community must never allow the past atrocities associated with slavery to be a justification for hating a white person.

We in the black community have to deal with the past only as it can be made useful in helping us in the present and in the future.

For many blacks today, our past has become an anchor, not a launching pad. We can't move forward because we're paralyzed and fixated on pointing to past pains.

Interestingly, the pain we often point to that prevents us from moving forward isn't any pain that was inflicted upon us personally. I've always found the stories of Frederick Douglass, Booker T. Washington, and George Washington Carver fascinating. All were born slaves. All understood fully the miseries of slavery from firsthand accounts. Yet, in each of their retellings of their stories, they share such hope for themselves, for the black community, and for all of America.

Surprisingly, they are not bitter, as one might imagine. They certainly had reasons to be. Instead, Douglass wrote, "From my earliest recollection, I date the entertainment of a deep conviction that slavery would not always be able to hold me within its foul embrace; and in the darkest hours of my career in slavery, this living word of faith and spirit of hope departed not from me, but remained like ministering angels to cheer me through the gloom. This good spirit was from God, and to him I offer thanksgiving and praise."[5]

Where's the angst? Where's the victim mentality? Where's the constant spewing of hate-filled words against this country? You won't see it.

In fact, each of these great men and many more came out of slavery and got busy contributing to society, being engaged in a useful employment, and bringing their fellow brothers and sisters along with them. They found passion in what they did. They did it all with a grateful heart that they were their own masters. Mothers and fathers, let me ask you: Do you want your sons to grow up to be another Frederick Douglass or the newest, hottest foulmouthed rapper to achieve fame?

Like anything in life, we must learn to fashion what has happened to us in the past in such a way that it propels us forward. We can't be so injured that we stop dead in our tracks. We must find the unconquerable spirit of Frederick Douglass, a self-taught slave who became an advisor to President Abraham Lincoln and was appointed as the minister resident to Haiti by President Benjamin Harrison. Or become the insatiable mind of Booker T. Washington, who slept under a staircase because he needed to save money to get to college. He would later establish Tuskegee Institute. Or find the resolve of Betsy, who thought enough of herself to seek a better life for her and her child.

Frederick Douglass said, "If there is no struggle, there is no progress. Those who profess to favor freedom, and yet depreciate agitation, are men who want crops without plowing up the ground. They want rain without thunder and lightning. They want the ocean without the awful roar of its many waters. This struggle may be a moral one; or it may be a physical one; or it may be both moral and physical; but it must be a struggle. Power concedes nothing without a demand. It never did and it never will."[6]

What is our demand today?

To the black community: America is our inheritance. We must stand up and fight to preserve her. Our fight starts with knowing who we are and embracing our identity as Americans. But our fight doesn't end there. We must also learn to fight with our vote.

We have nothing to lose. We have everything to gain.

THANK YOU,
LITTLE BLACK GIRL

Thank You, Little Black Girl.

Although, I've never met you, I can identify with your pain.

Thank You, Little Black Girl.

I can see you running through the bushes panting and screaming as massa calling out your name.

Thank You, Little Black Girl . . .

For never giving up, your father was snatched away and mine
just simply chose to give up.

Thank You, Little Black Girl.

I will never forget your sacrifice.

I will live and be free to spite the chains that were on your feet.

Thank You, Little Black Girl.

I will never forget.

I will carry forth your legacy and be accursed if I get beset

with the ignorance and the foolishness that often plagues
our community.

1 in 2 Black children growing up fatherless, how can that be?

There are no more chains on our feet or lashes on our back.

We don't have to work from sun up to sun down picking cotton
to make someone else's hat.

That was your present reality

It's our legacy.

You paid the real cost and now we get to walk in
the inheritance that you bought

Because of you, we now have a choice.

We can be all that we set our minds to be.

Yet, we're often choosing to be so much less than you
dared a little slave girl like you could even be.

Forgive us, Little Black Girl

For not living up to redeem the price that you paid.

There were so many ways out and yet you continued to be
strong and here we stand as part of your seed.

Here is my pledge to you and to my posterity:

I promise to aspire to be all that I can be, by putting forth the
effort to secure all that you had dreamt for me.

Thank You, Little Black Girl.

ACKNOWLEDGMENTS

I am eternally grateful to my late grandparents—Grandma Hattie, Granddaddy Charles, and Grandma "Tut." They showed me what it means to be loved and to love others. I am because of them. I miss their gentle hands of instruction. I am the fruit of their labor.

To my very first best friends—my brothers. John and Tyrone, I am so proud of you both. I could not have asked for better brothers. You two were my very first audience as I was forming my thoughts on politics and the black culture. Thank you for putting up with me and for never saying a harsh word although I knew you vehemently disagreed at times. We've endured so much together. To see how you two have thrived in life makes me one proud big sister.

Mom, I love you. Your perseverance has not gone unnoticed. You never gave up, and the apple has not fallen far from the tree. I am my mother's child.

I must acknowledge my literary agent, Nick Harrison. You are amazing! Your calm tone never wavered even when the voice in my head grew weary. Thank you for the many late-night phone calls and early-morning editing sessions to see me across the finish line.

I can never forget my editorial director, Kate Hartson. "I appreciate you" doesn't seem like enough. I am so grateful for your kindness and your work ethic. You are inspiring. Thank you for picking up my proposal and allowing me to realize a dream.

I would be remiss if I didn't thank my many aunts and uncles, specifically Uncle Herbert and my late Auntie Sherry. I'm grateful for your many conversations, your kindness toward me, and your love for my family. When I had less than nothing, you two opened up your arms, your doors, and your wallets. I have not forgotten. Thank you.

Most of all, I am grateful to God. Your thoughts and plans concerning me are precious and overwhelming at times. I am so grateful for Your kindness and Your mercy. Thank You for giving me a dream and for bringing the right people into my path at the right time. You are an awesome God.

NOTES

INTRODUCTION

1. Frederick Douglass, *The Narrative of the Life of Frederick Douglass* (Arcturus Holdings Limited, 2018), 62.

1. NOTHING TO LOSE, EVERYTHING TO GAIN

1. https://www.washingtonpost.com/news/post-politics/wp/2016/08/22/donald-trump-to-african-american-and-hispanic-voters-what-do-you-have-to-lose.

2. National Women's Law Center, "National Snapshot: Poverty among Women and Families, 2018," https://nwlc-ciw49tixgw5lbab.stackpathdns.com/wp-content/uploads/2018/09/National-Snapshot.pdf.

3. National Women's Law Center, "National Snapshot: Poverty Among Women and Families, 2018," https://nwlc-ciw49tixgw5lbab.stackpathdns.com/wp-content/uploads/2018/09/National-Snapshot.pdf.

4. https://www.fatherhood.org/father-absence-statistic.

5. https://www.bjs.gov/content/pub/ascii/dudsfp04.txt.

6. https://www.ncjrs.gov/pdffiles1/ojjdp/grants/250753.pdf.

7. https://trib.com/opinion/columns/williams-how-important-is-today-s-racial-discrimination/article_2762f4b4-c0ab-561f-9acf-c26dc3c3b82b.html.

8. https://www.nytimes.com/2008/06/15/us/politics/15text-obama.html.

9. https://www.cdc.gov/nchs/data/nvsr/nvsr64/nvsr64_06.pdf.

10. Burgess Owens, *Liberalism or How to Turn Good Men into Whiners, Weenies and Wimps* (Post Hill Press, 2016), 117.

11. Burgess Owens, *Liberalism or How to Turn Good Men Into Whiners, Weenies and Wimps* (Post Hill Press, 2016), 105.

12. https://blackdemographics.com/population/black-regions.

13. http://www.pbs.org/race/000_About/002_04-background-03-08.htm.

14. https://www.people-press.org/2018/03/20/1-trends-in-party-affiliation-among-demographic-groups.

15. https://www.epi.org/publication/50-years-after-the-kerner-commission.

16. https://www.epi.org/publication/50-years-after-the-kerner-commission.

17. https://www.urban.org/urban-wire/mapping-black-homeownership-gap.

18. https://www.bestplaces.net/voting/city/minnesota/minneapolis.

19. https://www.bjs.gov/index.cfm?ty=pbdetail&iid=812.

20. https://www.tulsaworld.com/news/trending/for-the-first-time-ever-most-new-working-age-hires/article_5b9f7c26-6369-5075-a9ac-e19b72e69685.html.

21. https://www.cnn.com/2019/09/06/economy/black-unemployment-rate/index.html.

22. https://www.ed.gov/news/press-releases/secretary-devos-issues-full-forgiveness-hbcu-hurricane-relief-loans.

2. LIVING OUTSIDE OF THE LIBERAL BOX

1. https://www.foxnews.com/entertainment/kathy-griffin-calls-for-doxing-students-in-viral-video-shame-them.

2. https://mobile.wnd.com/2019/01/adults-owe-covington-kids-an-apology.

3. https://www.yahoo.com/entertainment/vulture-writer-covington-students-just-153137522.html.

4. https://sputniknews.com/us/201901231071756514-us-students-taunting-native-american.

5. https://www.realclearpolitics.com/video/2019/01/22/behar_covington_catholic_incident_happened_because_were_desperate_to_get_trump_out_of_office.html.

6. https://www.washingtontimes.com/news/2014/nov/4/michelle-obama-tells-blacks-to-vote-democrat-its-t.

7. https://www.youtube.com/watch?v=oaAUbceI9cM; https://dailycaller.com/2014/11/04/michelle-obamas-closing-argument-to-black-voters-dont-think-vote-for-democrats.

8. Dr. Seuss, *Happy Birthday to You!* (Random House, 1959).

9. Shakespeare, *Othello*, act 1, scene 3.

10. https://www.dailysignal.com/2019/08/28/new-york-times-1619-project-has-key-error-about-our-founding.

11. https://www.breitbart.com/the-media/2019/08/16/new-york-times-staffer-racism-is-in-everything-foundation-of-all-of-the-systems-in-the-country.

12. https://www.cnn.com/2017/09/27/politics/michelle-obama-women-voters/index.html.

13. https://www.nytimes.com/2009/07/12/magazine/12ginsburg-t.html; https://thefederalist.com/2014/09/24/ruth-bader-ginsburg-really-wants-poor-people-to-stop-having-babies.

14. https://time.com/3823073/time-100-photos-behind-the-scenes.

15. https://www.glamour.com/story/ruth-bader-ginsburg.

16. https://newrepublic.com/article/119610/new-republic-cover-featuring-ruth-bader-ginsburg-american-hero.

17. https://www.theatlantic.com/magazine/archive/2019/01/ruth-bader-ginsburg-feminist-hero/576403.

18. https://www.imdb.com/title/tt7689964.

19. https://www.census.gov/newsroom/press-kits/2019/detailed-estimates.html.

20. https://www.kff.org/medicaid/state-indicator/medicaid-enrollment-by-raceethnicity.

21. https://www.census.gov/newsroom/press-kits/2019/detailed-estimates.html. Black = 15,517,400 on Medicaid versus 42,564,000 total black population (36 percent); White = 29,253,700 on Medicaid versus 195,530,000 (15 percent).

22. https://www.breitbart.com/politics/2019/04/29/planned-parenthood-and-black-lives-matter-leaders-partner-for-womens-new-deal-movement-ahead-of-2020.

23. https://www.plannedparenthoodaction.org/planned-parenthood-new-york-city-action-fund-inc/blog/this-black-history-month-stand-for-black-lives.

24. H. C. Black, *Black's Law Dictionary*, 6th ed. (Springer, 1994), 1523.

3. I'M BLACK…BUT I'M NOT A DEMOCRAT

1. https://www.washingtonexaminer.com/washington-secrets/feds-kushners-criminal-justice-reform-working-blacks-benefit-overwhelmingly.

2. https://www.politico.com/story/2018/11/28/tim-scott-gop-taxes-opportunity-zones-990788.

3. https://www.washingtonexaminer.com/opinion/op-eds/sen-tim-scott-opportunity-zones-are-really-working.

4. Booker T. Washington, *Up from Slavery* (Digireads.com Publishing, 2016), 52.

5. https://www.cnn.com/politics/live-news/trump-mexico-tariffs-immigration-2019.

6. https://www.pbs.org/newshour/world/iran-still-top-state-sponsor-terrorism-u-s-report-says.

7. https://www.forbes.com/sites/modeledbehavior/2017/05/28/guaranteeing-everyone-a-job-is-harder-than-it-sounds.

7. Frederick Douglass, *The Narrative of the Life of Frederick Douglass* (Arcturus Holdings Limited, 2018), p. 62.

4. WHAT DOES IT MEAN TO BE BLACK IN AMERICA?

1. The term "culture of poverty" derived from the work of a number of urban sociologists. Prominent among them was Oscar Lewis, author of *La Vida* (Vintage, 1965).

2. https://www.census.gov/quickfacts/fact/table/clevelandcityohio/PST045216.

3. http://www.businessinsider.com/jay-z-hillary-clinton-concert-2016-11.

4. https://censusreporter.org/data/table/?table=B17001&primary_geo_id=16000US3916000&geo_ids=16000US3916000,05000US39035,31000US17460,04000US39,01000US.

5. https://www.mediaite.com/tv/melissa-harris-perry-on-rachel-dolezal-it-is-possible-that-she-might-actually-be-black.

6. https://www.dol.gov/oasam/programs/history/moynchapter1.htm.

7. Roman. I. vii.

8. W. E. B. Du Bois, *The Souls of Black Folk* (Millennium Publications, 2004), 5.

9. https://ucr.fbi.gov/crime-in-the-u.s./2018/crime-in-the-u.s.-2018/tables/expanded-homicide-data-table-1.xls.

10. https://www.washingtonpost.com/graphics/2018/national/police-shootings-2018.

11. https://www.washingtonpost.com/graphics/2018/national/police-shootings-2018.

12. Fox & Friends, "Youth Football Team Kneel in Kaepernick-Inspired Protest," https://www.youtube.com/watch?time_continue=8&v=T7E2LmsKiTg.

13. Frederick Douglass, *The Narrative of the Life of Frederick Douglass* (Arcturus Holdings Limited, 2018), 67.

5. CULTURE OF POVERTY

1. Bruce J. Schulman, *Lyndon B. Johnson and American Liberalism* (Bedford/St. Martin's, 2007), 104.

2. https://www.washingtonexaminer.com/news/texas-father-blocked-from-stopping-gender-transition-of-son-james-7-to-girl-called-luna.

3. https://www.cdc.gov/nchs/fastats/marriage-divorce.htm.

4. https://dailycaller.com/2017/08/30/exclusive-paul-ryan-condemns-antifa-as-a-scourge-on-our-country.

5. https://www.realclearpolitics.com/video/2019/01/04/new_democratic_congresswoman_rashida_tlaib_on_trump_were_going_to_impeach_the_motherfcker.html.

6. https://www.washingtonexaminer.com/news/rashida-tlaib-were-going-to-impeach-the-mfer-dont-worry.

7. https://www.usatoday.com/story/news/politics/2019/09/27/rep-rashida-tlaib-sells-impeach-mf-shirts/3793470002.

8. https://www.foxnews.com/us/massachusetts-judge-who-helped-illegal-immigrant-escape-ice-arrest-indicted-federal-authorities-say. https://www.cnn.com/2019/08/13/us/massachusetts-judge-suspended-with-pay/index.html.

9. https://www.washingtonexaminer.com/news/dozens-of-documents-indicate-ilhan-omar-lived-with-ahmed-hirsi-while-claiming-to-be-married-to-ahmed-elmi. https://nypost.com/2019/08/27/inside-ilhan-omars-tangled-web-of-relationships/.

10. https://www.justicedemocrats.com/issues.

11. https://www.youtube.com/watch?v=1h5iv6sECGU.

12. https://nypost.com/2019/04/14/pelosi-rips-aoc-says-her-posse-in-congress-is-like-five-people.

13. American Community Survey. https://www.census.gov/newsroom/press-releases/2016/cb16-210.html.

14. https://www.nbcnews.com/politics/2020-election/kamala-harris-pulls-out-south-carolina-criminal-justice-forum-over-n1072371.

15. https://www.cnbc.com/2019/03/13/most-shocking-allegations-of-the-25m-college-admissions-scandal.html.

16. https://www.ibtimes.com/college-admissions-scandal-update-lori-loughlins-husband-allegedly-admitted-guilt-2853852. https://www.justice.gov/usao-ma/investigations-college-admissions-and-testing-bribery-scheme.

17. Booker T. Washington, *Up from Slavery* (Digireads.com Publishing, 2016), 27–28.

18. https://www.sacbee.com/news/local/education/article234218847.html.

19. https://www.collegetuitioncompare.com/edu/131159/american-university/tuition.

20. https://www.apmreports.org/story/2016/08/18/remedial-education-trap.

21. http://ccrc.tc.columbia.edu/media/k2/attachments/what-we-know-about-developmental-education-outcomes.pdf.

22. Daniel Moynihan, *The Negro Family: The Case for National Action* U.S. Department of Labor: Office of Policy Planning and Research, March 1965.

23. Bruce J. Schulman, *Lyndon B. Johnson and American Liberalism* (Bedford/St. Martin's 2007), 125.

24. https://dailycaller.com/2019/09/05/exclusive-ted-cruz-antifa-ocasio-cortez-boston.

25. https://www.berkeleyside.com/2018/08/08/eric-clanton-takes-3-year-probation-deal-in-berkeley-rally-bike-lock-assault-case.

26. https://www.huffpost.com/entry/white-nationalist-charlottesville-virginia_n_598e3fa8e4b0909642972007.

27. https://www.nytimes.com/1991/11/07/us/the-1991-election-louisiana-bush-denounces-duke-as-racist-and-charlatan.html?login=email&auth=login-email.

28. https://www.washingtontimes.com/news/2019/feb/5/david-duke-endorses-tulsi-gabbard-2020-presidentia/

29. https://www.wayfair.com/v/about/social_responsibility.

30. https://www.npr.org/2019/06/22/734923655/opinion-the-filthy-and-uncomfortable-circumstances-of-detained-migrant-children.

31. https://www.usatoday.com/story/news/nation/2019/06/26/wayfair-walkout-hundreds-protest-sales-migrant-detention-centers/1569622001.

32. http://www.foxbusiness.com/politics/2017/11/28/warren-lied-about-native-american-heritage-to-get-harvard-job-varney.html.

33. https://www.cbsnews.com/news/warren-explains-minority-listing-talks-of-grandfathers-high-cheekbones.

34. https://www.bing.com/videos/search?q=trump+navajo+code+talker+pocahontas&&view= detail&mid=466AF4230E57F508CCB9466AF4230E57F508CCB9&rvsmid= EBD1DC3F1FA1BA9B424FEBD1DC3F1FA1BA9B424F&FORM=VDMCNR.

35. Booker T. Washington, *Up from Slavery* (Digireads.com Publishing, 2016), 83.

36. https://www.usatoday.com/story/news/politics/2019/07/10/dc-mayor-muriel-bowser-trumps-july-4-speech-emptied-security-fund/1692760001.

37. https://www.usnews.com/opinion/articles/2016-08-14/donald-trumps-american-exceptionalism-is-the-ideology-of-arrogance.

38. https://www.newyorker.com/magazine/2016/11/21/making-america-white-again.

39. Moynihan, Daniel. *Maximum Feasible Misunderstanding*. The Free Press, 1970, 1969. pp. xxxiii.

6. THE PATRIOTISM OF SLAVES

1. Henry Wiencek, *An Imperfect God: George Washington, His Slaves, and the Creation of America* (Farrar, Straus and Giroux, 2003), 41.

2. Frederick Douglass, *The Narrative of the Life of Frederick Douglass* (Arcturus Holdings Limited, 2018), 66.

3. White, Deborah Gray, *Ar'n't I a Woman? Female Slaves in the Plantation South.* (W.W. Norton & Company Ltd., 1985), 45.

4. —. *Ar'n't I a Woman? Female Slaves in the Plantation South.* (W.W. Norton & Company Ltd., 1985), 44.

5. —. *Ar'n't I a Woman? Female Slaves in the Plantation South.* (W.W. Norton & Company Ltd., 1985), 43.

6. —. *Ar'n't I a Woman? Female Slaves in the Plantation South.* (W.W. Norton & Company Ltd., 1985), 43.

7. Daniel Moynihan, *The Negro Family: The Case for National Action* U.S. Department of Labor: Office of Policy Planning and Research, March 1965.

8. Henry Wiencek, *An Imperfect God: George Washington, His Slaves, and the Creation of America* (Farrar, Straus and Giroux, 2003), 198–199.

9. Henry Wiencek, *An Imperfect God: George Washington, His Slaves, and the Creation of America* (Farrar, Straus and Giroux, 2003), 199–200.

10. https://www.nytimes.com/2017/01/10/us/politics/obama-farewell-address-speech.html.

11. Mary Webster, *The Federalist Papers* (Merril Press, 1999), 202.

12. https://www.founders.archives.gov/documents/Adams/99-02-02-3102.

7. THE BLACK HARBINGER OF AMERICA'S FUTURE

1. I will use certain labels interchangeably: white liberals, the Left, progressives, white bureaucrats, and the Democrat Party.

2. https://www.businesswire.com/news/home/20190923005500/en/Woman-Owned-Businesses-Growing-2X-Faster-Average-Businesses.

3. https://www.forbes.com/sites/instituteforjustice/2015/01/29/hair-braiding-and-occupational-licensing/#416b64ef5dbd.

4. https://www.whitehouse.gov/briefings-statements/remarks-president-trump-working-lunch-governors-workforce-freedom-mobility/.

5. https://www.essence.com/news/simone-biles-breaks-another-record-21-medals.

6. https://www.indystar.com/story/news/2017/02/12/legislator-seeks-untangle-hair-braiding-regulations/97102728/.

7. https://youtu.be/QwIU7iUfhow.

8. https://www.washingtonpost.com/news/post-nation/wp/2017/08/13/one-group-loved-trumps-remarks-about-charlottesville-white-supremacists.

9. Bayard Rustin, "The Failure of Black Separatism," *Harper's Magazine* (January 1970): 124–125.

10. https://www.usatoday.com/story/news/politics/elections/2019/04/23/bernie-sanders-voting-rights-boston-marathon-bomber-buttigieg-harris/3548232002/.

11. Daniel Moynihan, *Maximum Feasible Misunderstanding* (Free Press, 1970), xiii–xiv.

12. Daniel Moynihan, *Maximum Feasible Misunderstanding* (Free Press, 1970), xvi.

13. Theodore Roosevelt, letter to Richard M. Hurd, January 3, 1919, Library of Congress, Theodore Roosevelt Papers: Series 3: Letters Sent, 1888–1919; Subseries 3A: Carbon Copies of Letters Sent, 1894–1919; vol. 198, 1919, January 1–February 5.

14. "Black Americans: A Profile," Bureau of Census Statistical Brief, March 1993.

15. United States Census Bureau, "Historical Living Arrangements of Children, November 2018." https://www.census.gov/data/tables/time-series/demo/families/children.html.

16. https://trib.com/opinion/columns/williams-how-important-is-today-s-racial-discrimination/article_2762f4b4-c0ab-561f-9acf-c26dc3c3b82b.html.

17. https://trib.com/opinion/columns/williams-how-important-is-today-s-racial-discrimination/article_2762f4b4-c0ab-561f-9acf-c26dc3c3b82b.html.

18. https://blackdemographics.com/cities-2/new-york-nj-ny.

19. "Black Americans: A Profile, Bureau of Census Statistical Brief," March 1993.

20. "Black Americans: A Profile, Bureau of Census Statistical Brief," March 1991, https://www.census.gov/prod/1/statbrief/sb93_2.pdf.

21. https://www.wsj.com/articles/SB10001424052748704881304576094221050061598.

22. https://www.capitalismmagazine.com/2004/08/war-on-poverty-revisited.

23. "Center for Disease Control and Prevention, Abortion Surveillance—United States 2010," November 29, 2013, http://www.cdc.gov/mmwr/preview/mmwrhtml/ss6208a1.htm.

24. http://www.numberofabortions.com/.

25. https://www.census.gov/data/tables/2018/demo/race/ppl-bc18.html.

26. https://www.washingtontimes.com/news/2018/aug/14/chelsea-clinton-roe-v-wade-added-three-and-half-tr.

27. https://www.washingtontimes.com/news/2018/sep/14/chelsea-clinton-unchristian-end-legal-abortion.

28. https://www.nbcnews.com/politics/congress/nancy-pelosi-border-wall-immoral-expensive-unwise-n749841.

29. https://dailycaller.com/2019/01/30/virginia-governor-northam-abortion.

30. https://www.realclearpolitics.com/video/2018/09/18/sen_hirono_on_kavanaugh_men_need_to_shut_up_accuser_needs_to_be_believed_and_i_believe_her.html.

31. https://www.breitbart.com/entertainment/2018/12/19/11-year-old-dances-gay-bar.

8. YES, RACISM EXISTS … IN DEGREES. WHAT DO WE DO ABOUT IT?

1. "Exhibit Traces History of Voting Rights Act," http://www.foxnews.com/story/2005/08/04/exhibit-traces-history-voting-rights-act.html.

2. "Iconic Selma Bridge Has a Racist Backstory," https://www.usatoday.com/story/news/2015/03/07/selma-bridge-racist-backstory-kkk/24537069.

3. https://www.phillyvoice.com/exclusive-watchdog-group-finds-offensive-social-media-posts-32-police-officers-montco.

4. https://thehill.com/policy/technology/393747-netflix-fires-chief-communication-officer-for-using-n-word.

5. https://www.washingtonpost.com/politics/2019/01/24/florida-secretary-state-resigns-over-blackface-photos.

6. https://www.freep.com/story/money/business/michigan/2016/01/29/ad-agency-ceo-fired-after-racist-e-mail-reported/79521974.

7. https://www.newsweek.com/michelle-obamas-proud-remarks-83559.

8. https://www.newsweek.com/michelle-obamas-proud-remarks-83559.

9. https://www.washingtonpost.com/news/fact-checker/wp/2015/03/19/hands-up-dont-shoot-did-not-happen-in-ferguson.

10. https://www.foxnews.com/opinion/kneeling-nfl-players-should-stand-up-and-work-with-president-trump-to-achieve-their-goals.

11. https://www.cnn.com/2018/08/20/us/unc-silent-sam-confederate-statue/index.html.

12. https://www.huffpost.com/entry/safe-spaces-college-intolerant_b_58d957a6e4b02a2eaab66ccf.

13. https://www.washingtontimes.com/news/2018/may/17/evergreen-college-students-back-it-no-white-people.

14. https://www.sanluisobispo.com/opinion/letters-to-the-editor/article105797216.html.

15. https://www.thedailybeast.com/trump-is-a-racist-if-you-still-support-him-so-are-you.

16. https://www.miamiherald.com/opinion/opn-columns-blogs/leonard-pitts-jr/article211963789.html.

17. Booker T. Washington, *Up from Slavery* (Digireads.com Publishing, 2016), 13.

18. Booker T. Washington, *Up from Slavery* (Digireads.com Publishing, 2016), 14.

19. Fredrick Douglass, *The Narrative of The Life of Fredrick Douglass*, (Arcturus Holdings Limited, 2018), 66.

20. https://www.flagusa.org/wp-content/uploads/2018/11/FLAG-Patriotism-Report-11.13.2018.pdf.

21. https://www.flagusa.org/wp-content/uploads/2018/11/FLAG-Patriotism-Report-11.13.2018.pdf.

22. David Limbaugh, *Guilty by Reason of Insanity: Why The Democrats Must Not Win.* Pg. 279. (Regnery Publishing, 2019), 279.

9. THE IMPORTANCE OF THE BLACK VOTE

1. https://foxbaltimore.com/news/project-baltimore/6-baltimore-schools-no-students-proficient-in-state-tests.

2. https://www.msn.com/en-us/news/politics/winners-and-losers-from-night-1-of-the-second-democratic-debate/ar-AAF6IOy.

3. https://dailycaller.com/2019/07/27/trump-baltimore-disgusting.

4. https://www.nytimes.com/1996/09/19/us/gop-tries-hard-to-win-black-votes-but-recent-history-works-against-it.html.

5. https://www.breitbart.com/entertainment/2019/06/27/watch-late-night-hosts-scorched-beto-orourke-for-speaking-spanish-at-debate; https://news.vice.com/en_us/article/43j8kn/the-democrats-terrible-spanish-ranked.

10. SOCIALISM IS SLAVERY

1. Daniel Moynihan, *The Negro Family: The Case for National Action*. U.S. Department of Labor: Office of Policy Planning and Research, March 1965.

2. https://www.forbes.com/sites/timworstall/2017/08/17/venezuelas-starving-people-are-now-eating-the-zoo-animals-the-parisians-had-the-german-excuse/#541c4d0cd2cc.

3. Milton Friedman and Rose Friedman, *Free to Choose* (Harcourt, 1980), 95–96.

4. https://www.washingtonexaminer.com/weekly-standard/michelle-will-steal-your-pie.

5. https://www.forbes.com/sites/kathleenhowley/2019/09/01/obamas-buying-marthas-vineyard-estate-from-boston-celtics-owner/#255310965300.

6. https://www.foxnews.com/politics/bernie-sanders-americans-will-be-delighted-to-pay-more-in-taxes-for-free-health-care-education.

7. https://www.theatlantic.com/magazine/archive/2019/10/black-athletes-should-leave-white-colleges/596629.

8. Frederick Douglass, *The Narrative of the Life of Frederick Douglass* (Arcturus Holdings Limited, 2018), 58–59.

9. Doris Kearns Goodwin, *Lyndon Johnson and the American Dream* (St. Martin's Press, 1991), 66.

10. Doris Kearns Goodwin, *Lyndon Johnson and the American Dream* (St. Martin's Press, 1991), 66.

11. https://ijr.com/warren-decriminalize-illegal-border-crossings-elected-president.

12. Doris Kearns Goodwin, *Lyndon Johnson and the American Dream* (St. Martin's Press, 1991), 67.

13. Doris Kearns Goodwin, *Lyndon Johnson and the American Dream* (St. Martin's Press, 1991), 54.

14. https://www.propublica.org/article/living-apart-how-the-government-betrayed-a-landmark-civil-rights-law; Doris Kearns Goodwin, *Lyndon Johnson and the American Dream* (St. Martin's Press, 1991), 55.

15. https://www.jbhe.com/2011/10/a-racial-breakdown-of-financial-aid.

16. https://www.youtube.com/watch?v=3-WubMXqTYY.

17. http://www.cliveden.org/the-chew-family.

18. Bruce J. Schulman, *Lyndon B. Johnson and American Liberalism* (Bedford/St. Martin's, 2007), 104.

19. Henry Wiencek, *An Imperfect God: George Washington, His Slaves, and the Creation of America* (Farrar, Straus and Giroux, 2003), 268.

20. https://www.fcc.gov/general/lifeline-program-low-income-consumers; http://www.foxnews.com/politics/2015/07/16/obama-announces-plan-for-high-speed-internet-in-low-income-homes.html.

21. https://feelthebern.org/bernie-sanders-on-education.

22. https://www.nytimes.com/2019/06/24/us/politics/bernie-sanders-student-debt.html.

23. https://www.nytimes.com/2019/06/24/us/politics/bernie-sanders-student-debt.html.

24. Bruce J. Schulman, *Lyndon B. Johnson and American Liberalism* (Bedford/St. Martin's, 2007), 102.

11. A LESSON FROM THE JEWS: MOURN, FIGHT, MOVE ON

1. https://shavei.org/tzvi-khaute-from-manipur-to-israel.

2. http://legisworks.org/congress/72/publaw-428.pdf.

3. https://www.usatoday.com/story/opinion/2017/11/27/sexual-harassment-fund-exposes-congress-editorials-debates/898008001/

4. Doris Kearns Goodwin, *Lyndon Johnson and the American Dream* (St. Martin's Press, 1991), 64.

5. https://www.jpost.com/Israel-News/Israel-Air-Force-gets-first-Ethiopian-pilot-574791.

6. https://www.timesofisrael.com/ethiopian-born-beauty-queen-visits-native-homeland.

12. MY HOPE FOR THE BLACK COMMUNITY

1. https://www.usatoday.com/story/opinion/2019/07/19/condemn-trump-racism-but-not-students-who-support-him-column/1745220001.

2. https://www.foxnews.com/transcript/teachers-attend-white-privilege-conference-on-taxpayers-dime.

3. http://www.washingtontimes.com/news/2017/jul/2/oregon-house-passes-free-abortions-bill-reproducti.

4. https://www.usatoday.com/story/news/politics/2016/05/12/feds-schools-transgender-bathrooms-letter-title-ix/84311104.

5. https://www.usatoday.com/story/news/education/2019/05/16/college-admissions-college-board-add-adversity-score-sat/3692471002.

6. https://www.usatoday.com/story/news/education/2019/05/16/college-admissions-college-board-add-adversity-score-sat/3692471002.

7. https://www.nationalreview.com/2018/10/political-correctness-problem-according-to-80-percent-of-people.

8. https://www.nationalreview.com/2018/08/skinny-eyebrows-declared-cultural-appropriation.

9. https://www.nationalreview.com/2018/03/god-bless-you-microaggression-against-muslims.

10. https://www.nationalreview.com/2017/08/chair-size-microaggression-new-school.

11. https://www.nationalreview.com/2017/07/city-councilman-hosing-poop-covered-sidewalks-might-be-racially-insensitive. https://www.seattletimes.com/seattle-news/crime/judges-complain-its-unsafe-unsanitary-outside-county-courthouse-in-seattle/

12. https://www.nationalreview.com/2019/06/desmond-napoles-gender-identity-ideology. https://www.dailywire.com/news/11-year-old-boy-dressed-drag-dances-gay-men-bar-amanda-prestigiacomo

13. https://www.youtube.com/watch?v=1kVdHr7sR0o.

14. https://www.cnsnews.com/new/article/63838.

15. https://abcnews.go.com/International/video/iran-hints-nuclear-deal-amid-death-america-chants-28895145.

16. https://www.reuters.com/article/us-nuclear-iran-israel-statements-timeli/timeline-israel-and-iran-statements-idUSTRE62S1E520100329.

17. https://www.reuters.com/article/us-iran-nuclear/irans-president-attacks-obama-on-nuclear-threat-idUSTRE6362IJ20100407.

18. https://www.reuters.com/article/us-nuclear-iran-israel-statements-timeli/timeline-israel-and-iran-statements-idUSTRE62S1E520100329.

19. http://www.breitbart.com/texas/2016/07/12/livewire-nation-gathers-honor-5-slain-dallas-area-police-officers.

20. https://abcnews.go.com/GMA/Weekend/dying-homeless-man-stopped-mugging-sidewalk/story?id=10471047.

21. https://www.bostonglobe.com/opinion/2015/07/21/planned-parenthood-videos-should-appall-even-pro-choice-advocates/TsR6dAxo82rQkLFD7W72lN/story.html.

22. https://www.nytimes.com/2017/01/23/world/trump-ban-foreign-aid-abortions.html.

23. https://www.cnn.com/2010/WORLD/americas/04/19/mexico.abortion/index.html.

24. C. S. Lewis, *The Abolition of Man* (HarperOne, 1974), 65.

13. WE ARE VICTORS, NOT VICTIMS

1. https://www.youtube.com/watch?v=S-AKUNpcLRg.

2. https://www.newsweek.com/kamala-harris-donald-trump-border-wall-us-mexico-2020-budget-1358091.

3. https://www.westernjournal.com/rashida-tlaib-suggests-americans-launch-hunger-strike-shut-ice.

4. https://www.breitbart.com/politics/2019/03/11/hawaii-democrat-lawmakers-repeal-or-amend-second-amendment.

5. Frederick Douglass, *The Narrative of the Life of Frederick Douglass* (Arcturus Holdings Limited, 2018), 62.

6. http://mentalfloss.com/article/92216/20-powerful-quotes-frederick-douglass.